Social Security Law in Chile

Social Security Law in Chile

Emilio Morgado-Valenzuela
Hugo Cifuentes-Lillo

This book was originally published as a monograph in the International Encyclopaedia of Laws/Social Security Law.

Founding Editor: Roger Blanpain
General Editor: Frank Hendrickx
Volume Editor: Willy van Eeckhoutte

Wolters Kluwer

Published by:
Kluwer Law International B.V.
PO Box 316
2400 AH Alphen aan den Rijn
The Netherlands
E-mail: lrs-sales@wolterskluwer.com
Website: www.wolterskluwer.com/en/solutions/kluwerlawinternational

Sold and distributed by:
Wolters Kluwer Legal & Regulatory U.S.
920 Links Avenue
Landisville, PA 17538
United States of America
E-mail: customer.service@wolterskluwer.com

ISBN 978-94-035-4007-8

e-Book: ISBN 978-94-035-4017-7
web-PDF: ISBN 978-94-035-4027-6

The Authors

Emilio Morgado-Valenzuela was born in Santiago (Chile) on 4 December 1933. He is a Lawyer (School of Law, University of Chile) and Doctor Honoris Causa at the University of Bordeaux I (France). Currently, he is an international and national adviser on labour law, labour relations and social security. He is also a member of the Labour Chapter's Arbitral Panel in the United States-Chile Free Trade Agreement, as well as a Non-National Arbiter of the Labour Chapter in the Free Trade Agreement between the USA, Central America and the Dominican Republic. He was also the Vice President of the International Society of Labour Law and Social Security (South America), and – in two opportunities – he has been a Member of the Executive Committee of the International Industrial Relations Association (now called ILERA). He also presided over the Chilean Labour Relations Association and is a Member of the academic 'Group of the Nine'. He is also an Honorary and Former President of the Iberoamerican Academy of Labour Law and Social Security and of the Chilean Society of Labour Law and Social Security. Further, he is a member of the Latin American Institute of Labour Law. Also, he is an 'Honorary Member' of the Labour Law Association of Murcia (Spain), the Costa Rican Association of Labour Law, the Colombian 'Collegium' of Lawyers Specialized in Labour Law and Social Security; the Peruvian Society of Labour Law and Social Security, and the Peruvian Association of Labour Relations. From 2007 to 2008, he was a Member of the Presidential Advisory Council on Labour and Equity, designated by President Michelle Bachelet. From 1970 to 1994, he was an Official of the International Labour Organization: first in charge of an ILO's technical cooperation project in Panama (1970), then held office as the ILO Regional Advisor on Labour Law and Labour Relations (Lima, 1974–1985); then as Director of the ILO Office for Central America and Panama (San Jose, 1985–1989); then as the Director of the Inter American Center for Labour Administration (Lima, 1990–1991); and finally as the Deputy Regional Director of the ILO's Office for Latin America and the Caribbean (Lima, 1991–1994). From 1970 to 1973, he was a Senior Labour Adviser in the Organization of American States (Washington D.C.). He is the author of specialized books and monographs published in American and European countries. He has received the grade of 'Commander' under the Ordem de Merito Judiciario do Trabalho-Brazil (Labour Tribunal's Merit Order) and the same honorary degree under the Labour's Order in Peru ('Orden del

Trabajo'). Widower of Lola Maúrtua-Cárdenas, father of Patricia (Associated Professor of Architecture at North Carolina State University, (Raleigh, USA) and Lucía (dentist and scientific researcher), and grandfather of Paula Camino-Morgado (Bachelor in Law).

Hugo Cifuentes-Lillo is Lawyer, Doctor of Law (Complutense University, Madrid), Professor of Social Security Law at the Catholic University of Chile. He is also a member of the Chilean Society of Labour and Social Security, and a member of the Iberoamerican Academy of Labour Law and Social Security. Among others, he has published (in Spanish): Pension System Reform (Inter-American Center for Social Security Studies, 2004); Feasibility to Make Obligatory the Independent Workers' Affiliation to the Pension System (with F. Walker), *Chilean Labour Review*, 2005; General Characteristics of the Chilean Social Security System, *Chilean Labour Review*, 2005; Needed Reform to Chilean Social Security *Chilean Labour Review*, 2005; Project of Law Improving the Pension System: Main Institutional Aspects, *Economy and Administration. Faculty of Economy and Business*, 1997; Multilateral Ibero-American Convention: Social Protection and Migration: XVII Ibero-American Summit; *Chilean Labour Review*, 2007; Labour Accidents: Assignation of Responsibilities and Prevention, *Chilean Labour Review*, 2007; General Aspects of Law 20.255, Establishing a Social Prevention Reform, *Chilean Labour Review*, 2008 (with F. Walker), and Social Security (Part General and Pensions), with Pablo Arellano Ortiz y Francisco Walker Errázuriz). President of the Chilean Social Prevention Users Commission. Head of the Supervisory Public Agency of Social Security (1992–1994). Labour Advisor for the State Bank since 1996. Delegate of Chile to the Ibero-American Social Security Organization since 2003. Titular Member of the Iberoamerican Academy of Labour Law and Social Security and Member of the Chilean Society of Labour Law and Social Security. Married to María Emma Ovalle de la Cuadra (Librarian) and father of Javier and Ignacio (University professionals).

Table of Contents

List of Abbreviations

AUGE	Social Prevention Explicit Minimum Health Guaranteed Programme
BSIP	Basic Solidarity Invalidity Pension
CAPREDENA	Social Security Institution for the Armed Forces
CCAF	Institutions to Compensate Family Allowances
CENABAST	Central Supply of the National System of Health Services
CLP	Chilean Peso
COMPIN	Preventive Medicine and Disability Commission
D	Decree
DFL	Decree with Force of Law
DIPRECA	Social Security Directorate for the Police Force
DLR	Deferred Life Rent
DW	Dependent Worker
EAA	Economic Association Agreement
ECA	Economic Complementation Agreement
ENC	Ergonomic National Commission
FONASA	National Health Fund
FTA	Free Trade Agreements
ILO	International Labour Organization/International Labour Office
ILR	Immediate Life Rent
ILR-PW	Immediate Life Rent with Programmed Withdrawal
IOS	Institute of Occupational Safety
IP	Invalidity Pension
ISAPRE	Social Prevention Health Institutions
IW	Independent Worker
L	Law
LD	Law Decree
LIC	Life Insurance Company
LR	Life Rent
MH	Ministry of Health

List of Abbreviations

MLSP	Ministry of Labour and Social Prevention
MTU	Monthly Tax Unit
OAP	Old Age Pension
OAS	Organization of American States
OECD	Organization for Economic Co-operation and Development
PFA	Pension Fund Administrator
PHI	Public Health Institute
PW	Programmed Withdrawal
SOP	Superintendency of Pensions
SP	Survivor Pension
SPI	Social Prevention Institute
TR-DLR	Temporal Rent with Deferred Life Rent
UGP	Universal Guaranteed Pension
UF	(Unidad de Fomento) A variable economic indicator
UFA	Unemployment Fund Administrator
UN	United Nations
UNDP	United Nations Development Programme
USD	United States Dollar
USSP	Undersecretariat of Social Prevention
VCSPS	Voluntary Collective Social Prevention Savings
WE	Wage Earner

Note. In 2023, on 30 April, the value of one USD was 792.79 Chilean pesos; the value of one UF was 35.838 Chilean pesos, and the value of one MTU was 63.074 Chilean pesos.

General Introduction

§1. General Background

I. Chile: A Portrait

1. Chile is located in the southwestern part of South America, from latitude 17° 30' S to latitude 90° S. The country borders Peru to the north, the South Pole to the south, Bolivia and Argentina to the east, and the Pacific Ocean to the west. It is considered to be a tri-continental country (South America, Antarctica, and Oceania). Chile is a very long and narrow country, with an average width of 150 km.

The Chilean continental extension is 4,239 km (8,000 km if the Chilean Antarctic is taken into account). Chile's South American continental surface is 755,917 km^2, its insular surface is 181 km^2, the Chilean Antarctic surface is 1,250,000 km^2 and its maritime surface is 3 million m^2. Chile's climate is dry and warm in the north, Mediterranean-like in the central valley, and temperate, cold, and rainy in the south, which is dotted with lakes, volcanoes, and old-growth forests. In the extreme south, there are hundreds of windswept islands separated by canals, straits, and seas. Its population is 19,458,000. The principal language is Spanish, but Mapudungun, Quechua, Rapa Nui and other languages are also spoken by native ethnic groups. The population is mainly of European and mixed-race descent.

2. The Republic of Chile is a representative democracy with a presidential regime. The president is elected for a four-year period (without the possibility of re-election to a second consecutive term). The Congress has two branches: the Senate (with thirty-eight elected Members representing nineteen electoral Districts) and the Chamber of Deputies (with 120 elected Members representing sixty electoral Districts). The Judiciary is composed of a Supreme Court, Courts of Appeals and Tribunals. There are sixteen Administrative Regions, with each of them being comprised of Provinces (fifty-six in total), each of them integrated by Local Governments called Municipalities (346 in total).

3. Chile's main economic resources are mining (copper, iron and molybdenum), fishing, agriculture, forestry, cattle, wines, fruits, cellulose, methanol and wood products.

4. In 2022, Chile's main commercial partners were China, the United States of America (USA), Japan, South Korea, Brazil, The Netherlands, Taiwan (Formosa), Canada, and Peru. Since the nineties, Chile has signed Free Trade Agreements

(FTA) with the following countries and entities: Australia (2005), Brazil (2022), Canada (1997), Central America (2002: Costa Rica, El Salvador, Guatemala, Honduras and Nicaragua), China (2006), Colombia (2009), South Korea (2004), EFTA (2004: Iceland, Liechtenstein, Norway and Switzerland), Hong Kong (2014), United States of America (2004), Malaysia (2012), Mexico (1999), Panama (2008), Peru (2009), Thailand (2015), Turkey (2011), Uruguay (2018), Vietnam (2014).

Chile has also Economic Association Agreements (EAA) with Japan (2007), the P4 (2006: New Zealand, Singapore and Brunei Darussalam), the European Union (Austria, Belgium, Bulgaria, Cyprus, Croatia, Denmark, Estonia, Finland, France, Germany, Greece, Hungary, Ireland, Italy, Latvia, Lithuania, Luxembourg, Malta, Netherlands, Poland, Portugal, Slovakia, Slovenia, Romania, Czech Republic, Spain, Sweden) and the United Kingdom (2021).

Economic complementation agreements (ECA) have been signed with Bolivia (1993), Cuba (2008), Ecuador (2008), MERCOSUR (1996: Argentina, Brazil, Paraguay, Uruguay and Venezuela), and Venezuela (1993).

Chile has also signed – with Colombia, Peru and Mexico – the Alliance of the Pacific, a commercial protocol. With India and Indonesia, there are agreements of partial or integral scope. With Argentina exists a commercial agreement. Chile is also a Member Country of the Organization for Economic Co-operation and Development (OECD).

In February 2023, the Comprehensive and Progressive Agreement for Trans-Pacific Partnership (CCTPP) was ratified and signed in 2018 between Australia, Brunei Darussalam, Canada, Chile, Japan, Malaysia, Mexico, Peru, New Zealand, Singapore and Vietnam.

Finally, it must be stressed that in some FTA and EAA agreements, there exist labour clauses regulating obligations with the purpose of impeding trade agreements that should be used as an excuse to diminish the content of protection established in the national legislation of the Parts in the agreement. Commonly, in those labour clauses, special mention is made to the ILO international standards, the ILO Constitution, and the ILO Declaration of the Fundamental Rights and Principles at Work (1998).

5. According to the ILO's publication 'Labour Overview 2013. Latin America and the Caribbean', it is needed to point out some conclusions derived from the statistical information corresponding to the period 2011–2013:

(1) The Gross National Product (GNP) presented an increase of 5.5% in 2011 and 5.6 in 2012, while in 2013, the GNP was 4.4%. In those years, the average GNP in Latin American and the Caribbean was 4.6%, 2.9% and 2.7%.
(2) The Chilean urban rate of participation was 59.5% in the third trimester of 2012 and 59.4% in the same period of 2013. The female rate of participation, as compared with the corresponding male rate, was 62.4% (2012) and 66.2% (2013).
(3) In Chile, the male's unemployment rate was 5.5% (2012) and 5.3% (2013), while the female's unemployment rate was 8.1% (2012) and 7.0% (2013). In turn, the occupation rate for males was 68.7% (2012) and 67.9% (2013). For females, those rates were 43.7% (2012) and 44.2% (2013).

(4) Finally, in Chile – taking into account the age factor – for persons aged from 15 to 24 years, the unemployment rate was 16.1% (2012) and 15.7% (2012), and their occupation rate was 31.3% (2012) and 30.5%. Those aged 25 or more years had an occupation rate of 62.2% (2012) and 62.5% (2013).

The recent ILO publication *'Labour Overview 2021. Latin America and the Caribbean'*, prepared by the ILO Regional Office for Latin America and the Caribbean, provides information on the employment situation in Chile, which I incorporate in the following Tables.

Table 1 Average Annual National Unemployment Rates by Sex (2014–2021)

	National	*Male*	*Female*
2014	6.5	6.1	7.5
2015	6.3	5.8	7.0
2016	6.7	6.3	7.2
2017	7.0	6.5	7.5
2018	7.4	6.7	8.3
2019	7.2	6.7	8.0
2020	10.7	10.5	10.9
2021			
1st quarter	8.2/10.4	7.1/9.9	9.7/11.0
2nd quarter	12.2/9.5	12.6/9.3	11.7/9.7
3rd quarter	12.3/8.4	12.8/8.3	11.6/8.6

Source: ILO: Labour Outlook 2021. Latin America and the Caribbean, p. 186.

Table 2 Average Annual Unemployment Rates by Age Group (2014–2021)

	15–24	*25 and More*
2014	16.4	5.1
2015	15.3	5.2
2016	15.5	5.6
2017	17.4	5.8
2018	17.7	6.2
2019	18.5	6.1
2020	24.1	9.5
2021		
1st quarter	19.17/23.5	7.0/9.2

	15–24	*25 and More*
2nd quarter	28.2/22.27	11.0/8.4
3rd quarter	27.1/17.0	11.2/7.7

Source: ILO: Labour Outlook 2021. Latin America and the Caribbean, p. 191.

Table 3 Average Annual National Employment Rates by Sex (2014–2021)

	National	*Male*	*Female*
2014	57.9	69.6	46.7
2015	58.1	70.0	46.7
2016	58.0	69.4	47.0
2017	58.3	69.4	47.7
2018	58.3	69.2	48.0
2019	58.3	68.7	48.4
2020	50.1	60.3	40.3
2021			
1st quarter	57.3/51.4	68.1/62.2	47.0/41.1
2nd quarter	45.6/50.6	55.1/60.9	36.4/40.7
3rd quarter	46.8/52.3	56.2/63.8	37.7/42.2

Source: ILO: Labour Outlook 2021. Latin America and the Caribbean, p. 206.

Table 4 Average Annual National Employment Rates by Age Group (2014–2021)

	15–24	*25 and More*
2014	30.6	64.8
2015	30.5	64.9
2016	29.7	64.7
2017	29.0	65.0
2018	28.2	85.0
2019	26.5	65.1
2020	20.0	56.4
2021		
1st quarter	28.6/20.9	63.4/57.6

	15–24	*25 and More*
2nd quarter	15.8/19/5	51.8/56.8
3rd quarter	16.2/21.4	53.1/58.5

Source: ILO: Labour Outlook 2021. Latin America and the Caribbean, p. 211.

Table 5 Wage Indicators: (i) Average Real Monthly Wage Index by Sex, and (ii) Average Real Monthly Wage Index in Public and Private Sectors (2014–2020)

	2014	*2015*	*2016*	*2017*	*2018*	*2019*	*2020*
(I)							
Men	101.3	103.5	103.8	105.8	108.8	109.5	110.2
Women	106.7	107.9	104.4	112.5	115.6	115.9	125.7
(II)							
Public Sector	107.3	112.5	105.1	111.6	111.1	115.1	114.3
Private Sector	100.4	101.6	103.2	104.5	107.9	107.3	110.6

Source: ILO: Labour Outlook 2021. Latin America and the Caribbean, p. 257.

Table 6 (I) Index of the Real Minimum Wage and Ratio of the Nominal Minimum Wage; and (II) As a Percentage of the Nominal Wage of the Urban Private Sector. Years 2014–2020 (2012= 100%)

	2014	*2015*	*2016*	*2017*	*2018*	*2019*	*2020*	*2020/2021**
(I)	108.8	111.7	117.1	120.7	123.6	128.6	133.3	3.5/0.3
(II)	45.2	43.9	44.8	45.6	45.8	46.9	47.9	–/–

*Year-on-year change in the average real minimum wage January/February.
Source: ILO: Labour Outlook 2021. Latin America and the Caribbean, p. 262.

6. In its Human Development Report 2021, the United Nations Development Programme (UNDP) presents the following main human development indicators referred to Chile:

- Index: 0,851.
- Rank: 43.
- Health (life expectancy at birth): 80.2 years.
- Education (expected schooling years): 16.4.

- Income/Composition of resources (Gross National Income per capita): USD 23,261.
- Inequality (inequality-adjusted HDI): IHDI 0.709.
- Gender (Gender Development Index): GDI 0.963.
- Work, employment and vulnerability (Employment to population ratio, ages 15 and older): 58.2.
- Human Security (homicide rate per 100,000 people): 4.4.
- Trade and Financial Flows (exports and imports– % of GDP): 56.8.
- Mobility and Communication (Internet users– % of population): 82.3.
- Environmental sustainability (Carbon dioxide emissions per capita): 4.7 tonnes.
- Demography (Total population): 19.5 million.
- Socio-economic sustainability (Skilled labour force): 71.3% of labour force.

Recently, in its Human Development Report 2020–2021 (Overview: Uncertain times, unsettled lives: Shaping our future in a transforming world), the UNDP published the following information referred to Chile, ranked as a country with a 'very high human development index':[1]

- HDI rank: 42.[2]
- Value 2021: 0,855.
- Inequality-adjusted HDI (IHDI).
- Value 2021: 0,722 Over all loss: 15.6%. Difference from HDI rank 2021: -8.
- Gender development Index: Value 2021: 0.967. Group 2021: 2.
- Gender inequality Index: Value 2021: 0.187. Rank: 47.

II. Preliminary Concepts

7. The Chilean social security system contains institutions corresponding to three different conceptual frameworks: social prevention, social security, and social protection approaches.

Nevertheless, in Chilean legislation, technical and academic studies and reports, and in practical use, to some extent, the expressions 'social prevention', 'social security' and 'social protection' are considered to be synonyms.

First of all, the expression '*prevision social*' is strongly related to concepts linked to social risks, such as anticipation, prevention, counteraction, foresight, and preclusion of such risks. In Chile, the Ministry in charge of these matters is the Ministerio de Trabajo y Previsión Social (Ministry of Labour and Social Prevention).

1. UNDP: 2021–2022 Human Development Report, p. 24.
2. *Ibid.* The fifteen better ranked countries are: Switzerland (0.962), Norway (0.961), Iceland (0.959). Hong Kong, China SAR (0.952), Australia (0.951), Denmark (0.948), Sweden (0.947), Ireland (0.945), Germany (0.942), Netherlands (0.941), Finland (0.940), Singapore (0.939), Belgium (0.937), New Zealand (0.937) and Canada (0.936).

8. The Chilean social prevention system was based on compulsory social insurance. The initial legislation on these matters was also guided by the first ILO standards, which made reference to concepts such as 'protection' (as in the Maternity Protection Convention 3, in 1919); 'indemnity' (as in the Unemployment Indemnity (Shipwreck) Convention 8, in 1920); 'compensation' (as in the Workmen's Compensation (Accidents) Convention 17, in 1925); and 'insurance' (as in the Sickness Insurance (Industry) Convention 24, in 1927). As it is now known, the expression 'social security' was first used in 1946 in the Social Security (Seafarers) Convention 70 and reached a very important and influential role with the adoption of Convention 102: Social Security (Minimum Standards) in 1952.

Under the social prevention model, since the 1920s, the enacting of laws establishing obligatory social insurance to cover social risks replaced the old strategy of covering them through four main sources: (a) charity initiatives developed by individuals and charitable organizations, most of them guided by fraternal sentiments or religious beliefs; (b) reciprocal assistance, protection, and cooperation of mutual help societies affiliating persons of similar professional activities, jobs, and needs (which planted the seed of the trade unions to come); (c) individual savings; and (d) voluntary mercantile insurance contracted on an individual basis. In this insufficient approach, not all persons and risks were covered. On the contrary, social prevention was based, as has been mentioned, on the existence of obligatory social insurance covering certain risks and only salaried workers. From that point of view, coverage was insufficient.

9. In the 1950s, Chilean legislation on social risks began to move to a social security model protecting not only salaried workers but also other kinds of workers, non-workers, and other large population segments. This legislation has tended to be in accordance with the general ILO concept of social security: national compulsory and contributory or non-contributory social welfare programs based on the principles of universality (i.e., covering the whole of a country's population) and unified general coverage against the risks of illness, accidents, old age, unemployment, and loss of revenue caused by family responsibilities.

10. The social pension and public health reforms imposed in the dictatorship period (1973–1990) correspond to a return to a private insurance model. They do not totally suppress the previous forms of social prevention, and, to some extent, they have co-existed with them.

11. However, reforms that have taken place since the 1990s – particularly the 2008 Reform and the increase of its 'solidarity pillar' by the approval of the Universal Guaranteed Pension (UGP) Law in 2021– are moving Chilean social security policies to a social protection model as defined by the ILO ('a general term covering all guarantees against reduction or loss of income in cases of illness, old age, unemployment or other hardships, and including family and ethnic solidarity, collective or individual savings, private insurance, social insurance, mutual benefit societies, social security, etc'.). Clearly, there is also a trend to identify boundaries between social security and social protection.

§2. HISTORICAL BACKGROUND

I. First Initiatives until 1924

12. In the Republican era, the first initial modalities that provided protection against social risks were individual programmes of charity, followed by collective efforts of mutual aid workers' organizations in the mid-nineteenth century (Mutual Societies), as well as some socially oriented programmes of religious organizations.

The legislative treatment of social protection began in 1898 with the enactment of a law establishing an old-age pension system for public employees. As part of political efforts to attend to the so-called social question that had existed in Chile since the middle of the nineteenth century, in September 1924, eight 'social' laws were approved by Congress, among them Laws 4054 and 4055.

13. Law 4054 introduced an obligatory social insurance system for blue-collar workers; apprentices; artisans or artists working at home; persons performing in streets, squares, and commercial establishments; small merchants; and industry owners with low incomes. It also allowed voluntary affiliation if legal requirements were fulfilled. Benefits were mainly financed with contributions of employers, workers, and the State. Affiliated workers could extend access to medical and pharmaceutical services to their dependant relatives. This insurance covered the following benefits: (i) medical care and necessary therapy, including hospital services; (ii) a monetary subsidy beginning on the fifth day after a medical condition was diagnosed; (iii) professional services and a monetary subsidy for female workers for pregnancy and childbirth; (iv) monetary aid for funeral costs; and (v) a pension for invalidity.

14. Law 4055 regulated labour accidents. The regulations mainly related to: (i) the definition of a labour accident; (ii) the employers' responsibility and the owners' subsidiary responsibility; (iii) the determination of economic entities covered by this Law; (iv) the determination of funds needed for the implementation of this Law; (v) the kind of benefits, assistance, indemnity payments, and pensions to be established in cases of occupational diseases and labour accidents; (vi) the financing and administration of this insurance; (vii) judicial procedures; (viii) preventive and inspection activities; and (ix) objectives of the system.

II. Normative Development (September 1924–September 1973)

15. In the period from 1925 to 1973, the 1924 legislation was followed by many Laws, Law Decrees (LD), and Decrees with Force of Law, as shown in Annex 2.

III. Normative Development (September 1973–March 1990)

16. During the non-democratic military regime (11 September 1973 to 10 March 1990), reforms were established that did not follow the rules set forth by the 1925 Constitution on procedures for the enactment of laws with the intervention of an elected Congress.

Those reforms can be classified into two groups: (i) reforms that in practice prepared for the intensive reforms of 1980, and (ii) the fundamental, substantive, and deep reform contained in LD 3500, supplemented by LD 3501, both of November 1980.

The first principal reform laws were the following:

(1) LD 307 (1974), creating the Single Fund for Family Allowances.
(2) LD 603 (1974), establishing a Single Unemployment Subsidy System.
(3) LD 2448 (1979), making uniform some matters in the existing pensions systems, such as the minimum age to be pensioned (men at age 65 and women at age 60).

In turn, LDs 3.500 and 3.501 inspired and guided reforms that took place until March 1990.

IV. Normative Development since March 1990

17. The main reforms approved since Chile's return to democracy are incorporated in the corresponding analysis of matters referred to in this monograph, especially in Annex 3 to 5.

§3. Sources of Social Security Law

18. The main regulations for social security matters are contained in the Constitution, international conventions, laws, decrees, adjudications, and collective conventions. In addition to these are the official opinions expressed by public institutions in charge of the general supervision over private and public organizations of social insurance and social security, as well as opinions of national and international scholars and academics specializing in social security and related matters.

I. Constitution

19. Since Chile's first independent government (1810), constitutional texts were enacted in 1812, 1818, 1822, 1823, 1826, 1828, 1833, 1925 (reformed in 1971), and 1980 (mainly reformed in 1989 and 2005). Now, we are in a second process of reform in the period 2019–2023.

20. When initial labour and social insurance legislation was approved (September 1924), the 1833 Constitution was in force. It did not contain provisions on labour or social security matters. A new Constitution was approved in 1925. Article 10 of this Constitution established guarantees protecting labour, industry, and welfare activities, especially those in housing and economic living conditions, giving each inhabitant a minimum of welfare funds appropriated to attend to his or her personal and family needs. It also established the State's duties to take care of public health and sanitary welfare, as well as to make a yearly assignment of sufficient funds to maintain a national health service.

21. These 1925 constitutional rules were replaced in 1971 by the following rules under the general title of 'Right to Social Security':

(1) The State will adopt all measures oriented to the satisfaction of social, economic, and cultural rights needed for the free development of human personality and dignity, the integral protection of the community, and be prone toward equality in the distribution of gross national income.
(2) Laws must especially cover risks related to: (i) the loosing, suspension, or non-self attributable diminution of the individual capacity to work; (ii) the death of a family head; (iii) the unemployment due to non-attributable causes; (iv) diseases in general and particularly occupational diseases and labour accidents, through preventive and curative medical care and rehabilitation; (v) pregnancy and maternity; and (vi) the right to family allowances.
(3) The State has to maintain social insurance for labour accidents, thus assuring the professional risks of workers. It is a State's duty to take care of public health and sanitary welfare in the country. Annually, the State has to assign sufficient funds to maintain a national health service.

22. The 1980 Constitution replaced previous constitutional normative development by the following, established in Article 19 Number 18, which relates to social security rights, particularly on the following subjects:

(1) Laws regulating the right to social security will be passed following the system of a 'qualified quorum' (with the approval of an absolute majority of Deputies and Senators, that is, fifty % and at least one more).
(2) State activities are to be directed to guarantee all inhabitants access to basic uniform benefits administered by public or private institutions.
(3) The law can establish obligatory contributions.
(4) The State will supervise the appropriated exercise of the right to social security.

The Constitution also assures the right to health protection (Article 19 Number 9), establishing the following particular rights:

(1) The State protects free and egalitarian access to actions for the promotion, protection, and recuperation of health and the rehabilitation of individuals.

(2) The coordination and control of activities related to health rest with the State.
(3) It is the prime duty of the State to guarantee health assistance undertaken by public or private institutions as determined by law, which can establish obligatory contributions.
(4) Each person has the right to select the health system to which he or she wants to belong, whether it is State – or privately controlled.

Other constitutional rights related to social security include the following:

(1) The right to life and to physical and psychological personal integrity (Article 19 Number 1).
(2) The loss of social security rights cannot be imposed as a punishment (Article 19 Number 7(h)).

After declaring that basic issues concerning social health and social security regimes are matters of law, the Constitution establishes that the President of the Republic has the exclusive initiative to propose laws to determine, modify, establish, or increase pensions and, in general, to establish or modify laws on social security or affecting it, both in the public and private sectors (Article 62 Numbers 4 and 6).

23. On 18 October 2019, the rise in transport fares provoked a powerful student protest. This situation triggered a large part of the population to join the protest, denouncing various situations of inequality and demanding innumerable, varied, and immediate social, economic and political changes. To make matters worse, the mass protests evolved into a 'social explosion', giving rise to acts of violence in the main cities, which endangered the governability of the country.

To recover that peaceful governability, in November 2019, most of the political parties of the ruling coalition and the opposition concurred, signing an agreement that included the elaboration of a new Political Constitution of the State. To this end, the National Congress adopted a law establishing some basic rules to elect the members of a Constituent Convention through a citizen vote held in May 2021. Most of those elected represented groups of citizens who were not members of political parties, including numerous representatives of the original ethnic groups.

On 4 July 2021, the Constitutional Convention concluded its work and delivered the official text of the Proposal for a New Political Constitution, with 388 articles and 57 transitory provisions. With specific regard to social security – including care – the proposed text provided:

Article 45

1. Every person has the right to social security, based on the principles of universality, solidarity, integrality, unity, equality, sufficiency, participation, sustainability, and opportunity.
2. The law shall establish a public social security system, which provides protection in the event of sickness, old age, disability, survival, maternity and paternity, unemployment, labour accidents and professional diseases, and

in other social contingencies, labour lack or reduction of means of subsistence or capacity for work. In particular, it shall ensure the coverage of benefits for those engaged in domestic and care works.

3. The State defines social security policy. This will be financed by workers and employers, through compulsory contributions and general incomes of the nation. The resources with which social security is financed may not be used for purposes other than the payment of the benefits established by the system.
4. Trade unions and employers' organizations have the right to participate in the management of the social security system, in the manner prescribed by law.

Article 50

1. Every person has the right to care. It includes the right to care, to be cared for and to be cared by itself from birth to death. The State undertakes to provide the means to guarantee that care is dignified and carried out in conditions of equality and co-responsibility.
2. The State guarantees this right through a Comprehensive Care System, norms and public policies that promote personal autonomy and incorporate human rights, gender and intersectional approaches. The System has a state, parity, solidary and universal character, with cultural relevance. Its financing will be progressive, sufficient and permanent.
3. This System shall pay special attention to infants, children and adolescents, the elderly, persons with disabilities, persons in situations of dependency and persons with serious or terminal illnesses. It will also ensure the protection of the rights of those who exercise care work.

In September 2022, the draft of the new Constitution was submitted to a plebiscite. By a very wide margin of votes, the citizens rejected the constitutional proposal, mainly due to certain norms on the nature and structure of the State, the relations between the executive, legislative and judicial powers, the plurinational, multicultural and decentralized character of the State and the regulatory character of its articles.

24. However, as a result of extensive and intensive political negotiations, a new constitutional reform process is under way. On 7 May, the citizens who will be part of a new Constituent Commission will be elected. They will be responsible for preparing the new proposal for the Political Constitution, along with the participation of an Expert Commission and a Commission of Proposals' Admission, appointed by Congress.[3]

Undoubtedly, what concerns social security will be present in the new text that will be proposed for citizen approval in December of this year. If it is approved –

3. Invited by the well known Chilean Centre of Development Studies, Hugo Cifuentes-Lillo and Emilio Morgado-Valenzuela participated in the elaboration of a Proposal on Fundamental Rights and Duties on Labour and Social Security.

and the new norms require it – it will be necessary to reform the current legislation to harmonize it with the new constitutional parameters.

II. International Declarations and Standards

25. Chile's historical need to establish some common basic rights and duties regarding social insurance and social security matters to protect human rights and also to balance international commerce has made necessary the approval of internationally accepted standards and declarations of purposes. This need has been reinforced by new social mores derived from or related to the development of globalization.

Since the 1990s, Chile has achieved remarkable success in its efforts to be an active participant in the present climate of globalization. For that reason, international declarations on and standards for social security are an important source of law. Special importance is attributed to the International Labour Organization (ILO) conventions, United Nations (UN) declarations and pacts, the Organization of American States (OAS) declarations and conventions, the Ibero-American declarations and agreements, and bilateral conventions and agreements.

26. The International Labour Organization: ILO Conventions Ratified by Chile. As of 30 April 2023, the following ILO Conventions on social security and related matters ratified by Chile are in force:

(1) Unemployment Convention, 1919, number 2.
(2) Workmen's Compensation (Agriculture) Convention, 1921, number 12.
(3) White Lead (Painting) Convention, 1921, number 13.
(4) Equality of Treatment (Accident Compensation) Convention, 1925, number 19.
(5) Sickness Insurance (Agriculture) Convention, 1927, number 25.
(6) Old-Age Insurance (Industry) Convention, 1933, number 35.
(7) Old-Age Insurance (Agriculture) Convention, 1933, number 36.
(8) Invalidity Insurance Industry, etc.) Convention, 1933, number 37.
(9) Invalidity Insurance (Agriculture) Convention, 1933, number 38.
(10) Maternity Protection Convention (Revised), 1952, number 103.
(11) Radiation Protection Convention, 1960, number 115.
(12) Employment Injury Benefits Convention, 1964 (Schedule I amended in 1980, number 121).
(13) Maximum Weight Convention, 1967, number 127.
(14) Benzene Convention, 1971, number 136.
(15) Vocational Rehabilitation and Employment (Disabled Persons) Convention, 1983, number 159.
(16) Occupational Health Services Convention, 1985, number 161.
(17) Asbestos Conventions, 1986, number 162.
(18) Promotional Framework for Occupational Safety and Health Convention, 2006, number 187.

27. The United Nations: UN Declarations and Pacts. As a member of the UN, Chile attributes special importance to the Universal Declaration of Human Rights (December 1948). This Declaration states that every person, as a member of society, has the right to social security and to obtain – through national efforts and international cooperation – the satisfaction of his or her economic, social, and cultural rights indispensable to his or her dignity and the development of his or her personality, taking into account the organization and resources of each State.

This Declaration was followed by the International Pact on Economic, Social, and Cultural Rights (December 1966), which recognized the right of each person to social security.

28. The Organization of the American States: OAS Declarations and Treaties. Chile also places importance on the American Declaration of Human Rights and Duties, adopted by the OAS in 1948. It establishes the right of all persons to the protection of their health and welfare through sanitary and social measures related to food, clothing, housing, and medical assistance at a level in accordance with public and community resources. The Declaration also states that each person has the right to social security that protects persons against the results of unemployment, old age, and disablement that causes a physical or mental impossibility of obtaining resources for subsistence.

This Declaration has been followed by the American Convention on Human Rights (1969) and its Protocol of San Salvador (Additional Protocol to the American Convention on Human Rights – known as 'Pacto de San José', 1969 – in the area of Economic, Social, and Cultural Rights (1988).

29. Multilateral Agreements: Ibero-American Social Security Multilateral Convention. Among other multilateral agreements, particular recognition is assigned to the Ibero-American Social Security Organization (OISS) declarations and agreements, especially the Ibero-American Social Security Multilateral Convention.

After some preliminary efforts related to the establishment of an Ibero-American Social Security Code, the focus became the protection of social security rights and the needs of migrants and their families in the Ibero-American context. The Fifteenth Ibero-American Summit of Chiefs of State and Government (held in Salamanca, Spain, in 2005) decided to begin the process of planning for an Ibero-American Social Security Convention to protect migrant workers and their families. That decision was ratified in the Sixteenth Ibero-American Summit (held in Montevideo, Uruguay, in 2006). In turn, the Seventeenth Ibero-American Summit (held in Santiago, Chile, in 2007) unanimously approved the Ibero-American Social Security Multilateral Convention. A summary of its content is presented in Annex 1.

30. Bilateral Agreements. Taking into account the principle of universal coverage of social security rights, everyone's rights are protected without distinctions between national citizens and foreigners, residents and non-residents, or even their status as workers or non-workers.

The implementation of this principle creates a number of legal and practical problems in matters such as equal treatment, the recounting and addition of affiliation periods, the 'export' of pensions, the territorial application of laws, and administrative collaboration. These matters have unique significance with regard to migrant workers.

The prevention and solutions of these problems are dealt with through bilateral conventions and agreements, including administrative agreements.

In Chile, the following principal bilateral agreements are in effect: Argentina (1972), Australia (2004), Austria (1999), Belgium (1999), Brazil (1996), Canada (1998), Columbia (2009), the Czech Republic (2004), Denmark (1995), Ecuador (2008), Finland (2008), France (2001), Germany (1994), Holland (1997), Luxemburg (1999), Norway (1998), Peru (2004), Portugal (2000), the Province of Quebec (2000), Spain (1998), Sweden (1995), Switzerland (1998), the USA (2001), and Uruguay (1999).

III. Legislation

31. As established in the 1980 Constitution, only the President of the Republic can propose legislation on social security or related matters for both the public and private sectors. Laws on social security matters have to be approved, modified, or derogated with a qualified quorum (an absolute majority of members in the Chamber of Deputies and the Senate).

Under specific authorization of law, the Executive can enact Decrees with Force of Law, which have the same legal effects as a law. In turn, LDs are established by the Executive when democratic institutions are not in operation, for instance, during the military regime (11 September 1973–10 March 1990). Consequently, it is important to note that in the few periods of non-democracy in Chile, the Executive has approved LDs, that is, standards that have not been approved by Congress. Nevertheless, in certain situations, Congress can legally delegate to the Executive some legislative powers on specific matters, thus authorizing the enactment of Decrees with Force of Law.

IV. Regulation (Decrees)

32. To implement laws, the Executive enacts Decrees (Executive Orders) regulating standards fixed by legislation. They are signed by the President of Chile and the relevant Minister or Ministers.

V. Adjudication

33. Judicial cases are subject to a special, recently reformed procedure, which has been implemented since March 2008. The process contemplates two instances of adjudication. First-instance adjudications are dictated by Tribunals, and they can be appealed to the Courts of Appeals in charge of second-instance adjudications. These adjudications can be subject to a final exceptional judicial claim that is resolved by the Supreme Court.

It is important to note that there is a special procedure that is applied in cases involving the non-fulfilment of an employer's duties to deposit social insurance contributions deducted from an employee's remuneration.

Even though these adjudications produce effects only in relation to the parties involved in the judicial procedure, the principles and doctrine that give rise to the pertinent adjudication constitute a powerful tool to resolve similar future cases, thus creating judicial jurisprudence.

VI. Collective Agreements

34. Legal and practical constraints on collective bargaining in Chile preclude extended protection of labour and social security rights. As collective bargaining is mainly – and almost exclusively – practised at the plant level and it is not possible to bargain at the central or branch level, the percentage of covered workers and the scope of agreed-upon matters are limited.

Nevertheless, in large enterprises and in the presence of large trade unions, collective bargaining is important for fixing wages and labour conditions, including agreements related to the improvement of social insurance rights. This is the case, for instance, in the betterment of levels and conditions of agreed-upon additional contributions to Old Age Pensions (OAP), paid leaves for medical reasons, family and maternal allowances, and survivor benefits.

VII. Technical Opinions: Doctrine Derived from Public Institutions, Jurisprudence and Academics

35. In labour and social security matters, Chilean supervisory public institutions are in charge not only of inspection duties but also of interpreting pertinent laws, decrees, and collective agreements, if so required by either party. Moreover, they are also allowed to adopt general instructions for the fulfilment of social security and labour rights and duties.

In that sense, administrative opinions constitute a kind of non-judicial jurisprudence, and in practice, the corresponding administrative process plays an important role in diminishing the amount of cases presented to the courts. Moreover, some administrative institutions can legally try to reconcile the parties' interests, and even further, they are entrusted with the power to pronounce decisions with binding effects. In any event, parties can always present their cases to tribunals and the courts.

Of course, the opinions of scholars and academics are always a recurring tool used by judges, lawyers, employers and workers' representatives and governmental officials to support their arguments.

Part I. The Institutions

Chapter 1. Public Institutions

36. Chile's main public institutions are the Ministry of Labour and Social Prevention (MLSP) and its related institutions and the Ministry of Health (MH) and its related institutions. In their fields of activities, they are in charge of: (i) the preparation, implementation, and evaluation of labour and social security public policies and health matters; and (ii) the supervision of public and private institutions related to the implementation of those policies.

§1. Ministry of Labour and Social Prevention and Related Institutions

37. The institutions with the main responsibility for the social security system are: (i) the Ministry of Labour and Social Prevention; (ii) the Undersecretariat of Social Prevention; (iii) the Superintendency of Social Security; (iv) the Superintendency of Pensions; (v) the Social Prevention Institute and its Comprehensive Social Security Care Centres; (vi) the Institute of Occupational Safety and; (vii) the National Ergonomic Commission.

In addition to these governing bodies, there are two advisory institutions: the Social Prevention Advisory Committee and the Users' Committee.

Also, there are two related bodies within the scope of the Ministry of Defence and of Internal Affairs: (i) the Social Security Institution for the Armed Forces (CAPREDENA), and (ii) the Social Security Directorate for the Police Force (DIPRECA).

§2. Ministry of Labour and Social Prevention

38. The Ministry of Labour and Social Security is the highest body for collaboration with the President of the Republic in labour and social security matters. It is responsible for proposing and evaluating the corresponding policies and plans, studying and proposing the rules applicable to the sectors under its responsibility, ensuring compliance with the rules issued, allocating resources and supervising the activities of the respective sector. It has two undersecretaries: one for Labour and the other for Social Prevention.

§3. UNDERSECRETARIAT OF SOCIAL PREVENTION

39. This Undersecretariat has, in particular, the following functions and attributions:

(1) Advise the Minister in the elaboration of policies and plans corresponding to the field of social security, as well as in the strategic analysis, planning and coordination of the plans and actions of the public services of the sector.
(2) Study and propose to the Minister the rules and legal reforms applicable to the sector and ensure compliance.
(3) Evaluate the policies applicable to the sector in accordance with the instructions of the Minister.
(4) Carry out and promote the preparation of studies and research in the field of social security.
(5) To assist the Minister in the field of international relations in the field of social security and in Chile's participation in international organizations related to the subject.
(6) Define and coordinate the implementation of strategies to make the population aware of the social security system and facilitate the exercise of their rights in accordance with the policies defined in the matter.
(7) Promote strategies for the incorporation of independent workers into the compulsory contribution regime established in the LD. 3.500 of 1980.
(8) Administer the Fund for Social Security Education.
(9) Administratively assist the Social Security Advisory Commission and the Commission of Users of the Pension System.

The Undersecretariat for Social Prevention is responsible for administering the Fund for Education on the Pension System, created by Law 20.250, for the purpose of financially supporting projects, programmes, activities and measures for the promotion, education and dissemination of the pension system. The resources of the Fund are allocated through public competitions on the proposal of the Selection Committee.

The Committee is composed of the Chairman of the Committee on Users of the Pension System, a representative of the Undersecretariat for Social Prevention, a representative of the Superintendency of Pensions (SOP) and a representative of the Social Prevention Institute (SPI).

Regulations issued through the MLSP, also signed by the Minister of Finance, establish the rules for the administration and operation of the Fund, criteria for the allocation of resources, rules for the operation of the selection committee and all relevant rules.

At least 60%of the funds allocated annually must be allocated to projects, programs, activities and measures of promotion, education and dissemination for beneficiaries who do not reside in the Metropolitan Region, provided that there is a sufficient number of these projects, programmes, activities and measures that comply with the technical requirements established for that purpose.

The Fund is mainly constituted by the contribution that is contemplated annually in the Budget Law and the contributions that are received through international cooperation in any capacity.

§4. Superintendency of Social Security

40. The Superintendency of Social Security is a functionally decentralized public service with legal personality and its own assets, which liaises with the President of the Republic through the Undersecretariat for Social Prevention. Its domicile is the city of Santiago, without prejudice to the regional offices that the Superintendent establishes in other cities of the country. The Superintendent of Social Security is the Senior Chief of the Superintendency and has legal, judicial and extrajudicial representation of the Superintendency. The Superintendent is appointed by the President of the Republic. The positions of the Superintendency of Social Security are incompatible with any employment, function or commission in the entities it supervises.

The assets of the Superintendency shall consist of: (i) the contribution contemplated annually in the Budget Law; (ii) remedies granted by special laws; (iii) movable and immovable, tangible and intangible property transferred or acquired to it in any capacity; (iv) the fruits of their property; (v) the donations made to it and the inheritances and legacies that it accepts, which it must do with the benefit of inventory. Such donations and hereditary allowances shall be exempt from all taxes and from any levy or payment affecting them. Donations will not require the process of insinuation; (vi) the income it receives from the services it provides; (vii) the contributions of international cooperation that it receives in any capacity; and (viii) other resources established by law.

The Superintendency will be structured organically and functionally in the Prosecutor's Office, the Intendency of Safety and Health at Work and the Intendency of Social Benefits.

The Superintendency is responsible for supervising and controlling the social security and social protection systems, as well as the institutions that administer them, within the sphere of its competence and in accordance with the law.

41. The functions of the Superintendency are:

(1) To establish, in the administrative order, the interpretation of the legal and regulatory norms of social security of its competence.
(2) To issue circulars, instructions and resolutions to the entities subject to its supervision in so far as they are necessary for the exercise of the functions and attributions conferred on it by this law. It must also instruct the institutions subject to its supervision on the procedures for the proper granting of the corresponding benefits in each case within the scope of its competence. Previously, the Superintendency must convene a process of public consultation and receipt of comments unless, due to the nature of the matter in question or the opportunity in which the respective instructions must take effect, this instance

is not appropriate. This process will be carried out by electronic means or others that are established for that purpose. The comments received will be evaluated without being binding.

(3) Resolve the presentations, appeals and claims of users, workers, pensioners, employing entities, social security administrative bodies and other persons, whether natural or legal, in matters that are not of a litigious nature, within the scope of its competence.

(4) Advise the MLSP in matters within its competence and propose the legal and regulatory reforms that the technique and experience advise.

(5) Carry out studies and reports on medical, actuarial, financial, legal and other aspects, referring to matters within its competence.

(6) Systematize and propose the standardization of regulations on safety and health at work to achieve their uniformity through periodic reviews.

(7) To administer and keep updated the National Information System on Safety and Health at Work, which shall contain, at least, information on complaints of occupational accidents and professional diseases, diagnoses of occupational illness, examinations and evaluations carried out, ratings of accidents and diseases, and the corresponding prevention and control activities, ensuring the privacy of personal and sensitive data. The System shall also be integrated with information on occupational safety and health to be provided, in the manner and periodicity determined by the Superintendence, by the National Health Fund (FONASA), regional ministerial health secretariats, Preventive Medicine and Disability Commissions (COMPIN), health services, the Institute of Occupational Safety (IOS), social security health institutions, employers' mutual societies and the Directorate of Labour, entities that will be obliged to deliver the background information they must possess in accordance with their legal attributions. In the event that they do not have the background or do not comply with their referral within the established deadlines, said entities must inform in writing the reasons for this and indicate the term in which they will do so. In addition, the Superintendence may request the information available to the Social Security Data Information System administered by the Social Security Institute, as well as information that other public or private entities have in their possession and is necessary for the integration of the system.

Likewise, the System will incorporate information regarding persons who are assignees of a disability pension of any social security system, which the pension and social security entities must send monthly in the manner determined by the Superintendency. The Superintendency is responsible for providing access to the information contained in the National Information System to public entities that request it, exclusively within the scope of its competence. The Undersecretaries of Labour and Social Prevention shall have access to this system and to the information that may be necessary only for the exercise of their functions. In this case, the processing and use of personal data carried out by the Undersecretaries will be within the scope of their competence. These undersecretaries and their staff must keep absolute confidentiality and secrecy of the information of which they become aware and refrain from using such information for their own benefit or that of third parties. It shall be considered that the facts that constitute infringements of this provision seriously violate the principle of administrative probity without prejudice to the other sanctions and responsibilities that may apply.

(8) Advise the Ministry of Labor and Social Prevention in the evaluation and design of public policies in the areas of its competence, including the Public Policy on Safety and Health at Work, and propose the legal and regulatory reforms that are pertinent.

(9) Issue instructions to the administrative bodies of Law 16,744, in accordance with the provisions of the Public Policy on Safety and Health at Work, as appropriate, and supervise that these entities comply with them.

(10) Evacuate the technical reports requested by the courts of justice in matters within their competence.

(11) Ensure that the supervised institutions comply with the laws and regulations that govern them and with the instructions issued by the Superintendency without prejudice to the powers that may correspond to other oversight bodies.

(12) Examine, qualify and observe the accounting and financial statements of the entities fully subject to its audit, which, according to a general application established by the Superintendency, must be duly audited by external auditors registered in the register of external audit companies of the Superintendency of Securities and Insurance.

(13) Order the conduct of audits or, in qualified cases, instruct the sanctioning procedures to the supervised entities, proceeding to the application of the corresponding sanctions, without prejudice to the power to file complaints and lawsuits before the Public Prosecutor's Office and the corresponding courts for any responsibilities of this nature that affect them or their directors, executives or workers.

(14) To issue general instructions to the audited bodies, so that they publish, with the periodicity indicated by the Superintendency, sufficient and timely information of public interest, relative to their legal, economic and financial situation, as well as background information on the structure of corporate governance and superior administration that they possess, and publish statistics regarding social security systems within the scope of their competence.

(15) Prepare and publish the Annual Report of the National Occupational Health and Safety System, which will include the results achieved, the main milestones in the development of the National Policy on Safety and Health at Work, and the progress made in achieving the objectives, indicating levels of compliance with them and prospects for the future. In addition, collect, consolidate and systematize the information provided by the administrative bodies of Law 16.744 and the various public institutions with competence in matters of occupational health and safety, directly or through the National Information System on Safety and Health at Work. This report shall be sent to the MLSP no later than May of each year.

(16) Disseminate the technical and social principles of social security through the dissemination of the corresponding legal texts and the result of their application.
(17) To perform such other functions as may be entrusted to it by law.

42. The Superintendency of Social Security is the technical authority for the supervision of prevention institutions within the scope of its competence. Such supervision includes medical-social, financial, actuarial, legal and administrative orders, as well as the quality and timeliness of services. It has the following powers with respect to the institutions subject to its supervision:

(1) Modify and standardize accounting methods according to the most economical and modern technical systems.
(2) Establish the procedures that social security institutions must follow in the management of the funds and assets of these institutions, as well as the way to present the accounts, prepare inventories and everything that refers to the investment, management and disposal of those funds and assets.
(3) Order the realization of balance sheets, actuarial and accumulations; provide for the preparation of demographic statistics of interest to forecasting and establishing the biometric and financial bases of the balance sheets and analytical-mathematical forms in order to standardize all calculation methods that lead to the actuarial valuation of the assets and liabilities of the institutions under their control.
(4) Issue instructions for the best granting of benefits to the imposing.
(5) To establish the interpretation of social security laws and regulations and to order the institutions subject to their supervision to conform to this interpretation.

The Superintendency of Social Security is competent to investigate, examine, review and pronounce on all acts of the administrative and technical procedures of the supervised institutions, in the matters within its competence, and in the granting of benefits to their insured persons; establish whether the laws in force regarding investments and granting of benefits have been complied with and, in particular, know the expenses and investments of the entities fully subject to their supervision. The purpose of the examination of financial management shall be to analyse the assets of the institutions, both in terms of their purely economic aspect and their ability to respond to future profits.

The constitution of companies or subsidiary bodies of social security institutions subject to the comprehensive supervision of the Superintendency of Social Security must be authorized by that Superintendency. Likewise, these companies or subsidiary organizations shall be subject to the oversight and supervision of the Superintendence, without prejudice to the powers that correspond to other agencies.

In the exercise of its supervisory work, the Superintendency must always inform the respective entity about the specific matter subject to the audit and the relevant regulations, carrying out the procedures proportional to the object of the audit.

For the fulfilment of its functions and attributions, the Superintendency may inspect all the operations, assets, books, accounts, archives and documents of the institutions subject to its supervision and request from them or from their administrators, advisers, auditors or personnel, the background and explanations it deems necessary. Likewise, it may request the delivery of the documents or books or records that are necessary for inspection purposes without altering the normal development of the activities of the affected party. The Superintendency, by resolution, shall determine those books, files and documents of the audited entities that must be permanently available for examination at their home or at the main headquarters of their activity.

The Superintendency may also require the audited agencies to provide it with the information necessary to carry out its functions through electronic means, as well as to grant it access to the information systems held by these institutions, in the cases determined through its instructions and adopting all necessary measures to ensure the protection of the confidentiality of sensitive information. In addition, it may request a written statement or summon to testify the senior managers, representatives, administrators, directors, advisors, auditors and dependents of the entities or persons audited, in cases in which it deems it necessary for the fulfilment of its functions.

43. The Superintendent shall observe any agreement of the boards or councils of the supervised institutions that he considers contrary to the laws in force or to the interest of the institutions. This power must be exercised in writing and within a period of seven working days, counted from the date on which the receipt of the agreement is recorded in the Superintendency. The boards or councils of the entities whose agreements have been observed by the Superintendent in the interest of said entities may, with the votes of two-thirds of their members, insist on the said agreement, in which case it must be complied with. In any case, the audited entity must adopt all necessary measures to ensure proper compliance with the insisted agreement and must record the results thereof. It shall report such results to the Superintendence at such intervals as it may determine.

The audited entities must inform the Superintendency of any relevant event that may affect their management or the timely granting of the corresponding benefits within a maximum period of twenty-four hours from their occurrence, in accordance with the instructions that it has given for that purpose. In any case, by means of rules of general application, the Superintendence must expressly indicate the meaning and scope of the relevant facts that must be reported.

44. The Superintendency of Social Security is empowered to order audits or conduct disciplinary procedures for the public institutions under its supervision in order to prove the offences and responsibilities for the facts investigated without prejudice to the powers of the respective heads of services on the same subject. In the other audited entities, the Superintendence may order audits or instruct the pertinent sanctioning procedures to prove the infractions and the responsibilities that correspond to the facts investigated. However, if the facts under investigation refer to resolutions or payments of remuneration to the personnel of public institutions supervised by the Superintendence or to accounts of the same institutions, the authority to conduct proceedings shall correspond to the Office of the Comptroller General of the Republic, without prejudice, also, to the powers of the respective Heads of Service.

By the fact that a delegate of the Superintendent is constituted in a visit to an institution subject to the supervision of the Superintendency, the Chief of the institution and all his personnel remain under his/her authority only for the purpose of providing the data and reports that serve to carry out the investigations that allow to establish the conditions of operation of the office.

The advisors, directors, vice-presidents and administrators of the institutions subject to the supervision of the Superintendence are obliged to give a statement in cases where they are required and, if they do not do so, after application of the sanctioning procedure and by means of a well-founded resolution, a fine of up to UF 100 may be applied.

The Superintendent may require the supervised entities or the respective head of service to evaluate the suspension of their functions to the advisors, directors, vice presidents and administrators for up to thirty days as a preventive measure during the processing of a sanctioning procedure, when he/she considers that this measure is indispensable for the development and good result of the proceedings decreed. If the sanctioning procedures involve the responsibility of any advisor, director, vice president or administrator of the institutions subject to its supervision, the corresponding legal sanctions will be applied.

If, as a result of compliance with an agreement observed by the Superintendence, prejudice is left to the respective institution, the Superintendency shall initiate the corresponding sanctioning procedure. The resulting penalties shall be without prejudice to the criminal and civil liability of the advisors, directors, vice-presidents or administrators of the institutions subject to their supervision, who shall be jointly and severally liable, in accordance with the law, for any damage they have caused to the institution or to the beneficiaries of the social security schemes which they administer, for the application of the agreement insisted.

In the event of conducting audits, the audited institutions must inform the Superintendency of the results of the audits and the corrective measures applied, if necessary, as instructed by it.

45. The instruction of the sanctioning procedure will be carried out by an official of the Superintendency who will be called an instructor. This procedure will begin with a precise formulation of the charges, which will be notified to the alleged offender by a registered letter sent to the address that he has registered with the Superintendency, giving him a period of fifteen days to formulate the discharges. The filing of charges shall indicate a clear and precise description of the facts deemed to constitute an infringement and the date of their verification; the laws, regulations, statutes and other rules that govern them or the instructions or opinions issued by the Superintendency in exercise of its powers, and the sanction assigned. Once the disclaimers have been received or the period granted for this purpose has elapsed, the Superintendency shall examine the merits of the antecedents and may order the carrying out of the pertinent expert examinations and inspections and the receipt of the other appropriate evidence. The facts investigated and the responsibilities of the offenders may be proven by any means of evidence admissible by law, which will be assessed in accordance with the rules of sound criticism.

Once these procedures have been completed, the instructor of the sanctioning procedure will issue, within five working days, a well-founded opinion in which he will propose the acquittal or sanction that, in his opinion, corresponds to apply. Once the opinion has been issued, the instructor of the procedure will submit the background to the Superintendent, who will resolve it within fifteen working days, issuing a resolution based on which he will acquit the offender or apply the sanction, as the case may be. However, the Superintendent may order the performance of new proceedings or the correction of procedural defects, setting a deadline for such purposes. In this case, he/she must give a hearing to the person investigated. No person may be punished for acts that have not been the subject of charges.

After investigation of the facts, the Superintendency of Social Security may apply to the institutions subject to its supervision as well as to their directors, heads of service, general managers and executives related to the superior administration of the same – who incur in infractions of the laws, regulations, statutes and other norms that govern them or to their instructions or opinions issued in exercise of their legal attributions – the sanctions established in Article 28 of LD 3.538 of 1980. The fine will amount to UF 15.000.

In the event that said fine is applied to natural persons, the offender must be personally liable for it. The specific amount of the fine shall be determined by assessing the gravity and consequences of the act, the economic capacity of the offender and whether he has committed other infractions of any nature repeatedly. They shall be understood to be repeated infringements when two or more of them have been committed in the last twenty-four months.

In any case, the advisors, directors, vice-presidents and administrators of the institutions subject to the supervision of the Superintendency who have been sanctioned in accordance with the aforementioned Article 28 or are fined for repeated infractions may not be reappointed or elected in the positions indicated above, for a period of five years from the date on which the resolution applying the respective measure takes effect. The sanctions imposed shall be recorded in a public register kept for this purpose by the Superintendency of Social Security, which shall be disseminated by the means established by the Superintendent.

Against the disciplinary measures adopted by the Superintendent of Social Security, a complaint may be made to the Court of Appeals of Santiago within fifteen working days from its notification by registered letter. The claim will be processed with preference after a report from the Superintendency of Social Security, which must be sent within six working days. Once this period has expired, the court shall proceed to hear the case and decide without further formality. No appeal shall be lodged against the decision rendered by the Court.

§5. Superintendency of Pensions

46. Created in Law 20.250 as a decentralized public body with legal personality and its own assets, it is governed by said law and its organic statute. It liaises with the President of the Republic through the MLSP through the Undersecretariat for Social Prevention. The senior management and administration of the SOP are the responsibility of the Superintendent of Pensions, who is the senior head of the service and shall have the authority, powers and duties inherent in that capacity.

For all purposes, the SOP is considered the successor and legal continuator of the Superintendency of Pension Fund Administrators created by LD 3.500 of 1980, with all its rights, obligations, functions and attributions.

47. The SOP has, in particular, the following functions and powers:

(1) Exercise those assigned to the Superintendency of Pension Fund Administrators in LD 3.500 of 1980, in Decree with Force of Law (DFL) 101, of the same year, of the Ministry of Labor and Social Prevention and in other legal and regulatory norms in force.
(2) Exercise oversight and supervision of the Solidarity Pension System (SPS) of the granting and payment of the Universal Guarantee administered by the SPI. To this end, the Superintendency shall issue the necessary rules, which shall be binding on all institutions or entities involved in the aforementioned System.
(3) Supervise the SPI with respect to the benefit regimes of the provident funds and the Social Prevention Service, which it administers, with the exception of those referred to Law 16.744. Likewise, supervise the operation of the services that the SPI has subcontracted, when these are related to their line of business in the areas of competence of the Superintendency. For the purposes of the foregoing, it may require the sending of necessary information and documentation or have direct access to the dependencies and files of the service provider.
(4) Ensure compliance with the legislation regarding the process of classification of disability, both for members of the pension system established in LD 3.500 of 1980, to the taxpayers of the pension schemes administered by the SPI, and to the beneficiaries of the solidarity disability pension system.
(5) Coordinate with the institutions that are competent in matters of control of the declaration and payment of the social security contributions of LD 3.500 of 1980.
(6) To issue rules and give instructions of a general nature in the areas of its competence.
(7) Interpret administratively in matters within its competence the laws, regulations and other rules that govern the persons or entities audited.
(8) Ensure that the supervised institutions comply with the laws and regulations that govern them and with the instructions issued by the Superintendency, without prejudice to the powers that may correspond to other oversight bodies and the Office of the Comptroller General of the Republic.
(9) Carry out the technical and actuarial studies necessary for the exercise of its powers.
(10) Apply sanctions to its auditees for infractions of the legal or regulatory provisions that regulate them.
(11) Constitute and administer the Registry of Social Security Advisors.

(12) Advise the MLSP in the conclusion and execution of international agreements relating to social security matters, acting as a liaison body for them.
(13) Issue instructions to the Social Security Institute regarding the Social Security Data Information System.

§6. Social Prevention Institute

48. Law 20.255 created the SPI, a decentralized public service with legal personality and its own assets, under the supervision of the President of the Republic through the MLSP. Its purpose is, in particular, the administration of the solidarity pension system and the pension schemes administered by the Social Prevention Standardization Institute.

All the functions and attributions of the Social Prevention Standardization Institute, created by Law 3.502 of 1980, are transferred to the SPI, with the exception of those referred to Law 16.744. SPI will be considered, for all purposes, successor and legal continuator of the Institute of Social Security Standardization Institute, with all its rights, obligations, functions and attributions.

The SPI has the following functions and powers:

(1) Administer the solidarity pension system, grant the benefits it contemplates, cease or modify them.
(2) Administer the child bonuses for women established in Title III of Law 20.255.
(3) Administer the pension subsidy to young workers established in Title III of Law 20.255.
(4) Grant and pay family allowances to independent workers in accordance with the provisions of LD 3.500 of 1980.
(5) Carry out actuarial diagnoses and studies and those related to topics specific to their functions.
(6) Administer the pension systems of the provident funds and the Social Security Service as a legal continuator of the Social Security Standardization Institute, as well as the other benefits granted by said Institute, with the exception of those contemplated in Law 16.744.
(7) To enter into agreements with entities or legal persons of public or private law, whether or not they are for profit, that administer social security benefits so that the Comprehensive Social Security Care Centres can provide services to them. The prices and methods of payment for services shall be fixed by a joint supreme decree issued by the Ministries of Labour and Social Prevention and of Finance.
(8) Make informative publications within the scope of its competence.
(9) Conclude agreements with public and private organizations to carry out support tasks in the processing and information regarding the benefits of the Solidarity System.
(10) To grant UGPs, modify them, suspend them or cease them.
(11) Conclude agreements with public and private organizations to carry out support tasks in the processing, information and payment regarding the UGP.

The higher management and administration of the SPI is the responsibility of a National Director, who shall be the senior head of the service and shall have the authority, powers and duties inherent in that capacity.

49. Officials of this Institute must respect the confidentiality of the information to which they have access. Likewise, it is absolutely forbidden to offer or grant users under any circumstances other services than those indicated in the law, either directly or indirectly, being especially prohibited from suggesting a certain type of pension or recommending them to a Pension Fund Administrator (PFA) or Insurance Company that offers life annuities. Any violation of this rule will constitute a serious offence for the purposes of establishing its administrative responsibility, without prejudice, to the other sanctions that proceed in accordance with the law.

50. Comprehensive Social Security Care Centres of the SPI. The SPI is made up of a network of nationwide Comprehensive Social Prevention Care Centres, with the aim of providing information and processing services in social security matters to users of the pension system, facilitating the exercise of their rights.

The Comprehensive Social Prevention Care Centres have the following functions and attributions:

(1) Receive applications for old-age pensions for reaching the legal age, disability and survival submitted by members and beneficiaries of the Pension System established in LD 3.500 of 1980 and send them to the corresponding PFA for processing.
(2) Accept for processing the applications for granting the benefits granted by the SPI and inform of their granting, modification or cessation.
(3) Inform and respond to queries regarding the operation of the Pension System established in LD 3,500 of 1980, the granting and payment of UGPs and the Solidarity Pension System established in Law 20.255. Likewise, the Comprehensive Social Prevention Care Centres are authorized to receive and remit to the corresponding FPA for processing the claims presented by the affiliates or their beneficiaries of a survivor's pension.
(4) Issue certifications related to the regimes administered by the SPI and the benefits it grants.

By virtue of the agreements that the SPI concludes with entities or legal persons that administer social security benefits, the Comprehensive Social Prevention Care Centres may only carry out one or more of the following activities:

(1) Receive the applications for the benefits that said entities or legal entities grant and send them to the corresponding one.
(2) Issue the corresponding certifications to be made to said entities or legal entities.
(3) Pay the benefits granted by such entities or legal entities.
(4) Receive claims submitted by users regarding such entities or legal entities and send them for processing.

§7. Institute of Occupational Safety

51. In accordance with the provisions of Law 16.744 and its amendments, which establishes rules on occupational accidents and diseases, the administration of social insurance against risks of labour accidents and occupational diseases – in the form and conditions established in said law – all employers will be understood to be affiliated to the IOS, with respect to all its workers, unless they join a mutual society of employers.

Consequently, the administration of the insurance will be in charge of the Institute of Occupational Security (IOS) or of the mutual societies of employers, as appropriate, hereinafter referred to as the administrative bodies.

The IOS will administer this insurance, including the realization of activities to prevent risks of accidents at work and occupational diseases, with respect to the employing entities affiliated with it, their workers and the corresponding self-employed workers.

The IOS may contract the granting of medical benefits with health services, employers' mutual societies or other public or private health establishments.

For the health services referred to in Article 16 of DFL 1 (2005) of the MH, and for the experimental health facilities established by DFL 29, 30 and 31 (2000), all of the MH, it shall be mandatory to agree to the granting and provide such benefits when requested by the IOS, subject to the payment of rates established according to the tariffs in force.

Care agreements concluded by the IOS with public and private bodies shall be subject to the general contracting rules of the State and to the modalities, conditions and tariffs indicated in a regulation issued by the MLSP, signed by the Ministers of Health and Finance.

§8. Ergonomic National Commission

52. Law 19.404 (1995) modified LD 3.500 (1980) and established additional rules on OAPs, taking into account the performance of heavy work. Such types of work are defined as those whose execution accelerates the physical, intellectual, or psychological erosion in the majority of workers performing those jobs, thus causing ageing even though they do not constitute an occupational disease.

The law also ruled that the determination of heavy work and factors to be taken into account for that purpose will be totally applied and weighed by the Ergonomic National Commission (ENC) in relation to workers affiliated with the pension system created by LD 3.500 and to those affiliated to pension systems administered by the old Institute of Social Security Standardization Institute.

53. The Ergonomics National Commission is composed of: (i) a surgeon specializing in occupational medicine, who will chair it; (ii) a surgeon specializing in traumatology and orthopaedics; (iii) a civil engineer expert in occupational risk prevention; (iv) a civil engineer expert in industrial hygiene; (v) a university professional expert in ergonometry; (vi) a worker appointed by the most representative trade union centre in the country, who is or has been a member of a Joint Health and Safety Committee, and (vii) an employer appointed by the most representative employers' organization in the country, who is or has been a member of a Joint Health and Safety Committee.

For the purposes of applying old-age pension reductions and overpayments, the ENC must draw up – taking into account their physical, environmental, organizational and mental burden – a list of jobs classified as heavy and another with those that have been refused such quality. The Commission acts ex officio or at the request of the worker concerned, the employer or the respective trade union.

Against the resolutions issued by the aforementioned Commission, the employer or affected workers may complain within thirty working days before the Appeals Commission, which will be composed of three members who must have one of the professions and specialities required to integrate the National Ergonomic Commission. The period mentioned in the previous paragraph shall be counted from the notification of the corresponding resolution.

Both Commissions are financed with fiscal resources and their members are entitled to receive fees for their performance, with the exception of the indicated employers' representative. The members of the National Ergonomic Commission, excluding trade unions and employers representatives, and those of the Appeals Commission, are appointed by the Superintendent of Pensions, who will select them from a Public Registry kept by this Superintendency for these purposes and in the manner determined by the Regulations. The President of the ENC is appointed by the Minister of Labour and Social Prevention on the proposal of the Superintendent of Pensions.

The SOP shall supervise the National Ergonomic Commission and the Appeals Commission.

§9. Social Prevention Advisory Council

54. Law 20.255 (2008) – amended by Law 21.419 (2022) – created the Social Prevention Advisory Council, which is responsible for advising the Ministers of Labour and Social Prevention and of Finance on matters related to the Solidarity Pension System and the UGP. Its main functions are:

(1) Advise in a timely manner on the proposals for legal modifications of the parameters of the solidarity pension system and the UGP.
(2) Advise in a timely manner on the proposals for modifications to the regulations issued on these matters. When the Council issues an opinion on these proposals – or on those indicated above – the Ministers of Labour and Social Prevention and of Finance shall transmit this document to the National Congress in due course, together with the response they have formulated. In any case, if the opinion of the Council is not issued within the period indicated in the regulations, the corresponding bill may be presented or the regulatory modification made without considering it.
(3) Advise on the methods, criteria and general parameters that affect the granting, review, suspension and extinction of benefits contained in such regulations.

(4) To issue an annual report that shall be sent to the Ministers of Labour and Social Prevention and of Finance and to the National Congress, containing their opinion on the operation of the corresponding regulations. The opinions, pronouncements, studies and proposals of the Council are not binding and will be made available to the public within thirty calendar days after they have been delivered to the relevant authorities.

The Council is convened by its President at the request of any of the Ministers indicated or of two of its members. In any case, the Council may agree to the holding of periodic meetings and their frequency.

The Ministers of Labour and Social Prevention and of Finance have the right to be heard by the Council whenever they deem it appropriate and may attend its meetings.

The Undersecretariat for Social Prevention shall make available to the Council the background and technical studies complementary to those provided in accordance with the preceding paragraph, which it may require for the proper performance of its functions. In addition, the Council is empowered to request from public bodies the information necessary for the performance of their functions, and they will be obliged to deliver it whenever it is available.

The Council must keep the information it receives from such bodies confidential. It will access the data only in an unnamed way. Likewise, the information it receives must be of an indeterminate and indeterminable nature with respect to personal data.

The Council may also request information from agencies not under the MLSP, such as the Financial Market Commission, the Budget Directorate, the Ministry of Social Development and Family and the National Institute of Statistics. In the latter case, strict compliance must also be given to the statistical secrecy enshrined in Article 29 of Law 17.374. Anyone who violates the obligation of confidentiality established in the preceding paragraph shall be punished with the penalty of minor imprisonment in any of its degrees, without prejudice to administrative responsibility, when appropriate. The Chairman of the Board must implement a policy of treatment and use of confidential information.

For the performance of its functions, the Board may invite experts to testify and present their opinion to the directors on the matters that they require. These hearings may be public, as defined by the Council itself.

55. The Council has a Secretary appointed by it and remunerated by the Undersecretariat of Social Prevention (USSP). The Secretary shall coordinate the functioning of the Council, carrying out the tasks defined for this purpose in the regulations. In addition, the Undersecretariat for Social Security should provide the administrative support necessary for the proper functioning of the Council.

The Council is composed of:

(1) A Councillor appointed by the President of the Republic, who shall preside over it.
(2) Four Councillors appointed by the President of the Republic and ratified by the Senate, who shall hold office for six years.

The President of the Republic shall appoint as councillors persons with recognized prestige for their experience and knowledge in the field of Economics, Law and disciplines related to social security and the labour market.

The councillors appointed for ratification by the Senate shall be elected in pairs alternately every three years. These must be ratified by four-sevenths of the senators in office. For this purpose, the President shall make a proposal comprising two directors. The Senate must decide on the proposal as a unit.

The performance of the duties of councillors shall be incompatible with the exercise of single-person managerial positions in the management bodies of political parties. The members of the Board may not be managers, administrators or directors of a PFA, a Life Insurance Company (LIC), or any of the entities of the business group to which they belong while serving on the Council.

The Council takes its decisions for the majority of its members, and in the event of a tie, its President decides. The minimum quorum for the meeting shall be three members with voting rights.

The regulations, issued through the MLSP, also signed by the Minister of Finance, establish the rules necessary for the functioning of the Council and for the proper execution of the functions entrusted to it.

The members of the Council receive a tax charge allowance in pesos equivalent to 17 MTU for each session they attend, with a maximum of 51 MTU for each calendar month.

Councillors appointed with Senate ratification are irremovable. In the event that any of them ceases for any reason, a new director must be appointed by means of a unipersonal proposal of the President of the Republic for the remaining period.

The following are grounds for dismissal of councillors ratified by the Senate:

(1) The expiry of the period for which he was appointed.
(2) The resignation accepted by the President of the Republic.
(3) The survival of any cause of disability or incompatibility. A councillor who acquires a capacity that disqualifies him from performing the function shall automatically cease to hold office.
(4) Serious failure to comply with obligations as a councillor. Unjustified absence from three consecutive sessions shall be serious misconduct, without prejudice to others, so qualified by the Senate, by four-sevenths of its members in office, at the proposal of the President of the Republic.

§10. Commission of Users of the Pension System

56. Law 20.250 created the Commission of Users of the Pension System, composed of a representative of the workers, one of the pensioners, one of the public institutions, one of the private entities of the pension system and a university academic, who will chair it.

Its function is to inform the USSP and other public bodies in the sector about the evaluations that their representatives carry out on the functioning of the pension system and to propose education and dissemination strategies for said system.

A regulation, issued through the MLSP and also signed by the Minister of Finance, regulates the functions and composition of the Users Commission and the manner in which its members are appointed, its regime of prohibitions and disqualifications, grounds for cessation of their posts and the other rules necessary for its proper functioning. The members of the Commission receive a daily subsistence allowance equivalent to an amount of 6 UF for each session, with a maximum monthly limit of 12 UF.

§11. Social Security Institution for the Armed Forces

57. CAPREDENA is in charge of social security programmes for armed forces personnel. Its main functions are related to: (i) the payment of retirement and survivors' pensions, indemnities for years of service, and funeral aids; (ii) the payment of family allowances; (iii) access to health benefits, including subsidies; and (iv) access to social assistance benefits, particularly through its Social Assistant Department and the Solidarity Fund.

The right to receive these benefits is established by the Ministry of Defence, with the intervention of Personnel Divisions of each armed forces branch.

§12. Social Security Directorate for the Police Force

58. As a result of the creation of the public police entity called '*Carabineros de Chile*', in 1927, the Police Forces Social Security and Social Welfare Organization and the Police Section of the Army and Navy Pension Organization were merged, giving rise to the Chilean Police Social Security Organization (CAPRECA). Later, the personnel of the Criminal Investigation Service, the Identification Service, and the Penitentiary Services were incorporated into CAPRECA.

In 1974, CAPRECA's functions and affiliated personnel were transferred to the Department of Police Social Security of the Undersecretary of Chilean Police in the Ministry of Defence. Two years later, it received its actual denomination: Directorate for the Police Force (DIPRECA).

Its main functions are: (i) to collect and administer funds assigned to DIPRECA and (ii) to provide social security services and benefits, such as retirement pensions, medical and dental care, hospitalization, housing loans, and subsidies.

§13. Ministry of Health and Related Institutions

59. The institutions with primary responsibility for the social security system are: (i) the Ministry of Health; (ii) the Undersecretariat of Public Health; (iii) the Undersecretariat of Social Networks; (iv) the Superintendency of Health; (v) the Regional Ministerial Secretariats of Health; (vi) Health Services; (vii) the National Health Fund; (viii) the Institute of Public Health; and (ix) the Central Supply of the National System of Health Services (CENABAST).

§14. Ministry of Health

60. The MH will be responsible for formulating and monitoring health policies. Among others, it has the following functions:

(1) Exercise the stewardship of the health sector.
(2) To issue general rules on technical, administrative and financial matters to which the agencies and entities of the system must adhere to carry out activities of prevention, promotion, support, protection and recovery of health and rehabilitation of sick people.
(3) Ensure due compliance with health standards in matters such as hygiene and safety of the environment and workplaces without prejudice to the competence that the law assigns to other agencies.
(4) Formulate, evaluate and update the Universal Access System with Explicit Guarantees ('AUGE System').
(5) Establish the minimum standards to be met by institutional health providers, such as hospitals, clinics, doctors' offices and medical centres, in order to ensure that the services reach the quality required for the safety of the users.
(6) Establish an accreditation system for institutional providers authorized to operate.
(7) Establish a system of certification of specialties and subspecialties of natural persons who grant health benefits legally authorized to exercise their respective professions.

The Ministry is composed of the Minister, the Undersecretariat of Public Health, the Undersecretariat of Assistance Networks and the Regional Ministerial Secretariats.

§15. Undersecretariat of Public Health

61. In addition to advising and collaborating directly with the Minister, the Undersecretary must: (i) coordinate the actions of the FONASA and the Institute of Public Health; (ii) administer the finances provided by the State for public health policies; and (iii) execute directly public health activities with the participation of Regional Ministerial Secretariats.

§16. Undersecretariat of Assistance Networks

62. It is in charge of the articulation and development of the network for the integral care of people and the regulation of the provision of health actions. To this end: (i) proposes to the Minister rules, plans and programmes; (ii) ensures compliance and coordinates its execution by the agencies that make up the health system; and (iii) participates in the selection, appointment and development of the professional staff of the system. In addition, in the absence of the Undersecretary for Public Health, it subrogates the Minister of Health.

§17. SUPERINTENDENCY OF HEALTH

63. The Superintendency of Health is a functionally decentralized body with its own legal personality and assets, which is related to the President of the Republic through the MH. Its domicile is the city of Santiago, without prejudice to the regional offices established by the Superintendent in other cities of the country. For all legal purposes, it is a legal continuation of the Superintendency of Social Prevention Health Institutions (ISAPRE), created by Law 18.933. It is made up of the Intendency of Health Pension Funds and Insurance and the Intendency of Health Providers.

With regard to ISAPRE, the Superintendency has, *inter alia*, the following functions and attributions:

(1) Register Social Prevention Health Institutions.
(2) Interpret administratively, in matters of its competence, the laws, regulations and other rules that govern the persons or entities supervised, and issue instructions of general application and promulgate orders for their application and compliance.
(3) Supervise these institutions in the legal and financial aspects for the due fulfilment of the obligations established by law and those emanating from health contracts. The Superintendency shall issue instructions regulating the timing and manner in which the balance sheets and other financial statements shall be presented.
(4) Ensure that the supervised institutions comply with the laws and regulations that govern them and with the instructions issued by the Superintendency without prejudice to the powers that may correspond to other oversight agencies.
(5) To require that these institutions comply with the constitution and maintenance of the minimum guarantee and assets required by law.
(6) Issue instructions and determine the general accounting principles according to which the institutions must comply with the guarantee and requirements for the constitution and maintenance of the minimum patrimony.
(7) To issue general instructions to such institutions to publish in the media and, with the periodicity indicated by the Superintendency, sufficient and timely information of interest to the public, on their legal, economic, and financial situation. Such publications shall be made at least once a year.
(8) Issue general instructions that allow greater clarity in the stipulations of health contracts in order to facilitate their correct interpretation and monitor compliance.
(9) Ensure that the practical application of contracts concluded between health providers and Social Security Health Institutions does not affect the benefits to which the affiliate or its beneficiaries are entitled.
(10) To request from the State agencies the reports it deems necessary for the fulfilment of its functions.
(11) Prepare and disseminate indexes, statistics and studies related to institutions and the private health system.

(12) Require providers, whether public or private, to deliver the medical certification necessary to decide on the pertinence of benefits. The Superintendency must adopt the necessary measures to maintain the confidentiality of the clinical record. Persons who commit falsehood in the certification of illnesses, injuries, state of health on the dates of diagnosis or in benefits granted shall be punished with the penalties provided for in Article 202 of the Penal Code.
(13) Inspect all operations, assets, books, accounts, files and documents of the audited institutions and request from them or their administrators, advisors, external auditors or staff the background and explanations it deems necessary for its information. It may request the execution and presentation of balance sheets and financial statements on such dates as it deems appropriate. Likewise, it may request the delivery of any document or book or antecedent that is necessary for inspection purposes, without altering the normal development of the activities of the affected party. Except for the exceptions authorized by the Superintendency, all books, files and documents of the supervised entities must be permanently available for examination at the principal place of their businesses. In addition, it may summon to testify the representatives, administrators, advisers, external auditors and dependents of the entities or persons of the audited entities whose knowledge it deems necessary for the performance of its tasks.
(14) Impose sanctions.

§18. Regional Ministerial Secretariats of Health

64. In each of the regions into which the country is administratively divided, there is a Regional Ministerial Secretariat for Health headed by a Regional Ministerial Secretary.

Among other functions, these Secretaries are responsible for:

(1) Ensure compliance with the rules, plans, programmes and national health policies established by the authority. Likewise, adapt the plans and programmes to the reality of the respective region within the framework established for this purpose by the national authorities.
(2) Execute the corresponding actions for the protection of the health of the population from the risks produced by the environment and for the conservation, improvement and recovery of the basic elements of the environment that affect it, ensuring due compliance with the provisions of the Health Code and the regulations, resolutions and instructions on the subject.
(3) Ensure the proper execution of public health actions by the entities that make up the Care Network of each Health Service and, where appropriate, execute them directly or through the conclusion of agreements with the persons or entities that correspond.
(4) Collaborate, at the request of any public body in the health sector, in the implementation of procedures for receiving complaints. The procedures must be agreed upon with the aforementioned bodies.

(5) Evaluate the level of compliance with the goals set for municipal health management entities and their establishments.

§19. HEALTH SERVICES

65. They are the bodies created for the articulation, management and development of the corresponding assistance network and the execution of the integrated actions of promotion, protection and recovery of the health and rehabilitation of sick people.

These services are functionally decentralized state bodies with legal personality and their own assets. They depend on the MH, which supervises them and whose policies, regulations and general plans must be subject in the exercise of their activities. These Services are the legal continuators of the National Health Service and the National Medical Service for Employees.

§20. NATIONAL HEALTH FUND

66. FONASA is a public service, functionally decentralized, endowed with legal personality and its own assets. It depends on the MH for the purpose of submitting to the supervision of the latter in its operation and to whose policies, norms and general plans it must submit in the exercise of its activities.

Its headquarters is the city of Santiago, without prejudice to the offices that may be established in the different regions of the country. Its functions are:

(1) Collect, administer and distribute the resources indicated in the current legislation.
(2) Finance, in whole or in part, the benefits granted to the beneficiaries, in any of its modalities, by organizations, entities and persons who belong or not to the System or depend on it, whether public or private. Likewise, to finance, in the same terms, the acquisition of the equipment, instruments, implements and other elements of infrastructure required by the public establishments that make up the System. The financing of benefits may include the cost of replacing the capital. The Budget Law shall contemplate, in the budget of the FONASA, the resources that it may allocate to the financing of the agreements it enters into with agencies, entities and persons that do not belong to the National Health Services System, private and/or public, to provide certain benefits.
(3) Collaborate with the MH in the compatibility and financial consolidation of the budget projects of the Health Services and other agencies linked to that Secretariat of State with the overall Health budget.
(4) To know and resolve, in accordance with current regulations, the claims that its beneficiaries make, in accordance with the procedures established by the MH, without prejudice to the competence of other public bodies.

§21. Public Health Institute

67. The Institute of Public Health is a functionally decentralized public service endowed with legal personality and its own assets. It depends on the MH, is subject to the supervision of the latter in its operation and to whose policies, regulations and general plans must be subject in the exercise of its activities. The Public Health Institute (PHI) serves as a national laboratory and reference in the fields of microbiology, immunology, bromatology, pharmacology, imaging, radiotherapy, blood banks, clinical laboratory, environmental pollution and occupational health and performs the other functions assigned to it by law.

The PHI is the legal successor of the National Health Service in relation to the Bacteriological Institute of Chile and the National Institute of Occupational Health for patrimonial purposes. Its headquarters will be the city of Santiago, without prejudice to the centres that may constitute in the Regions.

It is responsible for:

(1) Exercising quality control of medicines, foods for medical use and other products subject to sanitary control; It controls the conditions of internment, export, manufacture, distribution, sale and use in any capacity, as well as the advertising and promotion of the same products.
(2) Controlling narcotic drugs and pharmaceutical products that cause dependence and other psychotropic substances likely to have a similar effect with respect to their importation and their licit use in the process of manufacturing pharmaceutical products.
(3) Developing biological products according to programmes approved by the MH.
(4) Providing assistance and advisory services to other agencies and public or private entities.
(5) Promoting and carrying out applied research work related to its functions.
(6) Developing training activities in the areas of its competence.
(7) Supervising compliance with quality standards and accreditation of the laboratories indicated in the law.

§22. Central Supply of the National System of Health Services

68. This Central is a functionally decentralized public service endowed with legal personality and its own assets. It depends on the MH for the purpose of submitting to the supervision of the latter in its operation and to whose policies, norms and general plans it must abide in the exercise of its activities.

CENABAST provides medicines, instruments and other elements or supplies that may be required by the agencies, entities, establishments and persons who are members or attached to the system. These functions are without prejudice to the power of the Health Services and other agencies or entities of the System to acquire such elements from other providers.

The Central is the legal continuation of the National Health Service in relation to the central supply of said service for patrimonial purposes.

Its headquarters is the city of Santiago, without prejudice to the offices that may be established in the regions of the country.

Its purpose is to provide medicines, pharmaceutical and laboratory items, surgical material, instruments and other elements and supplies that are required for the exercise of health actions.

To this end, CENABAST can:

(1) Acquire, store, distribute, transport, lease and sell these elements to the agencies, entities, establishments and persons that are part of the System, with the sole purpose of complying with the plans and programmes of the Ministry and other public agencies, whose institutional purposes include the realization of health actions in favour of their beneficiaries. The Central will be obliged to publish and keep updated on the prices of all the products it provides and the discounts it applies in the sale by volume.
(2) Maintain in stock an adequate amount of elements of the same nature, determined by the MH, necessary for the efficient fulfilment of its programmes.
(3) To meet the needs in the matters of its competence, the Supreme Government entrusts it to satisfy in case of national or international emergencies.
(4) Provide technical advisory services to other agencies and entities of the System.

Chapter 2. Private Institutions

69. In the following areas of the Chilean system exist private institutions: (i) family allowances compensations (CCAF); (ii) labour accidents and occupational diseases (mutuals and delegated administrators); (iii) unemployment (UFA); (iv) pensions (PFA); and (v) health care (ISAPRES)

§1. Institutions to Compensate Family Allowances

70. These institutions (in Spanish known as '*Cajas de Compensación de Asignación Familiar*') are non-profit organizations entrusted to administer services and benefits recognized to their affiliates, such as family allowances, subsidies for incapacity to work, and labour disabilities.

Affiliation and dissociation to a CCAF have to be agreed upon by an enterprise and its workers. The pertinent workers' agreement has to be decided by an absolute majority of the total number of workers in a meeting specially called for that purpose.

Its activities are mainly financed through commissions charged over administered funds.

Representatives of employers and employees participate in the administration of each CCAF.

§2. Mutuals and Delegated Administrators

71. Their creation is approved by the President of the Republic, who gives them the pertinent legal personality if they meet the following requisites:

(1) They have a total number of workers occupied in permanent work at members' enterprises that amounts to no less than 20,000.
(2) They have, directly or in association with another Mutual, appropriate medical services, including specialized services for rehabilitation.
(3) They carry out permanent activities directed to the prevention of labour accidents and occupational diseases.
(4) They are not directly or indirectly administered by institutions with profit aims.
(5) Their members have a solidarity responsibility for these Mutuals' obligations.

Enterprise membership to a Mutual covers all its workers. Members' enterprises are mutually binding obligations of the corresponding Mutual. Their membership and its termination are regulated by law.

Mutuals' administration wholly covers all insurance activities: prevention, medical care, rehabilitation, and monetary benefits.

Each Mutual is administered by a bipartite directory composed of three employer representatives and three worker representatives and their respective substitutes.

If the enterprise puts into action appropriate prevention steps with a relevant diminution of labour risks, additional or overcharged contributions can be reduced or eliminated. In this way, the accomplishment of this insurance objective is stimulated and promoted.

§3. Unemployment Insurance Administration

72. The administration of the unemployment regime is in charge of a company of Chilean nationality or agency of a foreigner incorporated in Chile, which will have as its exclusive object to administer two funds that will be called Unemployment Fund and Solidarity Unemployment Fund and grant and administer the benefits and insurance assistances established by Law 20.328 (2009), which amended Law 19.728 (2001), which established unemployment insurance and amended other legal regulations.

The Unemployment Fund Administrator (UFA) company must provide the following services:

(1) Collection of contributions and the payment regulated in Article 5 of Law 20.328.
(2) Payment in the Solidarity Unemployment Fund and in the respective Individual Accounts for Unemployment.
(3) Update of those accounts.
(4) Investment of resources.
(5) Payment of benefits.

The administration company will be of indefinite duration and will subsist until the expiration of the term of the management contract. Once the former is dissolved, the provisions on the liquidation of public limited companies in Law 18.046 (1981) will apply.

The administration company will be entitled to a remuneration established, on the basis of commissions charged to the contributors, which will be deducted from the contributions or from the Unemployment Funds. The base value of the aforementioned commissions will be determined in the contract for the provision of the administration service. However, the value of the commissions charged will be established as indicated in Article 42, and only workers who are contributing may be subject to the collection of commissions. These commissions will be exempt from Value Added Tax established in LD 825 (1974).

No natural or legal person that has not been constituted in accordance with the provisions of this law as an Unemployment Fund Administrator may arrogate to itself the quality of such or make use of documents containing names or other words that suggest that the business to which said persons are engaged are those of the UFA.

Offences shall be punishable by minor imprisonment in its minimum degree to minor imprisonment in its medium degree. In any case, if, as a result of these illegal activities, the public suffers harm of any kind, those responsible shall be punished with the penalties established in Article 467 of the Criminal Code.

When, in the opinion of the Superintendency, it can be presumed that there has been an infringement of the provisions of this article, it shall have the same powers of inspection with respect to the alleged offenders as its organic law confers on it with respect to its supervised institutions.

73. The administration service of the Unemployment Funds was awarded through a public tender. The bidding and awarding of the service was governed by the rules established in Law 20.328 and in the respective Bidding Rules that the Ministries of Labour and Social Prevention and of Finance approved by the Supreme Decree. Both Ministries carried out a prequalification process for bidders in order to ensure their technical, economic and financial suitability. They awarded the tender by evaluating the technically acceptable bids, taking into account, among others, the following factors: (i) the commission structure; (ii) the form of readjustment of the commissions; and (iii) the technical qualification for the provision of the service.

74. The minimum capital necessary for the formation of Unemployment Fund Administrator will be the equivalent of UF 20,000, which must be paid in cash and be subscribed and paid at the time the social deed is granted. In addition, that company must permanently maintain assets at least equal to the minimum capital required. If the estate is, in fact, reduced to an amount lower than the minimum required, the Company shall be obliged, whenever this occurs, to complete it within a period of six months. If it fails to do so, it will be declared a serious breach of its obligations under the law.

Investments and debts in companies that are related to the UFA will be excluded from the calculation of the minimum equity required of it.

When a sale of shares of the UFA to a third party or a minority shareholder reaches alone or adds to those already owning more than 10% of the shares of the aforementioned company, the acquirer must request authorization from the Ministries of Labour and Social Prevention and of Finance. The authorization may be denied by resolution based on the ability of the UFA to continue providing the services stipulated in the administration contract. Shares in such a situation and the acquisition of which has not been authorized shall not have voting rights.

The rules of Law 30.328, its regulations, the contract for the administration of the insurance, and additionally LD. 3.500, Law 18.046 and its regulations are applicable to the UFA. In addition, that company is subject to the same rules as those governing PFAs, in particular as regards the acquisition, holding, custody and disposal of financial instruments belonging to unemployment funds, as well as the rules on conflicts of interest. However, the UFA will be exempt from the constitution of reserve requirements and from all the obligations established in Articles 37 to 42 of LD. 3.500.

75. The UFA may enter into contracts for the provision of services with external entities, according to what is established in this regard by the Bidding Rules and the Insurance Administration Contract.

The UFA is overseen, controlled and supervised by the Superintendency of PFAs. In the event of non-compliance with its obligations by the management company, the Superintendency may impose on it the legally established sanctions.

During the term of the contract, the UFA must ensure the continuity of the provision of the service in conditions of absolute normality and in an uninterrupted manner. Failure to comply with this obligation will constitute a serious breach of the obligations of the UFA.

76. The UFA must maintain a database of workers subject to insurance, with the necessary records for the operation of the insurance that will include the general record of worker information, the movements of individual accounts for unemployment and the file of documents. In this regard, it has the responsibility of carrying out the processing of the Database of workers subject to the Insurance, only to fulfil the functions defined in the law and those established by the Superintendency through a general rule. The sole purpose of the Database will be to support the functions of the UFA and for the realization of technical studies by the Superintendency.

For the purposes of Law 29.328 (2021), which modernizes the Labour Directorate, the processing of data of workers subject to insurance is understood to be any operation or complex of operations or technical procedures, automated or not, that allow collecting, storing, recording, organizing, elaborating, selecting, extracting, confronting, interconnecting, dissociating, communicating, assigning, transferring, transmitting or cancelling data or using them in any other way. The Superintendency, by means of a general rule, will establish the necessary mechanisms to guarantee the control and safeguarding of the Database.

Once the administration contract has been terminated for any reason, the UFA that is providing the service must transfer to the new contractor the Database that allows the continuity of the operation of the insurance.

Anyone who, during the period of validity of the administration contract or after it, makes use of the information included in the Database maintained by the UFA for a purpose other than that established in this law shall be punished with the penalties of minor imprisonment in any of its degrees, without prejudice to the administrative sanctions that may apply.

For the development of the technical studies already mentioned, the Superintendency may request the information of the Database that is necessary for the fulfilment of the objectives established therein and in order to exercise control and supervision in the matters of its competence, being able to carry out the processing of personal data that this Base contains.

The staff of the Superintendency must keep absolute confidentiality and secrecy of the information of which it becomes aware in the performance of its functions, without prejudice to the information and certifications that it must provide in accordance with the law.

The SOP and the Directorate of Budgets must carry out an actuarial study every three years to evaluate the sustainability of Unemployment Insurance, especially the Solidarity Unemployment Fund.

Likewise, this study must be carried out each time a modification to the benefits granted by this insurance is proposed, except for the readjustment contemplated in Law 20.328. This study should consider an analysis of the contributions and uses of the Unemployment Funds, differentiated according to whether they are workers with an indefinite contract or with a fixed-term contract or for a specific task, work or service, in both cases considering workers in private homes. The actuarial study shall be public.

77. The UFA must keep separate accounts of the assets of each of the Unemployment Funds. The assets and rights that make up the patrimony of the Unemployment Funds will be unattachable and will be destined only to generate benefits in accordance with the provisions of this law, without prejudice to the provisions of Article 50.

The resources that make up the Unemployment Funds may be delivered as a guarantee to banks and clearing houses for operations with derivative instruments referred to in Article 45 of LD 3.500.

The investments made with resources from the Unemployment Funds and the Solidarity Unemployment Fund will have as their sole objective the obtaining of adequate profitability and security.

Each month that the real profitability of the Unemployment Fund and the Solidarity Unemployment Fund of the last six months exceeds the respective real profitability determined by the Investment Regime of the Unemployment Funds, considering the volatility of the difference between the profitability of the respective fund and its reference portfolio, the commission charged will be the base commission, increased by 10%. In any case, the increase in commission may not exceed 50% of the difference in profitability.

However, in each month in which the real profitability of the Unemployment Fund and the Solidarity Unemployment Fund of the last six months is lower than the respective real profitability determined by the Investment Regime of the Unemployment Funds, considering the volatility of the difference between the profitability of the respective fund and its reference portfolio, the commission charged will be the base commission already referred to, reduced by10%. In any case, the decrease in commission may not exceed 50%of the difference in profitability.

Without prejudice to the foregoing, when the unemployment and solidarity unemployment funds have less than thirty-six months of operation, the calculation of profitability will be carried out considering the period of operation of the Funds, provided that this is greater than twelve months.

The aforementioned calculations shall be made separately for each period of validity of the respective administration contract.

78. The administration contract will be terminated for the following reasons:

(1) Compliance with the term for which it was granted.
(2) Agreement between the Ministries of Labour and Social Welfare and Finance and the Administration Company.
(3) Serious breach of obligations by the UFA.
(4) Insolvency of the Administration Company.
(5) Those stipulated in the Bidding Rules.

The grounds indicated in numerals 1, 2 and 5 will give rise to a new tender for the service by the Ministries of Labour and Social Welfare and of Finance.

The aforementioned invitation to tender must be carried out with the necessary anticipation so that there is continuity between the contracts. The declaration of serious infringement of the obligations of the UFA or its insolvency shall correspond to the Superintendency and must be based on any of the grounds established in Law 20.328, Law 18.046, LD 3.500, the Bidding Rules or the Insurance Administration Contract.

The Ministries of Labour and Social Welfare and of Finance must call for a public tender within sixty days, counted from the declaration of the serious infringement or insolvency, in order to select the new UFA.

If any of the aforementioned situations occur, the ordinary administration of the company will cease, and the Superintendency will appoint a Provisional Administrator, who will have all the powers of the ordinary manager that the law and the statutes indicate to the board of directors, or to whoever takes his place. Said Administrator will have the duties and will be subject to the responsibilities established by Law 18.046. The Interim Administration may last up to one year.

Once the new contract for the administration of the Unemployment Insurance has been awarded, the Provisional Administrator will carry out the transfer of the Unemployment Funds and the records of the individual accounts, after which the precedent UFA will be dissolved by the sole ministry of the law. Subsequently, the liquidation of that administration company will be practised by the Superintendency.

The penalties of minor imprisonment in its medium degree to major imprisonment in its minimum degree, the directors, managers, attorneys-in-fact, liquidators, money desk operators and workers of the UFA, who by reason of their position and using privileged information that dealt with in Title XXI of Law 18.045 (1981), about the stock market:

(1) Perform an act by themselves or through other persons with the aim of obtaining a pecuniary benefit for themselves or for others through any operation or transaction of publicly offered securities.
(2) Disclose inside information relating to the investment decisions of the Unemployment Funds to persons other than those responsible for carrying out the acquisition and disposal of publicly offered securities for the account of or on behalf of the Funds.

The same penalty shall be suffered by the employees of the UFA who, being in charge of the administration of the portfolio and, in particular, of the decisions of acquisition, maintenance and disposal of instruments for the Unemployment Funds, exercise by themselves or through other persons, simultaneously the function of administration of other investment portfolios and who, having the same prohibition, violate any of the prohibitions set forth in Article 154 of LD 3.500.

§4. PENSION FUND ADMINISTRATORS

79. The Pension Fund Administrators (PFA – in Spanish called AFP) are companies whose exclusive purpose is to administer pension funds, grant and administer the benefits and insure assistances established by LD. 3.500 and its amendments. The PFA are obliged to maintain at least one Agency or Office at national level dedicated to the attention of the public.

The PFA collect the corresponding contributions and deposits from their members, pay them into their respective individual capitalization accounts and voluntary savings accounts, as appropriate, and invest these resources in accordance with the provisions of this law.

PFAs whose assets are equal to or greater than 20.000 UF may provide other PFA the aforementioned services in accordance with the instructions pointed out by the PFA that receives these services. They cannot include the investment of the pension resources of other PFA.

Likewise, the AFPs may form subsidiary companies that complement their business, subject to authorization of their existence issued by the Superintendent, provided that they provide services to natural or legal persons operating abroad or that invest in PFA or in companies whose business is related to social security matters, incorporated in other countries. When granting the requested authorization, the Superintendency shall exclusively ensure that the purpose of the subsidiary does not prejudice or impair the proper functioning of the PFA.

Subsidiary companies are subject to the supervision of the Superintendency with respect to compliance with the requirements established by law. For these purposes, the shareholder PFA must periodically provide the Superintendency, and in an extraordinary manner when it so requires, information on the subsidiary company and its investments without prejudice to the obligations to provide information imposed on these companies by other laws.

In turn, the PFA may set up subsidiary public limited companies in the country, subject to authorization of existence granted by the Superintendent, whose exclusive purpose is the administration of portfolios of social security resources of that or other PFA.

With respect to the aforementioned applications for authorization of existence, the Superintendency must decide within thirty days of their presentation. This period shall be suspended if the Superintendency, by written communication, requires additional information, modification or rectification of it and its background. The time limit shall resume only when the applicant has complied with the formalities in writing. In any case, the Superintendency must issue its pronouncement within a maximum period of six months. The decision refusing authorization must be well-founded. Once the defects have been corrected or the observations made have been addressed, the Superintendency must rule on the application, it being understood that it authorizes the existence of the subsidiary company if it does not do so within the aforementioned period of six months.

Under no circumstances may the PFA, their directors and dependents offer or grant to members or beneficiaries other pensions, benefits or benefits than those indicated in the law, either directly or indirectly, or even free of charge or in any other way. Notwithstanding the foregoing, these entities may process for their affiliates the obtaining of the Recognition Bonus.

80. The PFA may entrust the function of portfolio management of the resources that make up the Pension Fund to public limited companies of indefinite duration, whose exclusive purpose is the administration of the portfolio of social security resources, which must comply with the requirements already indicated. The cost of subcontracting will always be borne by the PFA.

These companies must prove a minimum capital of 20.000 UF, which must be subscribed and paid at the time the social deed is granted. In addition, they must permanently maintain assets at least equal to the minimum capital required. If its assets are, in fact, reduced to less than the minimum required, it is obliged, whenever this occurs, to complete it within six months. If it does not do so, the authorization of existence will be revoked, and it will be liquidated by the Superintendency of PFAs. Likewise, the Superintendency may revoke said authorization for serious infringement of law, regulations or the rules that are applicable to these companies.

In these companies, there will be separation of assets between their own resources and those administered. The assets and rights that make up the assets of the Funds managed by these companies are not attachable, except in cases legally authorized.

These companies are subject to the supervision of the Superintendency of Pension, which has the same powers with respect to them as it has in relation to the PFA.

81. The minimum capital necessary for the formation of a PFA will be the equivalent of 5.000 UF, which must be subscribed and paid at the time the social deed is granted. If the initial capital exceeds the minimum, the excess must be paid within a maximum period of two years, counted from the date of the resolution authorizing the existence and approving the statutes of the company.

The minimum capital required increases in relation to the number of affiliates who are incorporated into it. The required assets will be 10.000 UF when completing 5.000 affiliates, 15.000 UF when completing 7.500 affiliates, and 20.000 UF when completing the 10.000 affiliates.

If the assets of the PFA are, in fact, reduced to an amount lower than the minimum required, it will be obliged, each time this happens, to complete it within a period of six months. If it does not do so, the authorization of existence will be revoked, and the company will be liquidated.

82. The founding shareholders of a PFA must meet the following requirements:

(1) Have individually or jointly a consolidated net worth equivalent to the projected investment, and when it is reduced to a lower figure, report this fact in a timely manner.
(2) Not have engaged in serious or repeated conduct that may jeopardize the stability of the Administrator they intend to constitute or the security of the Funds they manage.

(3) Not to have taken part in actions, negotiations or legal acts of any kind, contrary to the laws, regulations or sound banking, financial or commercial practices which prevail in Chile or abroad.
(4) Not be in any of the following situations: (i) that it is a debtor subject to a current liquidation bankruptcy procedure; (ii) that in the last fifteen years, counted from the date of request for the authorization of the Administrator, has been a director, manager, main executive or majority shareholder directly or through third parties, of a banking entity, an insurance company of the second group or an Administrator that has been declared in forced liquidation or bankruptcy liquidation proceedings, as appropriate, or subject to provisional administration, in respect of which the Treasury or the Central Bank of Chile have incurred considerable losses. The participation of a person for a period of less than one year shall not be considered for these purposes; (iii) that registers protests of unclarified documents in the last five years in a considerable number or quantity; (iv) who has been convicted or is under indictment for any of the following offences: (a) against property or against public faith, or (b) against administrative probity, national security, tax crimes, customs, and those contemplated in the laws against terrorism and money concealing or laundering.
(5) A person who has been sentenced to an afflictive penalty or disqualification from holding public appointments or office.
(6) That any of the following measures have been applied, directly or through legal persons, provided that the time limits for claiming have expired or the appeals filed against them have been rejected by an enforceable judgment: (i) that its forced liquidation has been declared or its commercial activities have been placed under provisional administration, or (ii) its authorization to operate or exist or its registration in any registry required to operate or to make a public offering of securities, as applicable, has been cancelled for violation of law.

In the case of a legal entity, the requirements established shall be considered with respect to its controllers, partners or majority shareholders, directors, administrators, managers, and principal executives at the date of the request.

Any advertising or promotion of their activities carried out by the PFA must provide the public with the minimum information about their capital, investments, profitability, commissions and offices, agencies or branches, in accordance with the general rules established by the Superintendence of Pension, which must ensure that it is aimed at providing information that does not lead to misunderstanding or confusion, either in terms of the institutional or patrimonial reality or the purposes and foundations of the System.

83. The PFA must keep in their offices, in a place easily accessible to the public, an available extract containing the following information:

(1) Background of the Institution: (i) corporate name; (ii) domicile; (iii) date of deed of incorporation, resolution authorizing its existence, and registration in the Commercial Registry; (iv) board of directors and general manager; and (v) agencies and branches.

(2) General Balance Sheet for the last fiscal year and the statements of situation determined by the Superintendence of Pension. In any case, they must keep the last two states of situation available to the public.
(3) Amount of capital, pension funds, profitability fluctuation reserves and reserve requirements.
(4) Value of the contributions of each of the Pension Funds.
(5) Cost of commissions to be charged.
(6) Composition of the investment portfolio of each of the Pension Funds.
(7) Additional contribution percentage of each type of Fund. The part that is destined to the financing of the Administrator and that which is destined to the payment of the insurance must be reported separately.

A member may transfer the value of his contributions to another AFP, prior notice given to the one who is incorporated and to his/her employer, where applicable, at least thirty days in advance of the date on which the contributions of the month in which the notice is given. In the case of pensioned members, the notice must be given at least thirty days in advance of the date on which the pensions are due for the month following the month in which the notice is given. The transfer of the values corresponding to contributions owed by the employer and not paid on the date of the transfer referred to in the preceding paragraph shall be made as soon as these have been received by the Administrator of origin.

84. The PFA shall be liable for the damages caused to the affiliates in their individual capitalization accounts as a result of the timely non-fulfilment of their obligations, as well as for the instructions given by the affiliate to them in the exercise of the rights established by this law. Once the default has been proven and there has been a loss of profitability in any of the affiliate's accounts, provided that the Administrator does not make the corresponding compensation, the Superintendency may order the restitution of said loss to the respective individual capitalization account, according to the procedure established by a general rule. In the latter case, the PFA may claim against such determination.

Once the Administrator is dissolved for any reason, the liquidation of the Pension Funds and the Company will be carried out by the Superintendence of Pension, which will be invested with all the necessary powers for the proper realization of the assets of each of the Funds. During the process of liquidation of the Funds, the FPA may continue with the operations indicated in this law with respect to affiliates that have not been incorporated into another entity, even if the company is in liquidation.

During the liquidation process, the liquidator shall transfer the fees representing the balance of the personal accounts of each member to the FPA, to which each of them is incorporated. The instruments transferred will be excluded, for a period of six months, from the calculation of the minimum return that will be made for the FPA who receives the instruments.

The obligation of the State shall subsist until such time as the transfer takes place.

However, if the dissolution occurs due to the merger of two or more Administrators, neither they nor their respective Pension Funds will be liquidated. In the event of a merger, the authorization of the Superintendency of Pension must be published in the Official Gazette within fifteen days of its granting and will have the effect of merging the companies and the respective pension funds sixty days after the publication is verified, without prejudice to compliance with the other procedures established by law.

The publication must also contain the cost of additional commissions and contributions established by the entity resulting from the merger.

The merger may not reduce the balance in the individual capitalization account and, if applicable, the voluntary savings account of the affiliates.

§5. Social Prevention Health Institutions

85. The Social Prevention Health Institutions (in Spanish called *Instituciones de Salud Previsional – ISAPRES*) will finance health benefits and monetary assistance, charged to the contribution of the legal contribution for health or an agreed higher. That is their main purpose, as well as activities that are related or complementary to that purpose, which in no case may involve the execution of said benefits and benefits or participate in the administration of providers.

They must be constituted as legal persons and registered with the Superintendence of Health. Health Services and the bodies attached to the National Health Services System cannot register as *ISAPRES.*

These *ISAPRES*:

(1) Are supervised by the Superintendence of Health, without prejudice to the supervision or supervision to which they may be subject in accordance with the legal status that regulates them.
(2) Must provide sufficient and timely information to their members regarding the fundamental matters of their contracts, such as values of health plans, modalities and conditions of granting.
(3) May not enter into agreements with the Health Services for the granting of the agreed benefits. However, agreements may be concluded that specifically refer to the use of single-person rooms, intensive care units and emergency service care, which in turn may include the performance of surgical interventions or diagnostic and therapeutic support examinations.

    These agreements may be concluded by each Health Service with one or more Institutions, and in them, the values of these benefits will be freely agreed by the parties. In any case, neither the conclusion nor the execution of these agreements may be to the detriment of the care of the legal beneficiaries, who will always have preference over any other patient.

    Notwithstanding the foregoing, in cases of emergency care duly certified by a surgeon, the ISAPRES must pay directly to the Health Services the value for the benefits they have granted to their members until the patient is stabilized so that he/she is able to be referred to another healthcare establishment. If there is no agreement, the value will be corresponding to the tariff for non-beneficiaries and will be applied to all benefits actually granted.

The foregoing shall also apply in respect of emergency care, duly certified by a surgeon, provided by private-sector care establishments. The amount to be paid for the *ISAPRES* will be corresponding to the agreed amount. If there is no agreement, the prices established by the healthcare establishment that provided the care will be used.

In the situations indicated above, the *ISAPRES* may repeat against the member the amount that exceeds what they are entitled to pay under the agreed health plan.

(4) In all these cases, providers are prohibited from demanding from the beneficiaries of this law, money, checks or other financial instruments to guarantee payment or condition such care in any other way. Health providers may not consult commercial information systems of any kind, even with the consent of the patient, for the purpose of conditioning or restricting emergency care. For the purposes of the application of this standard, it will be understood that the *ISAPRES* have granted a loan to their contributors.

If the period of thirty working days has elapsed since the *ISAPRE* has paid the provider the value of the services granted, or the contributor has not paid said amount directly to the *ISAPRE*, the loan must be paid by the affiliate in equal and successive monthly instalments, which will include the adjustment according to the Consumer Price Index and an interest equivalent to the current interest rate for readjustable operations in national currency.

The monthly contributions may not exceed 5% of the remuneration or taxable income in the case of dependent, independent or pensioned members, nor an amount equivalent to the price of the contracted health plan in the case of volunteers.

86. Anyone who, without having the status of beneficiary through simulation or deception, obtains the established benefits, and the beneficiary who, in the same way, obtains a greater benefit than that which corresponds to him/her will be punished with minor imprisonment in its minimum to medium degrees. The same penalty shall be incurred by anyone who cooperates or facilitates by any means the commission of these crimes.

87. The interested entity must apply for registration to the Superintendence, providing all the pertinent background information required to prove compliance with the requirements established by law. In addition, it must:

(1) Inform the Superintendency of the identity of the partners, shareholders and their controllers, provided that they have a participation equal to or greater than 10% of the capital or have the capacity to elect at least one member of the board of directors.
(2) Prove that its partners, shareholders and controllers are not disqualified from being directors, managers, administrators, attorneys or legal representatives of an *ISAPRE*, as is the case of: (i) those who have been convicted of a crime that deserves an afflictive penalty, until the completion of the sentence; (ii) failed persons who have not been rehabilitated or those who are prohibited or unable to trade, and (iii) those who, within the five years preceding the

appointment, have been directors, managers, administrators, attorneys or legal representatives of a legal entity sanctioned by any Superintendency with the revocation of its authorization of existence, such revocation being firm, unless they have saved their responsibility in the manner prescribed by law.

The Superintendency must rule on the application submitted within a period not exceeding sixty days and may reject the one that does not comply with the legal requirements or does not accompany the required background. The decision rejecting registration must be founded and may be requested to be reinstated by the affected entity within a period of ten days from the date of its notification.

88. Persons who wish to develop the activity of sales agent must register in the registry kept by the Superintendence. Those interested must meet the following requirements:

(1) Be Chileans or foreigners living in Chile with a current immigration card.
(2) Be of legal age.
(3) Accredit sufficient knowledge about the system of Social Security Health Institutions.
(4) Be in possession of a high school license or equivalent studies.

It is forbidden to exercise, simultaneously, the functions of a sales agent in more than one *ISAPRE*, unless expressly authorized by the Superintendency. Failure by sales agents to comply with the obligations imposed on them by law, instructions of general application, resolutions and opinions pronounced by the Superintendency shall be punished by it with censure, a fine of up to fifteen MTU or cancellation of their registration in the register. Failure to pay the fine enables the Superintendency to cancel the registration.

89. At the time of submitting the registration application, a minimum capital actually paid, equivalent to 5.000 UF, must be accredited. When registered, *ISAPRES* must provide a guarantee equivalent to 2.000 UF. Likewise, they must maintain a net worth equal to or greater than 0.3 times their total debts. This ratio shall be reviewed monthly by the Superintendency. In any case, the assets may never be less than 5.000 UF.

90. The *ISAPRES* must appoint independent external auditors, who must examine the accounting, inventory, balance sheets and other financial statements and report in writing to the Superintendency. These auditors must be chosen from among those registered in the Register of External Auditors maintained by the Superintendency of Securities and Insurance and will be applicable, in general, the requirements, rights, obligations, functions and other attributions established in the Law on Corporations and its regulations. The external auditors shall be remunerated by the audited institutions.

The Superintendency may additionally require specific reports or any data or antecedent related to the fulfilment of its functions in the supervised Institutions and examine, in its own dependencies, such information or antecedents.

The *ISAPRES* must maintain a liquidity indicator of not less than 0.8 times the ratio between current assets and current liabilities. This list shall be reviewed monthly by the Superintendence. Notwithstanding the foregoing, the Superintendency must issue instructions of general application to establish the conditions of diversification, issuer and depositary of long-term and easily liquidated instruments, as well as the way in which they may be considered by the *ISAPRES*, to establish the aforementioned index.

91. The *ISAPRES* shall maintain, in any entity authorized by law to carry out the deposit and custody of securities, which for this purpose determines the Superintendency, a guarantee equivalent to the amount of the obligations indicated below:

(1) With respect to contributors and beneficiaries, the guarantee amount shall take into account the obligations for benefits payable, benefits in the process of settlement, benefits that have occurred and not reported, benefits in dispute, surplus contributions, excess contributions and contributions paid in advance.
(2) With respect to health providers, the guarantee shall consider the obligations arising from health benefits granted to contributors and beneficiaries of the Institution. The update of the guarantee may not exceed thirty days, for which the *ISAPRE* must complete it within the following twenty days until the total amount corresponding to the aforementioned obligations is covered. When the amount of the aforementioned obligations is less than the existing guarantee, the *ISAPRE* may request the Superintendence to reduce all or part of the excess.

The financial instruments for the provision of the guarantee are, *inter alia*, the following:

(1) Documents issued by the Central Bank of Chile or the General Treasury of the Republic.
(2) Time deposits in national currency with maturity of less than one year issued by banks.
(3) Quotas of mutual funds in short-term debt instruments with a duration of less than ninety days nominated in national currency.
(4) Demand Guarantee Slips issued by banks.
(5) Bank repurchase agreements legally backed by instruments.
(6) Credit agreements in CPL or UF endorsable units in which two or more banks concur, provided that the credit is due in less than one year from its subscription and that the debtor is classified by risk rating agencies registered in the Registry of the Superintendence of Securities and Insurance, at least, in risk 'category AA'.
(7) Time deposits, mortgage bills of credit, bonds and other debt or credit securities issued by banks.
(8) Quotas of mutual funds whose assets are invested in national securities or assets.
(9) Quotas of mutual funds incorporated outside the country.

(10) Quotas of mutual funds incorporated in the country whose assets are invested in foreign securities.
(11) Investment fund fees.
(12) Bonds, promissory notes and other debt or credit securities issued by public or private companies.
(13) Shares of public limited companies with stock market presence, in accordance with the requirements established by the Superintendence of Securities and Insurance through a general rule and classified as 'first-class shares'.
(14) Claims for health contributions owed by members or their employers in the percentage indicated by the Superintendency.

The *ISAPRE* must inform the Superintendency of its intention that part of the funds in the guarantee be used to pay certain obligations. If, after five working days, the Superintendency does not rule on such operation, it shall be understood that it may be carried out. Notwithstanding the foregoing, the funds covered by the guarantee and the documents representing these obligations may not be used to secure any other obligation. Any act performed in contravention shall be null and void. The guarantee is unattachable and, in no case, may be less than the equivalent, in national currency, of 2.000 UF.

In case of cancellation of the registration of an *ISAPRE*, the guarantee will be liquidated and paid exclusively by the Superintendence, even if the *ISAPRE* is subject to bankruptcy liquidation proceedings, and this guarantee is therefore excluded from the estate until it loses its non-seizure.

Part II. Contribution and Financing

Chapter 1. Main Areas of Protection

§1. HEALTHCARE

92. Salaried and Independent Workers (IWs) must contribute 7% of their social security taxable monthly remuneration or income, or the greater amount agreed upon in the corresponding health contract. Pensioners must also contribute 7% of their pension.

Law 20.531 has declared that beneficiaries of solidarity pensions (Law 20.255) are exempted from paying the 7% health's contributions, while other low income's pensioners have now to pay 5% of health contributions.

Under Law 19.381 (1995), surpluses resulting from the legal basic contribution and the agreed upon health plan, and the application of the legal basic contribution to payments of a sporadic nature, such as bonuses, are the property of the affiliated worker and increase his or her patrimony to be inherited, unless the affiliated worker decides to use them:

(1) To finance a better health plan.
(2) To cover contributions in case of unemployment.
(3) To finance health plans in the period between the date on which a request to receive a pension is presented and the date on which that request began to be operative.

In all these cases, there exists a limit of 10% of legal basic contributions corresponding to the past three months. Remaining surpluses are accumulated in the affiliated worker's account, earning interest and subject to readjustments. They can also be translated to another ISAPRE institution or to FONASA. When the labour contract ends, the affiliated worker must receive a report about existing surpluses.

§2. FAMILY ALLOWANCES

93. These benefits are financed by the State.

§3. Labour Accidents and Occupational Diseases

94. Protection in this field is totally financed by employers. There are three kinds of contributions: a basic contribution, an additional contribution, and an overcharged contribution.

The basic contribution amounts to 0.95% of the social security taxable remunerations.

The additional contribution is a varied one, which can range from 0.0% to 3.5%, depending on the activity performed and to 6.89% if specific serious risks are involved. The corresponding percentage is fixed through a Presidential Decree.

This contribution can be overcharged by a Mutual by no more than 10% if the employer does not comply with preventive and security rules determined by the Mutual.

Taking into account their nature, additional and overcharged contributions are temporary.

Their amount can be augmented, reduced, or eliminated, depending on the degree of proven advances experienced and on correcting the conditions that gave rise to the application of these extra contributions.

95. Besides these contributions, other financing resources are: (i) fines and interests applied by the Mutual; (ii) interest produced by the investment of reserves; and (iii) reimbursements due to the Mutual if an occupational disease or labour accident is a result of a fault or fraud of an employer or third party.

This contribution can be overcharged by a Mutual by no more than 10% if the employer does not comply with preventive and security rules determined by the Mutual.

Taking into account their nature, additional and overcharged contributions are temporary. Their amount can be augmented or reduced, or eliminated, depending on the degree of proven advances experienced and on correcting the conditions that gave rise to the application of these extra contributions.

Besides these contributions, other financing resources are (a) fines and interests applied by the Mutual, (b) interest produced by the investment of reserves, and (c) reimbursements due to the Mutual if an occupational disease or labour accident is a result of a fault or fraud of an employer or third party.

§4. Unemployment

96. This insurance is partly financed with employer's contributions of 2.40% of the social security taxable remunerations, with a limit of UF 90; the worker's contribution (0.6% of that remuneration), and if needed, financed by the Unemployment Solidarity Fund.

The employer (or the institution paying the corresponding subsidy) has to deduct the worker's contribution from the appropriate remuneration or subsidy. The resulting contribution has to be deposited in the AFC within the first ten days of the month following the one in which the remuneration or subsidy was earned. The failure of the fulfilment of these obligations is sanctioned with fines, payment of interest, and application of criminal penalties.

The employer also has to communicate the beginning and termination of each labour contract no later than fifteen days after such beginning and termination. The failure to comply with this obligation is sanctioned with fines.

§5. Old Age, Invalidity, and Survivor Pensions

97. Insured workers who – under conditions laid down by LD 3.500 – decide to remain affiliated with the old pension system pay contributions established in the corresponding old public social security institution. Their contributions vary from 18.84% of social security taxable monthly remuneration (affiliates of the old Social Security Service) to 21.84% of those remunerations (affiliates of the old Social Security Institution of White Collar Employees).

Workers affiliated with the new pension system have to pay the following contributions:

(1) A basic contribution: 10% of their social security taxable monthly remuneration or incomes (plus a 7% contribution to finance health services and benefits).
(2) An additional contribution: a variable percentage of their social security taxable monthly remuneration or rent established by the corresponding AFP. Its average amount is 2.42% of the above-mentioned remuneration.

Workers performing heavy work also have to pay 2% of their social security taxable monthly remuneration. Heavy work is legally defined as that causing a physical, intellectual, or psychological decline and promoting or advancing workers' ageing, even though such work does not cause occupational diseases. The National Ergonomic Commission can reduce this contribution to 1% in the case of semi-heavy work.

Workers can also pay voluntary contributions destined: (i) to increase the Individual Capitalization Account; (ii) to improve the future pension amount; or (iii) to anticipate the retirement age.

Other additional contributions are paid by workers who decide to have voluntary social welfare saving accounts of an individual or collective nature.

Chapter 2. Contributions for Public Sector Workers

98. As established in LD 3.500, its regulations are applicable to all kinds of workers in the private and public sectors. Thus, public workers' contributions are the same as those fixed for private sector workers. A similar regulation exists in regard to other social security benefits.

Before 1980, public sector workers were affiliated with special social protection bodies, such as those for public employees, journalists, Central Bank employees, and the State Railroad Company's employees. After the 2008 reform, they became affiliates of the PFA system unless they expressed their opinion to remain in the old system. In that case, they became covered by the Social Security Normalization Institute. Members of the armed forces and the police are affiliated with their special social protection bodies: the CAPREDENA and the DIPRECA.

Chapter 3. Government Funding

99. The State participates in the financing of almost all types of social welfare insurance and their corresponding services and benefits. According to their nature, the State's main contributions present varied modalities and conditions, which are summarized below.

§1. Health

100. Law 18.469 (1985) developed the constitutional right to be protected against health risks. It established free and equalitarian access to health promotional, protective, and recuperative activities, as well as to rehabilitation and the freedom to select the public or private system with which each person wants to be affiliated. Dependent institutions from the MH cannot deny care to those requiring their services, or to set conditions of such care upon fees and tariffs unless these payments are established by law.

Within the above-mentioned framework, the State mainly – totally or partially finances:

(1) Services and benefits to affiliates with low incomes or without incomes.
(2) AUGE services and benefits (AUGE is a programme of explicit guarantees on health).
(3) Maternity benefits, health activities, shared healthcare payments, and 'third age' benefits (older persons).
(4) Different tariffs fixed, taking into account the beneficiaries' income level, classifying them into four groups with free or preferent shared-payments.

§2. Pensions

101. The State's main contributions to the pension system are the 'recognition bonus' established by LD 3.500 and the financing of non-contributory pensions of the so-called solidarity pillar, principally established by Laws 20.255 and 21.419:

(1) Recognition Bonus. Under LD 3.500, during a given period of time, workers were allowed to decide whether to remain affiliated with the old system or to affiliate with an AFP. If the worker decides to be an AFP member, the corresponding old Social Welfare Institute, represented by the INP, has to deliver a document expressing a given monetary amount representing the worker's contributions paid in the old system. This document, called a recognition bonus, is handled by the corresponding AFP, and its amount becomes a part of the Individual Capitalization Account, thus being part of the worker's pension.

To be entitled to receive a recognition bonus, it is necessary that: (i) a worker has made at least twelve monthly contributions to one Social Prevention Institution between November 1975 and October 1980; and (ii) these contributions have not been used to obtain a previously given pension.

The recognition bonus is ready to be paid to the affiliate when: (i) he or she reaches the age to be pensioned; (ii) he or she has the right to receive a disablement pension; or (ii) he or she dies.

(2) Solidarity Pillar. The Solidarity Pensions System (SPS), also called the solidarity pillar, established by Law 20.255, complemented the general pension system governed by LD 3.500 (1980), financed with State contributions. Under the SPS, there existed a basic solidarity pension for old age (BSPOA) and a basic solidarity pension for invalidity (BSPI), as well as social contributions.

(3) Law 21.419 established the UGP, reforming Law 20.255, Law-Decree 3.500 and other legislation.

§3. Unemployment

102. The State makes contributions to the Unemployment Solidarity Fund, finances unemployment subsidies, and finance deficits experienced.

Through the National Training and Employment Service (SENCE), the State contributes to the financing of professional training and the functioning of local government (municipalities) job placement services.

§4. Family Allowances and Maternity Benefits

103. The State finances the total costs of these benefits.

Part III. Healthcare

Chapter 1. Field of Application

§1. Territorial Field of Application

104. This insurance is applied in the entire Chilean territory.

§2. Personal Field of Application

105. Health care protection covers: (a) those who are affiliated with FONASA or an ISAPRE, and (b) other beneficiaries determined by law.

Under Laws 18.469 and 19.350, the following persons are affiliated with the healthcare regime:

(1) Dependent workers in the public and private sectors. An affiliate with a labour contract agreed upon for a previously defined period of time or for a defined work or task to performed, who has contributed for at least four of the last twelve months, will maintain the condition of affiliation for another twelve months after the last contribution. The same extension is provided for those affiliates with daily contracts and at least sixty days of contributions in the last twelve months.
(2) Independent workers contributing to any social welfare regime.
(3) Persons contributing to any social welfare regime as voluntary contributors.
(4) Persons receiving social welfare pensions of any kind, or social welfare subsidies for labour disability or unemployment.

106. Following persons are legally considered to be beneficiaries:

(1) Affiliates of the regime, as described above.
(2) Dependent persons who are actually receiving a family allowance.
(3) Independent persons contributing to any social welfare regime as a voluntary contributor should be entitled to receive a family allowance as established for a dependent worker.
(4) Pregnant women who, although not being an affiliated person or beneficiary, receive medical care during the pregnancy and post-partum until six months

after the birth. Birth services include all medical care needed, as well as medical examinations, hospitalization, surgery, treatments, medications, and so on. Children also receive medical care until they are six years old.

(5) Persons receiving non-contributory welfare pensions.

(6) Indigents.

Chapter 2. Services and Benefits

107. Beneficiaries receive medical care services, monetary benefits and leaves.

§1. Medical Care

108. The main medical services are:

(1) Preventive medical care of diseases determined by the MH, such as tuberculosis, sexually transmitted diseases, cancer, glaucoma, diabetes, and chronic kidney failure.
(2) Curative medical care, including medical examinations, treatments, hospitalization, surgeries, medicines, and other health services required.
(3) Dental care.

These preventive and curative services are accompanied by activities to promote and protect the people and the environment.

§2. Monetary and Leaves Benefits

109. A monetary benefit is paid for a medical leave or maternity leave. The first legislation on monetary benefits for health risks dates from 1937. Currently, this matter is ruled by legislation enacted in 1978, 1985, 1990, and 2005.

Monetary benefits for medical leaves are of a temporal nature and end once the disease is officially declared to be non-recoverable, unless an individual or collective contract of labour establishes the worker's right to receive a medical subsidy during the entire leave.

Dependent and independent affiliated workers on medical leave for a total or partial disability to work because of a disease that does not constitute an occupational disease or labour accident receive a sickness subsidy, ruled by DFL 44 (1978, MTPS).

Dependent workers are entitled to monetary benefits for health risks if they have at least a six-month period of affiliation and a three-month period of contributions. In turn, IWs need to fulfil the following special requisites: (a) they must have twelve months of affiliation before the month in which the leave begins; (b) they must have at least six months of continuous or non-continuous contributions in the twelve-month affiliation period prior to the month of the beginning of the leave; and (c) they must have paid the contribution corresponding to the month before the one in which the disability took place.

The beneficiary maintains the right to receive family allowances. In turn, subsidies are considered to be income for the purpose of calculating contributions for pensions and medical care. However, for fiscal law, subsidies are not taxable.

For medical leaves not exceeding ten days, the first three days are not covered by the subsidy.

The medical leave subsidy is paid by the relevant Social Welfare Institution (FONASA, an ISAPRE, CCAF, or Health Service).

If the leave is the result of a disease-causing partial labour disability requiring partial leave, the employer has to pay for the time effectively worked.

The situation of IWs is detailed by Article 21 of Law 18.469. Concerning dependent workers, the subsidy amount is equivalent to the average remuneration – or subsidies, or both – over which contributions were made during a three-month period prior to the month corresponding to the beginning of the health leave. In the case of IWs, the health subsidy amount is the average rent – or subsidies, or both – over which contributions were made during the last twelve months preceding the month in which the labour incapacity began.

I. Maternity Leaves

110. Female workers are entitled to a maternity leave of six weeks before the birth of a child and twelve weeks after the birth and to receive the maternity subsidy. If, during the pregnancy, a disease linked to it occurs, the mother has the right to a supplementary maternity leave. If the birth takes place after the six-week leave period, this leave is extended until the date on which the birth occurs. If, after the birth, a disease is contracted, the twelve-week-after-birth period is extended as a consequence.

As of December 2006, the father has the right to a five-day paid leave, which he can distribute over the first month from the birth date. Under Law 19.670 (2000), if the mother dies during childbirth or in the twelve-week period after the birth, the father is entitled to use the remaining period of maternity leave and to receive the corresponding maternity subsidy.

As said, maternity protection includes the following main standards on maternity leaves: (i) women workers have a natal leave of six weeks before childbirth and twelve weeks after the childbirth takes place. In both periods, she receives a maternal subsidy; (ii) the father worker has a paid natal leave of five days. He can use the leave in a continuous way since the childbirth or distribute it during the first month of the childbirth; (iii) if the mother dies during the childbirth –or in the leave's period after the childbirth, the leave corresponds to the father or to the person who has assumed the responsibility of caring the child (who is also protected with 'fuero' and receive the corresponding subsidy).

111. Law 20.545 (October 2011) has modified the maternity protection's legislation incorporating the so-called parental postnatal leave.

Among other reforms to the postnatal leave contained in Law 20.545, it is interesting to point out the following ones:

(1) If the childbirth takes place before the beginning of the thirty-third week of pregnancy, or if the child's weight is under 1.500 gm, the postnatal leave will be eighteen weeks.

(2) In cases of childbirth of two or more children, the postnatal leave will be increased in seven days for each child born after the first one. If both circumstances occurred simultaneously, the duration of the postnatal leave will be the most extended one.

112. In November 2011, Decree 1433 (Ministry of Finances) regulated the application of Law 20.545 in the public sector, particularly in relation with: (i) the employee's right to return to work during the postnatal paternal leave, and (ii) the criteria to be used by public entities to determine the daily time-work of the women worker that have decided to return to their works.

Other matters ruled in the Decree are concerned with: (i) the amount of remunerations and subsidies to be received, and (ii) the financing of corresponding subsidies.

As established by Law 20.399 (November 2009), the worker (woman or man) that judicially has been assigned the personal care of a child minor than 2 years will also be titular of all rights established in Article 203 of the Labour Code (cradle and nursery rooms and services).

In addition to the previously mentioned protection measures, Law 20.682 (July 2013) established that from six weeks before childbirth until twenty-four weeks before childbirth, women are not obliged to serve as members of the electoral sites to receive the citizen's vote.

The daily amount of this subsidy cannot exceed the equivalent of a dependent worker's net monthly remuneration or/and subsidies in the three-month period prior to the seventh month preceding the leave's beginning, divided by 90 and incremented in 100% of the cost of living index corresponding to the period of seven months before the beginning of the leave beginning.

II. Other Leaves

113. To these basic leaves, the Labour Code also has established the following other main types of leaves and payments: (i) if a minor aged less than one year requires attention at home because of a serious disease, the mother (or the father if she has died) has the right to a leave and to receive a subsidy equal to the maternity subsidy. If both the mother and father are workers, the mother can decide which of them will use the leave and receive the subsidy. The same rights are applied in the case of an adopted child; (ii) if a minor under 18 years of age requires the personal attention of his or her father or mother because of a serious accident or a terminal disease in its final phase, or a serious and acute disease with the possible consequence of death, the mother has the right to a paid leave for a maximum of eighty hours a year, distributed to the minor.

The cost of this paid leave must be returned by compensating it with vacation time, overtime work, or any other way agreed upon by the parties. Its amount can be discounted from the monthly remuneration, in quotas of one day per month. If both the mother and father are workers, the mother can decide which of them will use the leave. The same rights are applied in the case of an adopted child; and (iii) a worker legally having the guardianship or custody of a minor for at least six months has the right to leave subsidies for no more than twelve weeks.

III. Common Rules

114. In all these cases, the established requisites and circumstances must be previously proved with official legal certifications.

To partially finance health services and benefits, there are different direct payments according to the following classification set forth in Law 18.469:

(1) Group A: Indigents, non-contributory pensioners and family allowance originators: Free of charge.
(2) Group B: Affiliated persons with monthly incomes not exceeding one Minimum Monthly Income (about USD 183), or exceeding not more than 1.46% of that income but being entitled to receive three or more family allowances: Free of charge.
(3) Group C: Affiliated persons with monthly incomes: (i) superior to one Minimum Monthly Income and exceeding not more than 1.46% of that amount but being entitled to receive no more than two family allowances, or (ii) superior to one Minimum Monthly Income and exceeding more than 1.46% of that amount but being entitled to receive three or more family allowances: A shared payment of 10%.
(4) Group D: Affiliated persons with monthly incomes higher than 1.46% of one Minimum Monthly Income but being entitled to receive no more than two family allowances: A shared payment of 20%.

115. These percentages can be altered in the case of medications, prostheses, and dental services. The difference between the contribution of the Fund and the cost of services received must be covered by the affiliate (shared payment). For that purpose – and also in the free election modality, affiliates can request loans from the Medical Loans Fund.

Chapter 3. The Social Prevention Explicit Minimum Health Guaranteed Programme

116. AUGE was established by Law 19.966 (2004). *AUGE* refers to a high-priority group of illness and health conditions and to a set of health services associated with them – of a promotional, preventive, curative, rehabilitation, or relief nature – accompanied by explicit guarantees related to the access, levels of opportunity, financial protection, and quality of services.

FONASA as well as *ISAPRES* are obliged to provide *AUGE* services and guarantees to their affiliates, under the following special conditions:

(1) These services and guarantees are not applicable if the affiliate decides to opt for the free election system or has a complementary plan besides the originally agreed-upon plan.
(2) Planning and verification of these services and guarantees must be performed under rules established by Law 19.966.
(3) Established explicit guarantees will be into effect for three-year renewable periods.
(4) Their application can be suspended during one month if a sanitary crisis arises.
(5) Service fees cannot exceed the average price (called the universal premium) fixed by a government decree.
(6) By means of 'additional financial coverage', the fulfilment of shared payments of related illness or health conditions covered by *AUGE* is guaranteed.
(7) Different deductible amounts have been established for affiliates classified in groups C or D of the previously mentioned Health System. For Group C, the deductible is the equivalent of twenty-one monthly contributions by event or a total of thirty-one monthly contributions if there are two or more cases in a twelve-month period. For Group D, the deductible amount is the equivalent of twenty-nine monthly contribution in each case, or forty-nine monthly contributions if there are two or more events in a twelve-month period. The deductible amount cannot exceed the equivalent of 181 UF. IWs classified in Group D have a deductible amount equivalent to twice their average monthly incomes.
(8) In the four-year period after the corresponding actions or omissions have occurred, affected persons can demand the payment of indemnities for 'moral damage' if infringements to *AUGE*'s regulations occur. The indemnity amount will be fixed by a judge, taking into account the seriousness of the damage, changes that have occurred in the plaintiff's life conditions, physical conditions, and age.

Law 16.966 also established a mediation procedure before taking such matters to a court. Mediation takes place in the Council for the State Legal Defence if public institutions are involved. If private institutions are involved, the process is in charge of a mediator agreed to by the parties. The mediation process lasts no more than sixty days.

Chapter 4. Conditions

§1. The Health Contract

117. Modalities and conditions of social welfare healthcare services and benefits are agreed upon by the *ISAPRE* and the affiliate in the corresponding health contract. This written contract has to contain clauses that at least refer to the following matters:

(1) The explicit guarantees about the access, quality, financial protection, and timing to receive services established in *AUGE*, governed by Law 19.966 (2004). Consequently, besides services and benefits set forth in the health contract, the *ISAPRE* must assure the fulfilment of *AUGE's* rights and obligations. These include the following: (i) restrictions on amounts, coverage, or exclusions cannot be applied to benefits referred to *AUGE*; (ii) prices and means of payment of benefits will be the same for all beneficiaries of the *ISAPRE*, without discriminations based on age or sex; (iii) the *ISAPRE* has to assure the application of explicit guarantees as of the first day after a six-month period since the publication of the corresponding Decree; and (iv) the affiliate can decide to terminate the health contract within sixty days after an explicit guarantee has entered into force or has been amended.

(2) An additional complementary plan to the above-mentioned explicit health guarantees, which must include: (i) the right of workers on leave (including independent workers) for total or partial disability not resulting from an occupational disease or labour accident to receive a health subsidy); and (ii) if needed, benefits that are not a part of these explicit guarantees, including co-shared payments, percentages of coverage, and amounts over which they will be applied. This plan has to contain at least the same services and financial coverage levels existing for the *FONASA* free election modality, as governed by Law 19.966 (2004). At the same time, it is not allowed to agree to a plan containing coverage for specific services inferior to those agreed upon in the plan for generic services. Finally, the agreed-upon levels of financial coverage cannot be lower than those existing in *FONASA*.

(3) A procedure to agree to modifications related to contributions, services, and benefits.

(4) Mechanisms to deliver services and benefits established by Law 19.996, and those agreed upon in health contracts.

(5) The price and means of payment of the health plan, and the 'reference table of tariffs' (valued role of services). The price can only be altered once a year, and the valued role of services has to include all services listed in the *FONASA* role, unless there is a previous authorization of the Supervisory of Health.

(6) Maximum amounts of benefits for each beneficiary or for one or more services. However, it is allowed to agree upon specific services valued at 25% lower than those services listed in the general agreed-upon plan. Clauses violating this prohibition are considered to be invalid.

(7) Restrictions to the risk coverage. However, they can only relate to pre-existing illnesses declared for a maximum of eighteen months before the contract was agreed upon. These restrictions cannot apply values of 25% lower than the coverage of the same service in the agreed-upon general plan. For this purpose, it is understood that pre-existing illnesses or pathologies are those that have been known by the affiliate and medically diagnosed before the subscription of the health contract or the incorporation of the beneficiary. In the case of pregnancy, it must be expressly written that the coverage will be proportional to the pending period until the birth of the child. Finally, in any case, waiting periods in which services and benefits cannot be demanded are not allowed, except services and benefits related to pregnancy and pre-existing illnesses.

(8) Agreed-upon exclusions related to plastic surgery for cosmetic purposes and other services with the same purpose. These exclusions do not include: (i) plastic surgery performed to correct congenital malformations or malformations that occurred at birth, or plastic surgery performed to repair deformities sustained from an accident; (ii) infirmary services practised on an individual basis; (iii) hospitalization for rest purposes, or health services related to the participation in wars or resulting from legally considered crimes if criminal responsibility arises; (iv) services covered by other laws with the same coverage level; or (v) non-declared pre-existing illnesses. However, five years after the subscription of the health contract (or the beneficiary incorporation), the *ISAPRE* has to provide care unless it proves that the affiliate had had one or more medical treatments related to the corresponding pathology in the above-mentioned five-year period and that the beneficiary concealed this.

The ISAPRE can also enter into health contracts with persons who are not paying contributions to a social welfare pension system.

118. In turn, health contracts are also governed by the following rules:

(1) They cannot be subscribed for a fixed term period or be terminated while they are in force, unless contractual obligations are not fulfilled or the parties have agreed to terminate it. Nevertheless, after a year of being in force, the affiliate can decide to terminate the contract through a communication given at least one month before the end of the corresponding year.

(2) The affiliate can present a claim to the Supervisory Agency of Health in the event of the ISAPRE's decision to terminate the health contract because of supposed non-fulfilment of the affiliate's contractual duties.

(3) The ISAPRE has to offer a new plan when it is required to do so by an affiliate if: (i) his or her job has been lost, or (ii) there is a permanent variation in the legal contribution or in the composition of the family group.

(4) Annually, the ISAPRE can review the health contract to adjust for adequate prices, the agreed-upon services, and the nature and amount of benefits. Changes cannot represent discrimination in the terms governed by law.

(5) Contractual benefits will also be applied to new dependants declared by the affiliate and originating from a family allowance.

119. Medical leaves have to be authorized by the corresponding ISAPRE. For that purpose, the ISAPRE has a three-workday period in which to accept the request after it has been presented. If the ISAPRE does not express its opinion in this period, the medical leave is considered to be approved.

If the ISAPRE rejects medical leave or medical certification, affiliates can present a claim to the corresponding COMPIN.

Under Law 19.650 (1999), in cases of urgent or emergency needs for medical care, duly certified by a surgeon, the ISAPRE has to pay directly to the health service the costs of services received by its affiliates, until he or she is stabilized. If the paid amount is higher than the due payment according to the health contract, the excess is considered a loan and has to be paid to the ISAPRE in monthly instalments not exceeding 5% of the social prevention taxable remuneration or rent.

Law 19.650 (1999) also establishes that health services are forbidden to demand previous payments or guarantees of payment by means of cash, checks or other financial instruments.

Part IV. Family Allowances

120. Chilean legislation on family allowances started with the enactment of Law 6.020 of 1937, which was only for white-collar workers. From 1973 to 1974, numerous laws established family allowances of different nature, beneficiaries, and amounts. Among these, it is important to note Law 11.051 (making it possible to pay family allowances directly to a worker's wife, and DFL 245 (1953), extending family allowances to blue-collar workers. It is also important to note that payment of family allowances to those workers had been previously introduced through collective bargaining.

Family allowances were administered by numerous social welfare public institutions existing at that time, as well as by private non-profit organizations: the Family Allowances Compensation Institutions (CCAFs), legally recognized in 1953.

121. Law Decrees of 1973 and 1974 and DFL 150 (1981) replaced the former system with a new system, whose main characteristics are the following:

(1) The covered population is comprised of dependent workers (wage earners), pensioned persons, and those receiving subsidies for unemployment or temporal incapacity if they are in charge of legally entitled persons.
(2) Administered funds come from the national budget (the Unique Family Allowance Fund).
(3) Public and private organizations participate in the administration of this system, for instance: (i) the INP (now the IPS), in connection with its own pensioned affiliates, or employees whose employers are not members of an Employer Mutual, or when said employees are receiving health or unemployment subsidies paid by State institutions or institutions recognized by the State, or by IWs entitled to this benefit as of 1 January 1974; (ii) Family Allowances Compensation Institutions regarding employees of their employers' members, even if these employees are receiving health or unemployment subsidies and are not affiliated with an ISAPRE; (iii) employers Mutuals; and (iv) AFPs, regarding their own pensioned affiliates, insurance companies in relation to pensioned persons having opted for a life pension and centralized and decentralized public services regarding their own employees.
(4) The general rule is that family allowances are paid by employers jointly with the monthly remuneration. Those payments are then compensated by the pertinent Social Prevention Institution.
(5) Beneficiaries of a survivor pension are only entitled to receive family allowances existing at the death of the covered person.

(6) A family allowance of a given beneficiary can only be claimed by one covered person, in only one social welfare regime, despite the fact that he or she might have more than one job (multiple employers).
(7) Beneficiaries must live at the expense of the covered person. Their incomes cannot be higher than 50% of the Monthly Minimum Income. This prerequisite is not applicable to orphans' pensions or to incomes related to work done in periods no longer than three months a year.
(8) The loss of qualification to be a beneficiary of this allowance has to be communicated to the administering institution within sixty days. Allowances received after that time period have to be returned and penal sanctions are applied.
(9) Allowances are paid monthly. The amount is proportional to the days worked by the covered person. If this amounts to twenty-five or more days, the allowance is paid for the whole month. It also cannot be the object of legal transactions or seized.
(10) Family allowances are not fiscally taxable or subject to social welfare contributions.
(11) The family allowance regime is controlled by the Superintendency of Social Security (SUSESO), which, among other duties, is in charge of the Unique Family Allowance System programme.

122. Under Law 18.020 (1981), besides this family allowance regime, there also exists a family subsidy for minors under 18 years of age, invalids of any age, pregnant women, and the mother of any of these who do not have resources or access to a family or maternal allowance.

This subsidy is administered by SUSESO, the SPI and local governments (municipalities). Administered funds come from the national budget (the Unique Family Subsidy Fund).

Following chapters will present the most important aspects of family allowances and also summarize the main characteristics of family subsidies.

Chapter 1. Field of Application

§1. Territorial Field of Application

123. Family allowance regulation is applied in the entire Chilean territory.

§2. Personal Field of Application

124. The family allowance system covers the following:

(1) Dependent workers (wage earners) in the public and private economic sectors.
(2) Independent workers (self-employed) affiliated with a social welfare regime.
(3) Dependent and IWs who receive benefits from social welfare regimes of labour incapacity, labour accidents, occupational diseases or unemployment.
(4) Pensioned persons of any social welfare regime.
(5) State institutions or private institutions, recognized by the State, in charge of orphans or abandoned children and invalids.
(6) Pensioned widows and the mothers of children of active or pensioned workers who receive benefits under Laws 15.386 and 16.711.
(7) Female workers regarding the maternal subsidy.

Chapter 2. Dependent Children and Other Beneficiaries

125. Under Chilean legislation, family allowances do not include only children as beneficiaries. It also covers other economically dependent persons if a covered person is also in charge of another person having some incapacity to produce sufficient income to afford his or her living expenses.

Thus, beneficiaries of a family allowance include the following:

(1) Wives who are in the charge of working husbands, as well as invalid husbands who depend on their working wives.
(2) Sons and daughters, including adopted ones, under 18 years of age, or 24 years of age if they are nor married and are studying in State institutions or private institutions with State recognition.
(3) Grandsons, granddaughters, and great-grandchildren if they are orphans of a father and mother or abandoned by them. The same prerequisites established for sons and daughters are applicable.
(4) Widowed mothers.
(5) Fathers, mothers, grandfathers, grandmothers, great-grandfathers or great-grandmothers over 65 years of age.
(6) Orphans or abandoned children, and invalids in the charge of State shelter institutions and shelter institutions with State recognition that take care of their breeding, education, and maintenance.

Chapter 3. Amount of the Benefits

126. The family allowance monthly amount for each beneficiary varies, depending on the income of covered persons. Thus, there is a scale of three levels of income and family allowance amounts:

(1) Annual incomes less than UF 144.448: a monthly family allowance of about USD 13.10 for each person in charge.
(2) Annual incomes from UF 144.448 to UF 282.929: a monthly family allowance of about USD 8 for each person in charge.
(3) Annual incomes from UF 282.929 and less than UF 441.274: a monthly family allowance of about USD 2 for each person in charge.

Persons with incomes over UF 441.274 are not entitled to receive family allowances. These amounts are increased by 100% in cases of physical or psychic invalidity.

127. In cases of female Wage Earners (WE), the amount of their income consists of the average remuneration received in the last three months previous to maternity leave beginning. However, this amount cannot exceed the equivalent of the average remuneration received in the three-month period previous to the seventh month prior to the beginning of maternity leave.

Concerning self-employed women, the amount of their income consists of the average income received in the six-month period previous to the beginning of maternity leave as compared with remuneration corresponding with the six-month period previous to the eight months prior to the beginning of maternity leave.

Chapter 4. Family Subsidies

128. Family subsidies were established by Law 18.020 (1981). Payment of these subsidies is in the charge of the SPI. However, the Departments of Social Development of corresponding local governments (Municipalities) have some participation in the processes of inscription, selection, and revision of covered person's cases.

Persons having the right to claim the payment of a familiar subsidy include the following:

(1) The mother of a minor of less than 18 years or, in her absence, the father, guardian or person who cares for a minor, if they do not have the necessary financial means to provide maintenance and breeding for the beneficiary, alone or together with the minor's family.
(2) Pregnant women claiming this benefit after the fifth month of pregnancy. To this end, the pregnant woman has to present a certification of pregnancy, including dates of conception and possible birth, provided by a physician or matron of a health service or other authorized institution.
(3) Persons in charge of mentally handicapped persons, claiming that they permanently are in charge of them.

Beneficiaries of this subsidy also include the following:

(1) Minors less than 18 years of age, if they: (i) live at expenses of the covered person; (ii) participate in pertinent health programs of the MH; (iii) accomplish educational obligations laid by law, if they are over 6 years of age: and (iv) do not have or receive monthly incomes or benefits equal or superior to the amount of the subsidy.
(2) Pregnant women, if they do not have or receive monthly incomes or benefits equal or superior to the amount of the subsidy.
(3) Mothers of beneficiaries if they, in general, meet the same prerequisites as minors.
(4) Mentally handicapped persons, if they, in general, accomplish the same prerequisites as minors.

The family subsidy is the same amount established for workers of low incomes: about USD 10 for each person in charge. However, the subsidy for mentally handicapped persons is about USD 20 for each person in charge.

Any beneficiary can have only one subsidy, despite the possibility of being claimed by two or more covered persons.

129. Law 21.550 (2023) – with state financing – granted an extraordinary contribution of CLP 60,000, to each beneficiary of the Permanent Family Contribution (regulated by Law 20.743), conferred to each originator of family subsidy or family allowance who has received it on 31 December of the previous year. Such extraordinary contribution will be paid by the SPI in a single instalment, starting in March 2023.

In its Title II, the aforementioned Law increased the amounts of the family and maternal allowance and the Single Family-Allowance, automating this subsidy.

§1. Family and Maternal Allowance

130. As of 1 May 2023, the family and maternal allowance of the Single System of Family Benefits will have the following values and sections, in CLP:

(1) 20,328 per load, for those beneficiaries whose monthly income does not exceed 429,899.
(2) 12,475 per load, for those beneficiaries whose monthly income exceeds 429,899 and does not exceed 627,913.
(3) 3,942 per load, for those beneficiaries whose monthly income exceeds 627,913 and does not exceed 979,330.
(4) Persons who have accredited or who prove family dependents, whose monthly income exceeds 979,330, shall not be entitled to the allowances referred to in this article.

§2. Family Subsidy Allowance for People with Limited Resources

131. Law 118.020, which establishes family subsidy allowances for people with limited resources, is amended as follows:

(1) As of 1 May 2023, the amount of the subsidy will be the amount of CLP 20,328 per month.
(2) The family subsidy allowance regulated in this law shall be granted automatically when its originators are children or adolescents under 18 years of age belonging to households classified into the 40% socioeconomically most vulnerable of the population, according to Article 5 of Law 20.379, which creates the intersectoral system of social protection and institutionalizes the subsystem of comprehensive protection of children '*Chile Crece Contigo*' ('Chile grows with you'). The Ministry of Social Development and the Family shall periodically verify compliance with the requirements for the granting of this subsidy and shall periodically verify the concurrence of the grounds for extinguishing the requirements for its granting or maintenance.

132. At the same time, Law 21.550 provides: (i) that this subsidy shall be incompatible with family and maternal allowances and with the family allowance granted in accordance with the other articles of this law; (ii) the Ministry of Social Development and Family shall inform the beneficiaries of the granting of the family allowance granted, by the most expeditious means; (iii) the beneficiary may renounce this subsidy at any time, a decision that must be communicated to the Ministry of Social Development and Family in the form and channels that it has establishes for it; and (iv) the Superintendency of Social Security will be responsible for the supervision of the granting, payment and termination regime indicated in this law.

§3. Electronic Family Pocket

133. From 1 May 2023 until 31 December 2023, a monthly contribution is granted for the purchase or to complement the payments of purchases of all types of products in food stores, in favour of the people causing the family and maternal allowance of the Single System of Family Benefits, and of the persons causing the family subsidy, provided that they receive such benefits for having an income equal to or less than the maximum limit established in Article 1 of Law 18.987.

The originators of the families that were users of the 'Security and Opportunities' subsystem, created by Law 20.595, will also be entitled to this contribution. For these purposes, the members of these families who meet the following requirements will be considered as the cause: (i) persons with disabilities, duly accredited; (ii) students with special educational needs of a permanent nature, who participate in the School Integration Programme of the Ministry of Education; (iii) students enrolled in educational establishments with special education modality recognized by the Ministry of Education; (iv) students aged 18 to 24 years 11 months; and (v) persons under 18 years of age. The Ministry of Social Development and Family shall be responsible for submitting to the SPI the payrolls of the originators and their beneficiaries referred to in this paragraph.

Each originator will be entitled to a contribution of CLP 13,500 per month, even if the respective beneficiary is covered by different pension regimes and performs different jobs. The originators will receive the same treatment even when they can be invoked or invoked in that capacity by more than one beneficiary. In the latter event, preference will always be given to the beneficiary's mother.

The aforementioned monthly contribution may only be used for the purposes and in the manner established by this law and its regulations and will not constitute remuneration or income for any legal purpose and, consequently, will not be taxable and will not be subject to any discount.

The contribution established in this Title will be a fiscal charge. Its payment will be made monthly by the SPI through contracted electronic means, generating the so-called 'Electronic Family Pocket'. For such purposes, it may enter into agreements with one or more public or private entities that also have a network of branches that guarantee the national coverage of the payment of this contribution granted by this law, including the Banco del Estado de Chile.

The beneficiary may use his or her Electronic Family Pocket in purchases made with the respective electronic means (mobile phone, for example) with a limit corresponding to the available balance. For this, you can decide when to apply it and whether to do it for the total balance or in a percentage of the purchase, as determined by the regulations. If there is a remaining balance at the end of each month, it will be accumulated for the following months.

A regulation issued by the MLSP, also signed by the Minister of Finance, shall regulate the application of this benefit in that not provided for in this Title.

The SPI will know and resolve the claims related to the matters of the contribution established by this Title, in accordance with Law 19.880, and in accordance with the rules issued by the Superintendence of Social Security, without prejudice to the powers of the latter.

The term to claim for the non-granting of the contribution referred to in this Title will be one year, counted from the month in which it should have been received.

The Superintendence of Social Security shall be responsible for supervising and controlling the granting and payment of the contribution regulated in this law.

Those who unduly receive the contribution established by this Title must return the sums unduly received, readjusted in accordance with the variation experienced by the Consumer Price Index determined by the National Institute of Statistics, or the institution that replaces it, between the month prior to that in which it was received and the one that precedes its restitution.

During the month of November 2023, the Ministry of Finance must send a report to the Finance Committees of the Honourable Chamber of Deputies and the Honourable Senate, giving a detailed account of the operation of the Electronic Family Pocket. This report shall include, at least, aggregated statistics on the number of beneficiaries of the contribution referred to in this Title, level of use, amounts used as a complement to purchases and any other relevant information available in relation to its implementation, which must be provided by the competent bodies, upon request of the Ministry of Finance.

Chapter 5. Other Maternity and Children's Benefits

134. The first relevant legislation dates from 1931. Maternity and child benefits involve labour law and social security law.

In addition to the corresponding social prevention legislation, the Chilean Labour Code contains the following principal protection measures that are in force:

(1) Non-discrimination for being pregnant.
(2) Prohibited work during pregnancy if they are considered to be harmful to the mother's health.
(3) Nursery rooms and services. Establishments employing twenty or more women of any age or civil status must have independent rooms where women can take care of child nutrition. The same obligation is applicable to industrial, commercial, and service centres. Employers can replace these obligations by paying the costs of authorized child care establishments and transportations costs of mothers to give personal attention to children under 2 years old.
(4) Protection against unlawful dismissals *(fuero).*
(5) Maternal leaves and additional leaves in specific situations.

135. It is important to point out that legal protection rules tend to be accompanied by collective labour agreements clauses. For instance, special payments for childbirth are commonly established in collective labour contracts resulting from collective bargaining in larger enterprises.

Particularly since March 2006, social protection policies have been increased and strengthened, giving special attention to child care for the betterment of their health, nutrition, preliminary stimulation, and education. These valuable activities are carried out through governmental and private efforts. The common denominator of these activities is to make it possible to provide equal opportunities for everyone, especially those with low incomes.

This trend has been maintained until today. For instance, Law 20.595 (2012) – known as the 'ethical family income'– regulated many bonuses, subsidies and special benefits to lower income families or persons in extreme poverty or in vulnerable situations.

Part V. Incapacity to Work

Chapter 1. Field of Application

§1. Territorial Field of Application

136. As a general rule, Chilean legislation on social welfare is applied in every part of the national territory.

§2. Personal Field of Application

137. Personal coverage is determined by rules established by legislation referred to: (i) common diseases and accidents, (ii) labour accidents and occupational diseases, and (iii) maternal leaves and working conditions related to maternity protection.

Chapter 2. Benefits

§1. Common Diseases and Accidents

138. Under Laws 18.469 and 19.350, as amended, the following affiliated persons can be considered entitled to benefits related to common diseases and accidents covered in the FONASA and ISAPRE regimes:

(1) Dependent workers of the public and private sectors. An affiliate with a labour contract signed for a defined period of time or to perform a defined work or task who has contributed for at least four of the last twelve months will maintain the status of an affiliate for another twelve months after the last contribution. The same extension is given to those affiliates with daily contracts and at least sixty days of contributions in the last twelve months.
(2) Independent workers contributing to any legal social welfare regime.

Beneficiaries receive medical care services and subsidized leave payments in cases of incapacity to work. They are also entitled to benefits of AUGE.

§2. Labour Accidents and Occupational Diseases

139. In this context, the incapacity to work can be related to: (i) partially invalid persons (those suffering a diminution of their capacity to work, allegedly permanent, and equal to or superior to 15% but less than 70%), (ii) persons affected by a permanent incapacity.

In the second case, Chilean legislation has established the following four degrees of permanent incapacity:

(1) Partial First-Degree (from 15% to 39% loss of capacity to work): The victim is entitled to be paid an indemnity of no more than 15% of his or her basic salary, according to the degree of lost capacity. The indemnity can be totally paid in cash or paid in monthly instalments, as decided by the affected person, who can also, at any time, demand to be paid the remaining indemnity in cash. That same indemnity will be received by the insured who, as a result of the related accident, has not suffered from an incapacity to work but has suffered an important mutilation or an evident deformity. However, if the mutilation or deformity has occurred to the victim's face, head, or genital organs, the victim will receive major indemnity.
(2) Partial Second-Degree (from 40% to 69% loss of capacity): the victim is entitled to receive an invalidity pension amounting to 35% of his or her basic salary.
(3) Total (70% or more loss of capacity): The victim has the right to receive a total invalidity pension.

(4) Grand Invalidity (an invalid person who requires help from others to achieve the realization of fundamental functions of life): the victim is entitled to a supplement to a total invalidity pension, amounting to 30% of his or her basic salary.

A pension's amount will be increased by 5% for each child (over 2 years of age) entitled to family allowances. In any case, these pensions can exceed 50%, 100%, or 140% of the basic monthly remuneration, taking into account the degrees of invalidity mentioned above.

§3. Maternity Protection

140. In addition to corresponding social welfare legislation, the Chilean Labour Code contains the following principal protection rules related to the incapacity to work:

(1) There are certain prohibited types of work and working conditions during the pregnancy period that are considered harmful to a mother's health. Among them are those obligating the pregnant woman: (i) to lift, drag, or push large, heavy weights; (ii) to expend undue physical efforts, including standing for long periods of time; (iii) to perform work at night; and (iv) to be declared non-appropriated by a competent authority. In all these cases, pregnant women must be transferred to a safe type of work without the diminishing of her remuneration.
(2) Maternal leaves and other additional medical leaves after childbirth are ordered because the mother has a disease related to childbirth.
(3) Special additional leaves are granted in cases of: (i) a serious disease of a minor less than one year old; (ii) a disease of a minor less than 18 years of age requiring the attention of the mother or father because of a serious accident or a disease able to cause the minor's death; and (iii) the care of a minor of six months of age or less (a leave of no more than twelve weeks).

In particular and exceptional cases, and according to conditions set forth by law, fathers can substitute for mothers for some of these leaves.

141. Self-Employed Person. The rules related to the incapacity to work regarding WEs are partially valid in relation to the self-employed, taking into account the special characteristics of self-employment, that is, employment without an employer. Nevertheless, the self-employed are entitled to some forms of the incapacity to worker's protection. Those rights are to be claimed at the relevant social welfare institution.

There is the legal presumption that a self-employed affiliate was contributing if death or an invalidity declaration took place after he or she has paid obligatory contributions for social welfare's taxable yearly rent amount or at least the equivalent for seven months of Minimum Income. In this case, he or she will have yearly coverage as of 1 May of the year when contributions were paid, until 30 April of the following year.

If the above-mentioned contribution amount is less than seven months of Minimum Income, a concerned affiliate will be covered during the number of months resulting from multiplying by 12 the existing relation between the number of contributions equivalent to the Monthly Minimum Income and 7, counted since 1 May of the year of paid contribution. Nevertheless, whichever contribution is paid, the affiliate will always be covered in May of the year when contributions are paid.

In case of a voluntary affiliate that has contributed the month before death or an invalidity declaration has made, to determine the additional contribution, the basic income will be calculated based on the maximum social prevention taxable rent: 60 UF legally readjusted.

Chapter 3. Certification of Incapacity to Work

§1. Common Diseases and Accidents

142. As has been mentioned, incapacity to work has to be certified by a competent person or institution, commonly medical doctors that have intervened or are involved in corresponding diagnoses or treatments.

§2. Labour Accidents and Occupational Diseases

143. As established by Law 16.744 (1968), the certification of labour accidents, occupational diseases, and derived invalidities have to involve concerned workers, employers, Bipartite Parity Committees on Hygiene and Safety, and medical doctors and institutions that have participated or are participating in the related diagnoses and treatments.

§3. Maternity Protection

144. The condition of being pregnant, as well as diseases related to pregnancy, childbirth or child health, has to be certified by a medical doctor. The duration of leaves has to be decided by the medical institution in charge of preventive or curative health. Leaves required because of a minor's disease or health condition need to be certified by concerned persons or institutions participating in the related diagnoses and treatments.

Part VI. Industrial Accidents and Occupational Diseases

145. The first partial attempt to approach this matter was a law enacted in 1916. A technical approach was developed in Law 16.744 (1968), still in force and with many amendments adopted to harmonize that Law with new needs arising from new work and production structures, conditions and organizations.

Objectives of social insurance for labour accidents and occupational diseases are to prevent those accidents and diseases and to provide medical and monetary services and benefits if, as a result of them, death or the suspension, reduction, or loss of the capacity to work occurs.

Insurance covers: (i) injuries suffered as a result of or in connection with work, causing incapacity or death, including those that occur in the direct route between home and the place of work and between that site and home (*in itinere* accidents); (ii) diseases directly caused by work or professional activities, causing incapacity or death; and (iii) death.

Affiliation with this insurance automatically results from the workers' affiliation with any Social Prevention Institution. This automatic affiliation takes place even if the employer has not paid or deposited corresponding contributions. Moreover, WEs are mandatorily and automatically covered by this insurance. By virtue of law, any person linked to an employer through a contract of employment is automatically covered by this insurance. If the employer fails to register a worker, he or she is personally responsible for any medical and monetary provisions and benefits due as a result of the accident, besides the corresponding labour, civil, and penal responsibilities and sanctions.

146. Under Law 20.123 (2006), owners of works, enterprises, and services have a subsidiary responsibility for the duties and obligations of their contractors and subcontractors. Equal responsibility lies with contractors in relation to their subcontractors' duties and obligations for these matters.

The share-out financial regime of this insurance is accompanied by the obligation to constitute a financial reserve that is not inferior to 2% and not superior to 5% of annual incomes.

As mentioned above, the insurance is administered by public and private institutions.

The public administrators of this insurance are: (a) the SPI, which replaced the INP as the legal successor of the old social prevention institutions originally in charge of the insurance's administration (such as the Social Insurance Service and Health Services that have replaced the old National Health Service).

The SPI is in charge of collecting contributions, declaring the right to indemnities and pensions, and providing payments. The Health Services are in charge of medical services and subsidies, with the possibility of contracting those duties with private health institutions.

Private administration exists in the cases of: (i) employers' Mutuals, and (ii) enterprises' delegated administrators.

147. Employers' Mutuals are private institutions, without profit aims, in charge of administering this insurance regarding workers of the affiliated enterprises. Their creation is approved by the President of the Republic, who gives them the pertinent legal personality if they meet the following requisites:

(1) They have a total number of workers occupied in permanent work at members' enterprises that amounts to no less than 20.000.
(2) They have, directly or is association with another Mutual, appropriate medical services, including specialized services for rehabilitation.
(3) They carry out permanent activities directed to the prevention of labour accidents and occupational diseases.
(4) They are not directly or indirectly administered by institutions with profit aims.
(5) Their members have a solidarity responsibility for these Mutuals' obligations.

Enterprise membership to a Mutual covers all its workers. Members' enterprises are mutually binding obligations of the corresponding Mutual. Their membership and its termination are regulated by law.

Mutuals' administration wholly covers all insurance activities: prevention, medical care, rehabilitation, and monetary benefits.

Each Mutual is administered by a bipartite directory composed of three employer representatives and three worker representatives, and their respective substitutes.

If the enterprise puts into action appropriated prevention steps with a relevant diminution of labour risks, additional or overcharged contributions can be reduced or eliminated. In this way, the accomplishment of this insurance objective is stimulated and promoted.

For judiciary purposes, the resolution applying a fine has the character of an Executive Order.

Chapter 1. Field of Application

§1. Territorial Field of Application

148. Corresponding legislation must be applied in the entire Chilean territory.

§2. Personal Field of Application

149. Under Law 16.744, Labour Accidents and Occupational Diseases insurance is obligatory for the following protected persons:

(1) All WEs in the private and public sectors, whatever their labour activities or the nature of the enterprise, institution, service, or person for whom they work, including workers engaged in home-aid services and apprentices, except some employees covered by another system (the police, for instance).
(2) Public employees in the State administration, local government (Municipalities) and decentralized State institutions.
(3) Students, covering those who suffer accidents as a result of or in relation to their studies or professional practices.
(4) Independent (self-employed) and familiar workers. For instance, by virtue of Law 16.744, some groups of workers have been incorporated, such as: (i) peasants receiving land assignations; (ii) newspaper street vendors; (iii) horseback riders who are independent professionals; (iv) taxi owners' conductors; (v) self-employed miners in small and informal undertakings (called *pirquineros*); (vi) magazine vendors; (vii) street commerce vendors; and (viii) non-industrialized fishermen.
(5) Trade union representatives.
(6) Members of Congress.

Chapter 2. Concept of Labour Accident

§1. Accident

150. Law 16.744 defines a labour accident as any damage or injury suffered by a person as a result of or on the occasion of work that causes incapacity or death. Not defined as labour accidents are those: (i) resulting from a force majeure totally not related to the performance of work or duties, and (ii) that are intentionally provoked by the victim.

Keeping in mind the nature of activities performed by beneficiaries of this insurance, damages are related to corresponding duties. For instance, in the case of students, trade union representatives, and Members of Congress, a labour accident is damage or injury suffered as a result of or on the occasion of the accomplishment of their duties as such, causing incapacity or death.

Under the Reforms of 1993 and 1997, the following are also considered labour accidents: (i) psychic or physical damages suffered by workers during work, enterprises; or (ii) tasks who have been the victims of theft, assault, or other criminal violence, as a result of or on the occasion of work; and (iii) damages suffered during professional training activities.

Lesions and injuries are insured if they are a result of an accident, that is, an unforeseen event, an event that is not expected, foreseen, or has been tried before. In other words, a cause-effect relationship must exist between the work done and the accident. This relationship can be of a direct or indirect nature. In the first case, the accident is a result of the work. In the second case, the accident results in connection with the work.

§2. Link to the Contract of Labour

151. As has been mentioned, a labour accident is any damage or injury suffered by a person as a result of or on the occasion of work. Thus, a link between the accident and the labour contract must exist. Consequently, events that occur as a result of a voluntary act of a victim are not labour accidents. Moreover, as said, Law 16.744 has established that accidents resulting from a force majeure totally not related to the work performed are not covered.

§3. Accident on the Way to Work

152. Chilean legislation has incorporated the notion of accidents on the way to work, also known as accidents *in itinere*, which are understood to be:

(1) Those taking place on the direct route between home and the work site and from there to home.
(2) Those taking place on the direct route between two workplaces, even if they depend on different employers. In that case, the labour accident is considered to be related to the workplace to which the victim was going.

The circumstance of an accident having taken place on the direct route from home to work, work to home, or workplace to workplace must be proven through a police report or other irrefutable means of proof.

Chapter 3. Concept of Occupational Diseases

153. Occupational diseases are those directly caused by the fulfilment of labour or professional duties that cause incapacity or death.

The following categories of factors are considered sources of occupational diseases: (a) chemicals, (b) physics, (c) biologics, and (d) dusts. In Chile, there is an official but not exclusive list of occupational diseases, included in LD 109 (1968) from the MLSP. Consequently, a pathology not included in that list but directly caused by work is declared an 'occupational disease', and covered by Law 16.744.

Among the diseases listed are: (a) alcoholism; (b) dermatitis; (c) carcinoma and pre-cancer dermatological damage; (d) pneumoconiosis; (e) bronchitis, pneumonia, emphysema, and pulmonary fibrosis; (f) bronchial asthma; (g) pulmonary or respiratory tract cancer; (h) urinary tract cancer; (i) leukaemia and aplastic anaemia; (j) central and periphery nervous system damage; (k) damage of sense organs; (l) motion organism; (m) handicapping neurosis; (n) handicapping laryngitis; (o) infectious diseases; and (p) malignant tumour of the pleura or peritoneum.

The official diseases list is reviewed yearly by the Supervisory Public Agency of Social Security.

Chapter 4. Medical Care

154. Medical services and monetary benefits regulation applies to both labour accidents and occupational diseases, which are classified in following categories based on their effects:

(1) Those causing temporal incapacity.
(2) Those causing partial invalidity.
(3) Those causing total invalidity.
(4) Those causing grand invalidity.
(5) Those causing death.

Free of charge, the following medical services are provided as of the time of the accident or disease diagnosis date, until total recovery is achieved:

(1) Medical, chirurgical, and dental attention in external establishments or at home.
(2) Hospitalization, if needed.
(3) Medicines and pharmaceutical products.
(4) Prostheses and orthopaedic devices, and their reparation.
(5) Physical rehabilitation and vocational retraining.
(6) Transportation costs and every other cost needed for receiving services and benefits.

Chapter 5. Degrees and Benefits

155. Incapacity to work gives rise to monetary benefit payments to victims of insured labour accidents and occupational diseases or to their survivors if the insured worker dies.

The amount of payments varies depending on the effects produced by the labour accident or occupational disease, as described below.

A daily subsidy equivalent to 80% of social welfare taxable remuneration or rents received in the last payment period, duly readjusted. Subsidies will not be affected by income taxes or by social welfare contributions. Subsidies will be paid during the period of all medical treatment until the affiliate's health recuperation or invalidity is declared.

The maximum period for paying subsidies is fifty-two weeks, extendable for another fifty-two weeks. Once the 52 or 104-week period is over, invalidity is to be declared.

If an affiliate refuses to follow the prescribed medical treatments or impedes the recovery of his or her heath, payment of subsidies can be suspended. That suspension can be claimed by the insured.

A person suffering a diminution of his or her capacity to work, allegedly permanent, equal or superior to 15% but less than 70%, will be considered partially invalid.

Chilean legislation establishes the following four degrees of incapacity:

(1) Partial First-Degree (from 15% to 39% loss of capacity to work): The victim is entitled to be paid an indemnity of no more than 15% of his or her basic salary, taking into account the degree of lost capacity. The indemnity can be totally paid in cash or paid in monthly instalments, as decided by the victim, who can also, at any time, demand to be paid the remaining indemnity in cash. In this case, the indemnity will be equivalent to thirty-day subsidies. The same indemnity will be received by the insured, who, as a result of the accident, has not suffered incapacity to work but has suffered a major mutilation or an evident deformity. However, if the mutilation or deformity has occurred to the face, head, or genital organs, the victim will receive the major indemnity.
(2) Partial Second-Degree (from 40% to 69% loss of capacity): The victim is entitled to receive an invalidity pension amounting to 35% of his or her basic salary.
(3) Total (70% or more loss of capacity): This gives the victim the right to a total invalidity pension, which amount is the equivalent of 70% of his or her basic salary.
(4) Grand Invalidity (an invalid person requiring to be helped by others to afford the realization of fundamental functions of life): This gives the victim the right to a complement to the total invalidity pension, amounting to 30% of his or her basic salary.

156. A pension's amount will be increased by 5% for each child (over 2 years of age) entitled to family allowances, who maintains the right to receive those allowances. In any case, these pensions can exceed 50%, 100%, or 140% of the monthly remuneration, taking into account the degree of invalidity mentioned above.

Payment of this pension can be suspended if the insured person does not agree to be submitted to duly ordered examinations, controls, or prescriptions, or refuses without justification to be submitted to ordered and needed procedures for his or her physical rehabilitation and professional retraining. The insured can present a claim against such a suspension.

As governed by Law 16.744 and its amendments, at any time, new evaluations, re-evaluations, and revisions can take place, especially if the invalid person suffers new labour accidents or occupational diseases (or other non-professional accidents and diseases).

Chapter 6. Death

157. If a labour accident or occupational disease produces the death of the active or pensioned affiliated worker, Survivor Pensions (SP) are recognized for a widow, sons and daughters, the non-married mother of children of the deceased, an invalid widowed husband, and – in their absence – ascendants and descendants receiving family allowances.

The following particular conditions have to be fulfilled in each case:

(1) Widow. A life pension to a widow who is over 45 years of age or an invalid of any age. The pension amount corresponds to the 50% of the basic pension that the victim should have received for total invalidity, or 50% of the pension that the insured worker was receiving until his death. If the widow is under 45 years of age, she receives that pension for one year unless she is in charge of children receiving family allowances. If after that extended period, she has become 45 years old, her pension becomes a life pension. A widows' right to a pension ceases if she marries again. However, in that case, if she was a receiving a life pension, she is entitled to receive once an amount equivalent to a two-year pension.
(2) Sons and/or daughters. If they are less than 18 years of age (or 23 if they are students), or invalids of any age, they receive a pension equivalent to 20% of the father's pension or the pension he should have received in case of total invalidity.
(3) Non-married mother of sons and/or daughters of the deceased. If she is single or a widow and was living in the charge of the deceased, she is entitled to receive a pension equivalent to 30% of that of a widow, calculated and governed in the same way as for a widow.
(4) Invalid widowed husband. If he has lived in the charge of his insured wife, he is entitled to a life pension under the same conditions laid down for an invalid widow.
(5) Other survivors. If none of above-mentioned survivors is present, ancestors receiving family allowances from the deceased are entitled to receive the pension. The pension amount is the same established for sons and daughters.

In any case, these SPs can jointly exceed 100% of: (i) a pension that the victim could have received if he or she had been rendered totally invalid, or (ii) a pension that was being received at the date of death.

Chapter 7. Prevention of Occupational Diseases and Labour Accidents

158. Chilean legislation gives special attention to the enforcement of policies and practises devoted to prevent professional risks (occupational diseases and labour accidents), which are mandatory for all parties concerned. The main regulation is contained in Law 16.744 and its amendments, as well as LDs developing and readjusting specific matters.

Primarily, workers and employers are obliged to take any needed steps to avoid those risks, in their own interests and fulfilling social and economic interests. For that purpose, legislation has established that, in each enterprise, the following duties are to be carried out:

A Bipartite Paritary Committee has to perform the following duties:

(1) To advise and instruct workers in the appropriate utilization of protection devices.
(2) To verify the accomplishment of prevention, hygiene, and security measures by employers and workers.
(3) To investigate causes of labour accidents and occupational diseases produced at the enterprise, as well as any other health problems affecting workers in a general or continuing way, allegedly originated by the utilization of phytosanitary or chemical products harmful to human health.
(4) To indicate the adoption of all hygienic and sanitary measures useful to prevent professional risks.
(5) To accomplish all other requested functions or missions.

Worker's representatives are designated by workers. They will be protected by labour fuero (protection of their independence and autonomy in the fulfilment of duties by prohibiting their unlawful dismissal or change of labour conditions).

Besides these rules, there exist additional rules to be implemented in economic activity branches, sectors, and subsectors. This is the case, for instance, in the mining and building industries.

159. Moreover, in mining, industrial, and commercial enterprises employing more than 100 workers, a Department of Professional Risks Prevention must be established and directed by a prevention expert.

160. Employers that engage a contractor or subcontractor to perform work, tasks, or services pertaining to their own economic activity must duly supervise the fulfilment of contractors' or subcontractors' duties related to the requirements of legislation on hygiene and security. To this end, such employers have to implement a system of labour safety and health management covering all involved workers, even when their labour relation's dependency, if the principal employer's workers together with contractors or subcontractors' workers total more than fifty.

Consequently, the principal enterprise has to prepare special rules for contractors' or subcontractors' enterprises, particularly, at least, the coordination of prevention activities for all involved employers, thus guaranteeing appropriate hygiene and security conditions for all related workers.

161. The relevant set of rules must also establish procedures to verify obligations of the principal enterprise as well as corresponding sanctions to that enterprise.

Likewise, as said, an enterprise must verify the constitution and functioning of: (i) a Bipartite Paritary Committee on Hygiene and Safety, and (ii) a Department of Professional Risks Prevention, if the total joint number of workers is equal or greater than twenty-five or 100 workers in the same workplace.

162. To enforce and supervise the due accomplishment of these obligations, legislation has given general or specific powers and duties to the following private and public institutions:

(1) Employers' Mutuals: They have to develop permanent activities of prevention through specialized services in charge of experts. As has been mentioned, Mutuals are authorized to impose additional contributions to require enterprises to establish preventive rules and practices.
(2) Labour Directorate: As an institution under the purview of the Ministry of Labour, it is in charge of inspection activities in this field. It also supervises the constitution and functioning of Bipartite Paritary Committees on Hygiene and Safety. It has the legal power to order the immediate suspension of an enterprise's working activities that it considers to constitute an impending danger to workers' health or lives.
(3) Health Services: As public institutions in charge of inspecting and supervising the prevention of risks, among other functions, they are empowered to: (i) impose sanctions against enterprises that do not appropriately accomplish their duties in this area; (ii) supervise risk prevention activities in charge of employers' Mutuals and enterprises with delegated administration; (iii) evaluate the suitability of any person to be considered a professional expert in risk prevention; and (iv) advise Bipartite Committees in their tasks to prevent risks.

In particular, the PHI, being the 'national laboratory and reference unit' in the area of occupational health, is in charge of functions such as advisory services and the proposal of prevention measures.

In turn: (i) the General Directorate of Maritime Territory and Merchant Marine is in charge of supervising risk prevention in ships, harbours, and maritime, river, and lake navigation; (ii) the National Mining and Geology Service is in charge of enforcing the observance of legislation on mining safety and risk prevention, especially rules contained in LD 140 (1992).

To improve the level of protection in safety and health at work, in 2011, Chile ratified the ILO Convention 187, on the promotional framework for safety and health at work (2006).

In the Preamble of the Convention, it is remembered: (i) that the protection of workers against occupational or common diseases and labour accidents is one of the ILO's objectives; (ii) the international standards established by the ILO Convention 155, on workers' security and health (1981); and (iii) the ILO's Programme of Decent Work. In its text, the Convention sets up the following obligations: (i) to promote the continuous improvement of safety and health at work, as a means to prevent lesions, diseases and deaths caused by work, through the implementation of a policy, a system and a national programme, in consultation with the most representative organizations of employers and workers; (ii) to adopt measures directed to progressively obtain a safety and healthy place of work; (iii) to periodically consult with the employers and workers most representative organizations, the measures to be adopted in order to ratify the ILO Conventions in security and health at work.

The elaboration of the national policy must take into account basic principles such as: (i) the evaluation of risks and perils at work and combating them, and (ii) the development of a national culture of prevention that includes information, consultation and formation.

On turn, the national system of safety and health at work must be established, maintained and developed in a progressive way, with consultations of the most representative organizations of employers and workers.

The system has to integrate: (i) the legislation, collective agreements and other pertinent tools; (ii) an authority or body – or authorities and bodies – responsible for the security and health at work; (iii) mechanisms to guarantee the accomplishment of national legislation, including labour inspection systems; and (iv) ways and means to promote cooperation in the level of the enterprise, between the direction and the employees and their representatives, as an essential element of prevention measures.

The system should also include: (i) one or more tripartite consultative bodies at the national level; (ii) information and technical advisory services; (iii) formation in matters of security and health at work; (iv) health services at work; (v) research on these matters; (vi) collection and analysis of information; (vii) collaboration with pertinent insurance or social security's regimes; and (viii) support to the progressive improvement of security and health little and medium enterprises and in the informal economy.

Finally, every ILO Member that ratifies the Convention has to prepare, implement, control and evaluate periodically a national programme, in consultation with the most representative organizations of employers and workers. Mainly, the programme has: (i) to promote the development of a national culture of prevention; (ii) to contribute to the workers' protection through the elimination of perils and risks to their maximum reduction; (iii) to include objectives, ends and indicators of progress; and (iv) to be supported by other national programmes and plans, to obtain the objective of a safe and healthy labour environment.

§1. PROCEDURES

163. The main procedure is related to the announcement (notification) of labour accidents and occupational diseases. In this regard, the following steps have to be observed:

(1) All accidents and diseases that can produce incapacity to work or death have to be announced by the employer to the corresponding insurance's administrator immediately after they have occurred. The same obligation is applicable to the victim or inheritors and to the medical doctor who has intervened in related medical services or diagnoses. Likewise, the relevant Bipartite Paritary Committee on Hygiene and Safety has to make that announcement.
(2) The announcement has to contain all needed information that has been legally established.
(3) The relevant insurance's administrator has to report to Health Services those notified accidents and diseases causing incapacity to work or death.

In addition to the above-mentioned announcement, in cases of fatal and serious labour accidents, the employer must immediately announce its occurrence to the relevant Labour Inspectorate and Regional MH's Secretary. Moreover, the employer has to immediately suspend the affected work and, if necessary, allow for the workers' evacuation. The suspension will be in force until the relevant authority authorizes it, after the deficiencies have been corrected.

Infringements to these rules are sanctioned with fines ranging from 50 to 159 Monthly Tax Units.

Chapter 8. Supplementary Benefits

164. Additionally, in case of the death of an insured or pensioned worker, there exists the death benefit paid by the appropriate pension system. That payment corresponds to a reimbursement of funeral costs of 15 UF (about USD 563) to the widow, the father or mother, or the son or daughter who has paid the funeral expenses.

If those costs were paid for someone not having legal family ties, the death payment will amount to real costs paid, up to 15 UF. This payment will be charged to the affiliate's individual capitalization account.

Pensioned workers for labour accidents or occupational diseases, who become entitled to receive an OAP, cease to receive the former pension and start receiving the OAP. In any case, the new pension can be less than 80% of the affiliate's basic monthly remuneration, which is taken into account to calculate the old pension, duly readjusted.

Chapter 9. No-Fault Insurance

165. Chilean legislation is in line with the no-fault or employer's objective responsibility. Thus, a worker has no obligation to prove the employer's responsibility for an accident. In turn, employers must transfer that objective responsibility to the insurance institution.

As has been mentioned, an employer's objective responsibility does not cover accidents: (i) resulting from a force majeure totally not related to the performance of work or duties, or (ii) intentionally provoked by the victim.

Chapter 10. Civil Liability

166. When an accident or disease is an employer's fault or the result of fraud or a third party's fault or fraud, criminal judicial case can be initiated, governed by the following special rules:

(1) The relevant insurance administrator can legally prosecute the employer or third party responsible for the accident to obtain the reimbursement of benefits and services that have been already delivered or are to be delivered.
(2) The victim and all other persons damaged as a result of the accident or disease can also prosecute the responsible employer or third party to pay all other legal indemnities to which they are entitled, including those related to moral damages.

As established in Law 17.744, if the accident or disease is a result of the non-excusable negligence of a worker, a fine will be applied, even if that worker was a victim of the accident.

167. Affiliates suffering an occupational disease are also entitled to the following:

(1) To be transferred by the relevant enterprise to workplaces not affected by the agent causing the disease.
(2) To be authorized to attend control examinations. The time used for that purpose will be considered effectively as work time for all legal purposes.

Part VII. Unemployment

168. The Unemployment insurance was established by Law 19.728 (2001), mainly reformed by Law 20.328 (2009).

Chapter 1. Protected Persons

169. The insurance applies to dependent workers who start or restart work activities after the entry into force of Law 19.728.

The beginning of the employment relationship of a worker not subject to insurance generates automatic incorporation into it and the obligation to contribute in the terms established in Article 5 of the law.

The provisions of this law shall not apply to: (i) workers subject to an apprenticeship contract; (ii) minors under 18 years of age until they reach that age; (iii) pensioners, unless the pension has been granted due to partial disability or they are workers in a private home.

The incorporation of a worker into insurance does not authorize the employer to agree, either individually or collectively, to a reduction in the amount of compensation for years of service referred to in Article 163 of the Labour Code.

The rights established in this Law are independent and compatible with those established for workers in Title V of Book I of the Labour Code – referred to the termination of the labour contract – without prejudice to the provisions of Article 13 of the Law, in the case of the imputation of part of the balance of the Individual Unemployment Account constituted by the contributions made by the employer plus its profitability, minus the corresponding administration costs, from which the insured can make withdrawals. In no case may the amount constituted by the contributions of the worker be taken into account.

Chapter 2. Benefits Financed from the Unemployment Individual Account

170. Insured workers are entitled to unemployment benefits if they meet the following requirements:

(1) That the labour contract has been terminated for any of the reasons indicated in Articles 159, 160, 161 and 163 bis, or by application of the first paragraph of Article 171, of the Labor Code.
(2) That the worker with an indefinite contract or the worker of a private home, regardless of the duration of his contract, registers in the Individual Account for Unemployment a minimum of twelve continuous or discontinuous monthly contributions, since his affiliation to the Insurance or from the date on which the last draft to which they would have been entitled under this law was due.
(3) In the case of a worker with a fixed-term contract or for a specific work, work or service, he or she must register in the Individual Unemployment Account a minimum of six continuous or discontinuous monthly contributions, from his affiliation to the Insurance or from the date on which the last draft to which they would have been entitled under this law was accrued.
(4) Be unemployed at the time of the application for the benefit.

171. If the contract is terminated for the reasons provided for in Article 161 of the Labour Code, the member is entitled to compensation for years of service provided for in the second paragraph of Article 163 of the Code, calculated on the last monthly remuneration, with a maximum limit of three hundred and thirty days of remuneration, unless agreed, individually or collectively, a superior, in which case the latter will apply.

The part of the balance of the Individual Unemployment Account constituted by the contributions made by the employer plus its profitability, minus the corresponding administration costs, from which the insured can make withdrawals, will be charged to this benefit. In no case may the amount constituted by the contributions of the worker be taken into account.

172. If the employment contract terminates by application of any of the causes indicated in numbers 1 and 2 of Article 159, in Article 160, or in the first paragraph of Article 171, all of the Labour Code, the benefit will consist of the withdrawal of the funds accumulated in the Individual Account for Unemployment.

173. Workers who terminate their employment relationship for any of the reasons indicated in numbers 4, 5 and 6 of Article 159 and in Article 161 of the Labour Code will have the right to make as many monthly transfers of their Individual Account for Unemployment as their balance of said Account allows them to finance, according to the percentages expressed in the second column of the following table.

Table 7 Months Average Percentage Remuneration (Last Six or Twelve Months Contributions)

First	70
Second	55
Third	45
Quarter	40
Fifth	35
Sixth	30
Seventh or higher	30

The amount of the unemployment benefit during the months indicated in the first column shall correspond to the percentage indicated in the second column, which refers to the average of the remuneration earned by the worker in the last twelve months, in which contributions are recorded prior to the end of the employment relationship for those who are hired for an indefinite period or for workers in private homes. In the case of workers with a fixed-term contract or for a specific task, work or service, the average of the remuneration accrued by him/her in the last six months in which contributions prior to the end of the employment relationship are recorded.

The last month of benefit to which the worker is entitled may be less than the percentage indicated in the preceding table and will correspond to the outstanding balance of the Individual Unemployment Account. In any case, if the last draft to which the worker is entitled is equal to or less than 20% of the amount of the previous draft, both drafts will be paid together. Notwithstanding the foregoing, in the case of workers who, complying with the established requirements, have chosen to receive benefits from the Solidarity Unemployment Fund, the amount of the benefits to which they are entitled will be governed by the provisions of Article 25.

The benefit will be paid for monthly payments due and will accrue from the day following the end of the contract.

The enjoyment of the benefit will be interrupted each time the status of the unemployed person is lost before exhausting all the drawings to which he is entitled.

174. Those workers who, having terminated an employment relationship, maintain another one in force or are hired in a new job before exhausting all the drafts of their Individual Account for Unemployment to which they are entitled will have the following options:

(1) Withdraw the amount corresponding to the benefit to which he would have been entitled in that month in the case of having remained unemployed.
(2) Keep such balance in the account.

In both cases, the worker will keep the unused balance in his account for the next period of unemployment. The balance maintained in the respective Individual Unemployment Account, increased with subsequent contributions, will be the new basis for calculating the benefit.

In the event of non-payment of contributions, the worker shall have the right to demand from the employer the payment of all the benefits that such non-compliance prevented him from receiving. This right is understood to be inalienable for all purposes and will not oppose the exercise of other corresponding actions. The judgment establishing the payment of benefits shall also order, by way of sanction, the payment of the contributions owed by the employer with the corresponding adjustments and interest.

175. In the event of the worker's death, the funds in the Individual Severance Account will be paid to the person or persons designated by the worker at the Administration Company. In the absence of an expression of will by the worker, such payment shall be made, in order of precedence, to the spouse or civil partner, children or parents of the deceased. These payments will be made if it is sufficient to prove, by the beneficiaries, their identity or the respective marital status.

If a worker retires, for any reason, he/she can dispose in a single draft of the funds accumulated in his Individual Unemployment Account.

176. Workers who are processing their pension application may transfer part or all of the balance of their Individual Unemployment Account to their individual capitalization account that they maintain in a PFA, in order to increase the capital to finance their pension. The Administration Company shall inform the Internal Revenue Service of the transfers of funds made in accordance with the preceding paragraph, in the manner and within the period determined by said Service.

177. Insurance affiliates who receive benefits charged to the Individual Unemployment Account or the Solidarity Unemployment Fund will maintain the status of affiliates to the regime of Law 18.469 (1985) –on the constitutional right to health and legal health benefits– during the period in which the respective monthly payments are accrued. The foregoing is without prejudice to the rules of disaffiliation contained in Law 18.933 (1990), regulating health benefits of the ISAPRES.

178. Those workers who are entitled to the benefits of the Solidarity Unemployment Fund, who at the time of being unemployed received family allowances as beneficiaries, will have the right to continue applying for this benefit for the same amounts they were receiving on the date of dismissal, as long as they receive monthly transfers in accordance with this law.

Chapter 3. Benefits Financed from the Solidarity Unemployment Fund

179. The remaining contribution of the employer referred to in Article 5, that is 0.8% and 0.2% of the taxable remuneration of the worker of indefinite term contract and fixed term contract, or for a specific task, work or service, respectively, and the State tax contribution referred to in the same article will enter a fund called Solidarity Unemployment Fund.

In the case of domestic workers, the remaining employer contribution will correspond to 0.8% of the worker's taxable remuneration, regardless of the duration of the contract.

180. Workers who meet the following requirements will be entitled to receive benefits from the Solidarity Unemployment Fund:

(1) Register twelve monthly contributions to the Solidarity Unemployment Fund since their affiliation to the Insurance or since the last draft to which they would have been entitled under this law was due, in the last twenty-four months prior to the month of the end of the contract. However, the last three contributions made must be continuous and with the same employer.
(2) That the employment contract terminates for any of the reasons provided for in numbers 4, 5 and 6 of Article 159 or Articles 161 and 163 bis, all of the Labour Code.
(3) That the resources of their individual unemployment account are insufficient to obtain a severance benefit for the periods, percentages and amounts indicated in Article 25 of the Law.
(4) Be unemployed at the time of the application.

Without prejudice to the provisions of the following article, a worker may not receive more than ten payments of benefits financed partially or totally by the Solidarity Unemployment Fund, in a period of five years.

The right to receive the benefit will cease by the sole operation of the law, once a new job has been obtained by the beneficiary.

181. As established in Article 25 of the Law on Unemployment Insurance, the amount of unemployment benefit during the months indicated in the first column from the table below shall correspond to the percentage of the average remuneration earned by the worker in the twelve months prior to the end of the employment relationship, indicated in the second column. The profit shall be assigned to the upper and lower values for each month, referred to in the third and fourth columns, respectively:

Months	*Average Percentage Respect to Remuneration Last 12 Months (%)*	*Superior* Value CLP	*Lower Value CLP*
First	70	525,000	157,500
Second	55	412,500	123,750
Third	45	337,500	101,250
Fourth	40	300,000	90,000
Fifth	35	262,500	78,750

182. In the case of workers hired for a fixed term, or for a specific task, work or service, the unemployment benefit will be extended until the third month, with the percentages and higher and lower values indicated in the following table:

Months	*Average Percentage Respect to Remuneration Last 12 Months (%)*	*Superior Value CLP*	*Lower Value CLP*
First	50	375,000	112,500
Second	40	300,000	90,000
Third	35	262,500	78,750

183. Beneficiaries who are receiving the fifth draft charged to the Solidarity Unemployment Fund shall be entitled to a sixth and seventh draft of benefit, whenever the national unemployment rate published by the National Institute of Statistics exceeds by one percentage point the average of said rate, corresponding to the previous four years published by that Institute, to be paid according to the following table:

Months	*Average Percentage Respect to Remuneration Last 12 Months (%)*	*Superior Value CLP*	*Lower Value CLP*
Sixth	50	375,000	112,500
Seventh	40	300,000	90,000

In the case of workers hired for a fixed term, or for a specific task, work or service, when the unemployment conditions already indicated are presented, and they are receiving the third draft, they will be entitled to a fourth and fifth draft with a benefit equal to that corresponding to the sixth and seventh month already evoked.

The aforementioned lower and upper values will be readjusted on 1 March of each year by 100% of the variation experienced in the previous calendar year by the

Consumer Price Index, determined by the National Institute of Statistics or by the agency that replaces it. In addition, these lower and higher values will be readjusted at the same time indicated above, in 100% of the variation experienced in the previous calendar year, the Real Remuneration Index determined by the aforementioned Institute. These values will be adjusted by the remuneration index indicated above, provided that their variation is positive.

In the case of workers who, during the last twelve months, have received one or more salaries corresponding to part-time work, an adjustment of the higher and lower values referred to in this article must be made in proportion to the average monthly working day of the last twelve months.

The foregoing provisions shall apply to domestic workers, subject to certain exceptions.

184. The responsibility of the Solidarity Unemployment Fund will operate once the resources of the Individual Unemployment Account have been exhausted.

The Solidarity Unemployment Fund may finance preparation programmes to facilitate the reintegration into the labour market of unemployed persons who are receiving the benefits indicated in the previous article and who have a low employability index. The National Training and Employment Service shall administer and supervise the aforementioned programmes financed with said Fund, without prejudice to the powers of the Superintendence of Pensions in relation to the supervision of the Administration Company with respect to the administration of the Solidarity Unemployment Fund.

The Solidarity Unemployment Fund will contribute to the mandatory individual capitalization account for pensions of the beneficiaries who have opted for said Fund, the amount equivalent to 10% of the unemployment benefit that corresponds to them receiving in accordance with Article 25. This contribution must be paid by the Fund Management Company and will not be subject to the collection of commissions by the corresponding PFA.

The total value of the benefits payable from the Solidarity Unemployment Fund in a given month may not exceed 20% of the value accumulated in the Fund on the last day of the previous month. If the total value of the benefits to be paid exceeds the percentage already indicated, the benefit to be paid to each affiliate will be reduced proportionally according to the total value of benefits that the Solidarity Unemployment Fund can finance.

Persons who obtain benefits from the Solidarity Unemployment Fund through simulation or deception and who similarly obtain a benefit greater than that which corresponds to them will be punished with minor imprisonment in its minimum to medium degrees. The same penalty shall apply to those who provide the means for the commission of such crimes. The foregoing, without prejudice to the obligation to return to the Fund the sums unduly received.

185. The beneficiary shall not be entitled to the benefits provided, or those granted shall cease, as the case may be and for each event of unemployment, if he/she does not effectively seek employment. For these purposes, the beneficiary will be considered not to be effectively seeking employment when:

(1) Do not register with the National Employment Exchange.
(2) Do not apply, repeatedly and without just cause, to an employment opportunity that is available as informed by the respective Municipal Office of Labour Intermediation or the National Employment Exchange.
(3) Not attend, repeatedly and without just cause, job interviews duly mediated by the same institutions referred to in the previous point.
(4) Reject, without just cause, an opportunity for intermediated employment or training offered by the respective Municipal Labour Intermediation Office or the National Employment Exchange.
(5) Reject, without just cause, a training grant offered and financed by the National Training and Employment Service.

186. For the purposes of the preceding paragraph, causes of similar entity shall be considered justified causes of the beneficiary, such as:

(1) Suffer from any illness or disability that prevents you from developing the job offered.
(2) Reside in a location distant from the place where the job interview is held, where the respective job must be performed or where the training offered is carried out.
(3) The employment or training scholarship offered is not related to the skills or abilities of the previous employment or causes a serious impairment of its employment status or its professional, university or technical studies.
(4) The employment offered does not allow him/her to receive a remuneration equal to or greater than 50% of the last accrued in the previous employment.

Notwithstanding the foregoing, a regulation issued by the MLSP, which must be signed by the Minister of Finance, shall establish the criteria and conditions for determining the pertinence of the justified causes referred to in this article, as well as the requirements, procedure and mechanisms to prove their concurrence and, in general, any rule for the correct application of this provision.

The benefit will accrue and be paid for monthly payments due and will not be subject to any social security contribution or taxes. Their enjoyment shall be incompatible with any remunerated activity.

Chapter 4. Provision of Work

§1. Intermediation

187. Law 20.328 also created the Labour Information System and the National Job Vacancies Agency (Bolsa Nacional de Empleo), designed to:

(1) Increase the employability of unemployed workers affiliated with Unemployment Insurance.
(2) Facilitate the labour reinstatement of the above-mentioned workers.

The Labour Information System provides labour market information. It is administered by the MLSP through its Undersecretariat of Labour.

The National Job Vacancies Agency facilitates the search and offer of vacancies to unemployed workers affiliated with Unemployment Insurance.

Registered unemployed workers can offer their labour services and will have access to relevant job vacancy information (through a database). In turn, registered employers can offer job vacancies and search for workers to fill those vacancies.

Among other duties, the Administrator of the National Job Vacancies Agency:

(1) Must communicate job vacancies and training opportunities to: (i) beneficiaries of the Solidarity Unemployment Fund, and (ii) those beneficiaries that have ceased receiving payments.
(2) Must maintain a database with all information necessary to appropriately perform National Job Vacancies Agency tasks.

The Administrator of the National Job Vacancies Agency is assigned through a public binding conducted by the MLSP and the Finance Ministry. The Administrator receives from the Solidarity Unemployment Fund remuneration (compensation payment), and it is obliged to meet corresponding Law 20.328 regulations.

§2. Vocational Training

188. Another important reform incorporated by Law 20.328 is authorizing the Solidarity Unemployment Fund to finance programmes designed to facilitate reinstatement in the labour market of unemployed workers receiving benefits described above, and, also, with a low employability level. These programmes are administered and supervised by SENCE.

Each year, no more than 2% of the total balance of the Solidarity Unemployment Fund can be assigned to these programmes, which are executed by the Labour Information Offices and private entities that accomplish requisites specially governed by the MLSP.

§3. Direct Work Provision

189. In connection with seasonal unemployment, there are governmental programmes to promote better levels of employment, especially in relation to seasonal and temporary workers.

Nevertheless, despite the significant efforts of government policies to improve the employment level, presently, the unemployment rate is almost 10%, mainly as a result of the financial and economic crisis that began in 2008 and as a result of the COVID-19 pandemic. To deal with this problem and to promote the betterment of the general economy, governmental policies are mainly focused on: (i) a large programme of public works to create jobs; (ii) the payment of subsidies for the employment of young workers; (iii) special measures to support medium, small, and micro-enterprises, taking into account the large percentages of jobs generated by them; and (iv) measures to prevent or diminish the precarious nature of labour contracts.

Part VIII. Pensions

190. Law Decree 3.500, adopted in 1980, established a new pension system. As of March 1990, its original text was modified by LDs 3.626 and 3.650 (both of 1981), and by Laws 18.072 (1981), 18.086 (1981), 18.137 (1982), 18.196 (1982), 18208 (1983), 18.225 (1983), 18.379 (1985), 18.398 (1985), 18.420 (1985), 18.481 (1985), 18.482 (1985), 18.520 (1986), 18.646 (1987), 18.681 (1987), 18.717 (1988), 18.753 (1988), 18.768 (1988), 18.798 (1989), 18.840 (1989), and 18.964 (1990).

After Chile's return to democracy, the following laws have been passed establishing new and important reforms to LDs 3.500: 19.177 (1992), 19.200 (1993), 19.247 (1993), 19.260 (1993), 19.301 (1994), 19.350 (1994), 19.389 (1995), 19.398 (1995), 19.400 (1995), 19.415 (1995), 19.469 (1996), 19.601 (1999), 19.641 (1999), 19.705 (2000), 19.768 (2001), 19.795 (2002), 19.895 (2003), 19.934 (2004), 20.023 (2005), 20.190 (2007), 20.210 (2007), 20.255 (2008), 20.255 (2008), 20.345 (2009), 20.455 (2010), 20.448 (2010), 20.531 (2011), 20.552 (2011), 20.720 (2014), 20.830 (2015), 20.956 (2016), 21.130 (2019), 21.133 (2019), 21.190 (2019), 21.276 (2020), 21.306 (2020), 21.309 (2021), 21.419 (2022) and 21.538 (2023).

Chapter 1. Pension System: Main Characteristics

§1. Uniqueness and Affiliation

191. According to LD 3.500 (1980), there is only one pension system for old age, invalidity, and survivors, which is compulsory and automatically applied to dependent workers engaged in labour contracts since 1 January 1983 and voluntarily applied to: (i) those dependent workers that were engaged in labour contracts before that date and decided to be affiliated with the new pension system, and (ii) those IWs voluntarily affiliated to a PFA.

Affiliation is a legal relationship between a worker and the Old Age, Invalidity, and SP's System, which gives raise to legally established obligations and rights, particularly the right to services and the obligation to contribute.

The affiliation is unique and permanent. It continues throughout an affiliate's life, even when he or she: (i) is not actively working, (ii) has one or more simultaneous or successive work activities, or (iii) changes to another Social Prevention Institution within the system. Each worker can only contribute to one PFA.

The beginning and termination of their workers' labour relations have to be communicated by an employer to the PFA to which they are affiliated in the twenty-day period following that labour relations' beginning or termination. In turn, a worker has to communicate to his or her employer the PFA with which he or she is affiliated in the thirty-day period following that labour relations' beginning or termination.

§2. Contributions

192. There are obligatory contributions and a set of voluntary contributions and deposits –of an individual or collective nature comprising the so-called voluntary pillar of the Chilean pension system.

§3. Obligatory Contributions

193. Affiliated workers, from minors to 65 years of age for men and 60 years of age for women, are obliged: (i) to contribute 10% of their social prevention taxable remunerations and rents in their individual capitalization accounts, and (ii) to pay an additional contribution to cover the PFA's financing and payment of the invalidity insurance premium.

This additional contribution is the same for all affiliates, except those not entitled to the invalidity and survivor insurance coverage that all PFA have to jointly contract to totally cover their obligations related to:

(1) Pensions of affiliates declared invalid by a First Medical Report.
(2) Additional contributions corresponding to: (i) the above-mentioned affiliates when they become entitled to an invalidity pension by a Second Medical Report, and (ii) affiliates declared totally invalid.

(3) Additional contributions due when an affiliate who has been declared invalid by a First Medical Report dies.
(4) Additional contributions due when a non-pensioned affiliate dies.
(5) Additional contributions due when an affiliate that has been declared invalid by a First Medical Report does not become entitled to an invalidity pension based on a Second Medical Report. This exemption is also applicable to: (i) independent workers' affiliates, and (ii) dependent workers' affiliates who are not in service because of their labour relation's termination or suspension, and for whom death or an invalidity declaration has occurred in the two-month period after their labour relation's termination or suspension, if those affiliates have a minimum of six monthly contributions in the year previous to the last month's day of their labour relation's termination or suspension.

Regarding dependent workers, the contribution to be paid for the invalidity and survivor insurance premium has to be assumed by the employer, except in cases of young workers receiving a social prevention subsidy.

194. There is another additional contribution related to heavy work (those types of work that accelerate physical, intellectual, or psychological erosion for the majority of workers performing them and thus provoke premature ageing, even though they do not give rise to an occupational disease). Heavy work is determined by the National Ergonomic Commission, which is entitled to reduce the initial employer and employee contributions (2% of social welfare taxable remuneration) to 1%. The resulting contributions will be applied over existing remuneration as of the first day of the month following the National Ergonomic Commission's decision.

§4. CONCEPT OF REMUNERATION

195. As established in the Labour Code, remuneration is a payment made in cash and any additional payments in kind but appreciable in cash – which the worker has to receive from the employer on the basis of the labour contract. In turn, a labour contract is an agreement by which a worker commits himself or herself to perform personal services under a dependent and subordinate relationship with an employer and the employer commits himself or herself to pay remuneration for those services.

By way of example, the following kinds of remuneration are enumerated by the Labour Code: wages, extra pay for overtime, commissions, gains' shares, and bonuses. Specifically, the Labour Code establishes that the following types of compensation are not considered remuneration: transportation allowances, cash deficit allowances, tool wear and tear allowances, meal allowances, per diem allowances, family allowances granted by law, discharging payments, and the refunding of expenses.

The monetary equivalence of remuneration paid in kind is determined by the SOP.

§5. Concept of Rent

196. Rent is the amount of money declared by an independent affiliate as a basis for his or her contribution's calculation. For that purpose, yearly rent amounts to 80% of rents considered to be taxable by the Tax Law.

§6. Maximum Limit of Remunerations and Rents

197. Monthly remuneration and rent have a limit of UF 60. For pension purposes, the variation experienced by the UF of the last November in comparison with the existing one in the previous year has to be considered. Resulting remuneration and rents after the application of the above-mentioned limit can be called social welfare taxable remuneration or social prevention taxable rent.

§7. Calculation of Contributions

198. To calculate the contribution to be paid by an affiliate working for more than one employer, all remuneration has to be considered. Regarding the financing of invalidity insurance, all concerned employers have to contribute in proportion to the social prevention taxable remuneration.

§8. Voluntary Individual Contributions

199. Each worker can make voluntary contributions to his or her own PFA individual capitalization account, or to any fund administered by the PFA with which he or she is affiliated.

§9. Voluntary Individual Savings Deposits

200. Workers can voluntarily deposit savings in the PFA with which they are affiliated. These deposits are not considered social prevention contributions for the purpose of the Tax Law.

Savings will be deposited in an individual savings account, independent of a worker's individual capitalization account. A PFA can charge commissions for the administration of these savings, and they can be subject to legal seizure.

A general rule will establish the number of withdrawals allowed to the affiliate every year (not less than four).

Independent affiliates can authorize the PFA to transfer funds from their savings accounts to their individual capitalization accounts: (i) to cover corresponding social prevention contributions, and (ii) to make other social prevention contributions in corresponding institutions. These will not be considered withdrawals.

Affiliates can totally or partially transfer their savings account funds to their individual capitalization accounts with the following two purposes: (i) to accomplish requisites to receive an anticipated pension, or (ii) to increase the pension amount. Any remaining surplus will be at the affiliate's free disposal.

A worker can also make social prevention Individual Saving Deposits offered by: (i) banks and financial institutions; (ii) mutual funds' administrators; (iii) life insurance companies; (iv) investment funds' administrators; (v) housing funds' administrators; and (v) any other institutions or savings plan authorized by the Superintendency of Banks and Financial Institutions (SBFI) and the Superintendency of Values and Insurance (SVI).

§10. Agreed-Upon Contribution

201. A worker can also deposit – in her or his individual capitalization account or in any fund administered by the PFA with which he or she is affiliated – contributions agreed upon with the employer and intended to finance an anticipated pension or to increase the pension amount.

The worker can also give instructions to the corresponding PFA for transferring agreed-upon deposits to an authorized institution. Moreover, the worker can give the employer instructions for directly making the above-mentioned transfers and deposits.

§11. Common Rules

202. Voluntary contributions, social prevention savings deposits, and agreed-upon deposits will not be considered in the calculation of the additional contribution related to old age and Invalidity Pension (IP) financing.

These voluntary contributions are also governed by the following legal provisions:

(1) Concerned affiliates are entitled to decide that the resulting resources will be: (i) totally or partially transferred to an authorized institution or a PFA, and (ii) simultaneously maintained in one or more PFA.
(2) Concerned affiliates can freely decide to totally or partially withdraw resources resulting from voluntary contributions or social prevention savings deposits. Regarding resources originating from deposits agreed upon with employers, a set of rules establishes the conditions and procedures to do so.
(3) A concerned PFA is authorized to charge commissions to affiliates for its administration and transfers of referred voluntary contributions, social prevention savings deposits, and agreed-upon deposits.
(4) Affiliates who meet the requisites to be pensioned can totally or partially transfer voluntary contributions, social prevention savings deposits, and agreed-upon deposits to their individual capitalization accounts, thus increasing the pensions' amount.
(5) The same transfer can be made, if an affiliate chooses, for an anticipated pension.

(6) If there are no beneficiaries to survivor' pension, the existing balance of referred resources will increase the general inheritance amount.
(7) Affiliates to any social prevention system administered by the SPI can voluntarily make social prevention savings deposits in a PFA or other authorized institution. They can also make agreed-upon deposits with corresponding employers. In turn, employers can make those agreed-upon deposits in the SPI to be transferred to a PFA or authorized institution. Both the PFA and the SPI can charge commissions to concerned affiliates as compensation for their administration and transfers.

§12. Voluntary Collective Social Welfare Savings Deposits

203. Law 20.255 established the modality called Voluntary Collective Social Prevention Savings (VCSPS).

VCSPS is a savings contract convened by an employer (on his or her own and with the representation of employees) and a PFA or other authorized institution to increase employees' social prevention resources. The contract's terms and conditions will be the same for all workers, and in any circumstance, the existence of benefits to favour only one or more but not all employees can be agreed upon. A period of required workers' affiliation in which the concerned workers have to maintain their contributions in the PFA or authorized institution can also be agreed upon. A PFA cannot impose the obligation to affiliate or transfer an employee's individual capitalization saving accounts to that PFA.

SBFI and SVI jointly establish a general rule setting forth requisites to be met by VCSPS contracts and plans, as well as pertinent procedures and functioning. This general rule must preclude arbitrary discrimination, especially through:

(1) Determining the minimum number or percentage of workers employed by the same employer – in relation to the total number of employees – needed to adhere to one or more savings contracts.
(2) Determining needed years of service in the enterprise to acquire ownership of the corresponding employer's contributions. Nevertheless, if a labour contract ends by a cause set forth in Article 161 (Labour Code), the employer's contributions will belong to the concerned worker. The Article establishes: (i) that an employer can terminate a labour contract invoking 'necessities of the company, establishment or service', such as those derived from their rationalization or modernization, productivity decreases, market changes, or changes in the economy that make necessary the labour contract's termination; (ii) that the employer can terminate the labour contract of workers who represent the employer – as under-managers, agents, or representatives – if in all these cases, workers are entitled at least to general administrative benefits. The employer has to notify such workers of the termination thirty days in advance, at least, unless he or she pays a special indemnity equivalent to the last month's remuneration. The same rules are applicable in relation to workers of the employer's exclusive confidence, this condition emanating from the nature

of assigned work; and (iii) that the employer can terminate the labour contract of workers contracted for home-aid services and are entitled to receive the special indemnity established by law.

The employer can offer each worker the opportunity to enter into one or more voluntary collective savings contracts. Workers can accept offered contracts or not, but they cannot propose modifications to them. Employer contributions have to be maintained in an equal proportion to employee's contributions. Nevertheless, the employer can fix a maximum contribution amount. If workers stop making contributions, the employer is not obliged to continue making contributions unless he or she has agreed to do so. An employer's obligation to contribute ceases once the worker decides not to continue being part of the savings contract.

Employers and workers are not obliged to contribute while monthly subsidies are paid on the occasion of a medical leave of any number of days.

Contributions will be incorporated in an individual account with separate registries of employer and worker contributions. Workers will be owners of their own contributions and also of the employer's contributions if they have fulfilled the seniority period established by the employer and the corresponding PFA or authorized institution.

These contributions will not be considered in the calculation of the additional contribution referred to in LD 3.500 (as reformed), with the understanding that the additional contribution is the amount (in UF) representing the existing difference between capital needed to finance the pensions plus a death payment, and the total amount accumulated in the affiliate's individual capitalization account, including the recognition bonus, upon the death of the affiliate or when a medical report declaring definitive invalidity goes into force.

Contributions can be deposited in either a fund administered by the PFA or in a savings plan of institutions authorized by SVI or SBFI. Investments of deposited funds are governed by law. Restrictions are established regarding investments in instruments issued or guaranteed by the employer or related persons.

A commission can be charged by the concerned PFA – or authorized institutions for the administration or transferring of savings accounts.

When a labour contract or savings contract terminates, or when a requirement established in the savings contract occurs, employees have to transfer the balance to a new VCSWPS plan or to an Individual Voluntary Social Prevention Savings plan (VISPS).

Controversies on these matters will be settled by labour tribunals.

§13. Payment of Contributions

204. The payment of contributions is governed by following main rules:

(1) Obligatory and voluntary contributions have to be declared and paid to the pertinent PFA by the employer, the IW, the voluntary affiliate, or the entity paying subsidies, as follows: (i) in the first ten days of month following the one in which contributions were due, or (ii) when a medical leave is authorized (or

the first workable day if the previously mentioned date falls on a Saturday, Sunday, or holiday). The due date is extended to the thirteenth day if payment is made through electronic means.

(2) For this purpose, the employer deducts the contribution from the affiliate's remuneration and also pays those that are obligatory for employers.

(3) Periods of labour incapacity do not interrupt employers' and workers' obligations to contribute. The institution in charge of paying subsidies has to deduct and deposit those contributions.

(4) Voluntary affiliates can pay monthly contributions or one payment for each month's rent or income, with a maximum of twelve payments.

(5) An employer or entity in charge of subsidy payments that does not pay on time their workers or subsidized contributions has to declare them to the PFA in the process established for their declaration and payment. If this obligation is not fully and legally accomplished, the Labour Directorate can apply a fine of 0.75% for each worker or subsidy. In the case of home-aid workers, the fine is 0.20 UF to 0.50 UF. In case of false or incomplete declarations, the Labour Directorate can initiate a judiciary process in a competent penal court. Employers have the opportunity to prove that the corresponding labour relation has terminated or is suspended.

(6) Unpaid contributions will be legally readjusted and will also be increased with penal interests.

(7) A concerned PFA is obliged to develop all needed legal actions to obtain the contributions' payments, duly readjusted and increased with the amount of legal interest. This obligation does not cease if the affiliate decides to move to another PFA.

(8) Judicial procedures establish appropriate treatment to causes related to these matters.

(9) Non-paid contributions (duly increased with readjustments and interest) are classified as a preferential credit in case of the employer's insolvency of bankruptcy.

(10) Non-accomplishment of an employer's obligation can impede that employer from receiving resources from public institutions or private institutions financed with public resources for productive promotion, if the employer does not previously prove that owed contributions, adjustments, and interest have been paid. In contrast, those employers that have timely made their contribution payments in the previous twenty-four months will be given priority rights to receive those public resources.

In connection to the great earthquake and associated tsunami that occurred on 27 February 2010, Law 20.446 (July 2010) was passed, establishing special modalities to facilitate the payment of social security contributions corresponding to remunerations paid – or that had to be paid – by employers, corresponding to the period January 2009 and May 2010. Law 20.446 established the procedures and specific requirements to be met by employers asking for the approval of agreements with the pertinent social security entity. Through those agreements, employers were exempted from paying overcharges usually applied in case of the late deposit of contributions. The agreed payment could be made in eighteen instalments. The employer's failure in the payment of three instalments, or in the payment or deposit of other social security contributions was sanctioned with the payment of the total owed contributions and deposits.

Chapter 2. Selection of Funds

205. As said, the exclusive purpose of the PFA is to administer pension funds and to grant and administer legally established revenues and benefits.

Each Administrator shall maintain five Funds – depending on the risks involved in their investments – which shall be called the Type B Pension Fund, Type C Pension Fund, Type D Pension Fund and Type E Pension Fund. Likewise, the Administrator may maintain an additional Fund, which will be called Type A Pension Fund, in which investments present less risks.

The total balances for compulsory contributions, agreed deposits and voluntary contributions, as well as the voluntary savings account and the indemnity savings account referred to in Article 165 of the Labour Code, may remain in different types of funds. In any case, the compensation savings account will be assigned to the Type C Fund, when the worker does not opt for any type of Fund.

Male members up to 55 years of age and women up to 50 years of age may opt for any of the Funds mentioned in the previous paragraph. In turn, male members from 56 years of age and women from 51 years of age, will not be able to opt for the Type A Fund, with respect to balances originated in compulsory contributions. Affiliates pensioned by scheduled withdrawal and temporary income and affiliates declared partial invalids by means of a first opinion may not opt for Type A or B Funds with respect to the aforementioned balances. These prohibitions shall not apply in respect of that part of the balances that exceeds the amount necessary to finance an early pension.

If, on reaching the age of 56, in the case of male members, and 51 years of age, in the case of women, their balance for compulsory contributions is in the Type A Fund, it must be transferred to any of the other Funds, within a period of ninety days, with the exception of that which exceeds the amount necessary to finance an early pension. In the event that the affiliate does not opt for any of the Type B, C, D or E Funds, within the aforementioned period, the aforementioned balances will be assigned to the Type B Fund gradually, in accordance with the provisions of paragraph six.

206. If at the time of affiliation to the system, the worker does not opt for any of the types of Funds, he will be assigned to one of those as follows:

(1) Male and female members up to 35 years of age will be allocated to the Type B Fund.
(2) Male members from 36 to 55 years of age and women from 36 to 50 years of age will be allocated to the Type C Fund.
(3) Male members from 56 years of age and women from 51 years of age, affiliates declared partial invalids through a first opinion and pensioned by the modalities of programmed retirement or temporary income, will be assigned to the Type D Fund.

When the participant has been assigned to a Fund and has not subsequently expressed his choice for any of them, the balances originated in mandatory contributions, voluntary savings accounts, agreed deposits and voluntary contributions, will be partially transferred to the corresponding Fund in accordance with the foregoing, in the opportunities and amounts indicated below:

(1) When the affiliate reaches the age to change its age tranche, 20% of its total balances must remain in the Fund corresponding to the new bracket.
(2) One year after reaching the age at which the affiliate changed age bracket, 40% of its total balances must remain in the Fund corresponding to the new tranche.
(3) Two years after reaching the age at which the participant changed age bracket, 60% of its total balances must remain in the Fund corresponding to the new tranche.
(4) Three years after reaching the age at which the affiliate changed age bracket, 80% of its total balances must remain in the Fund corresponding to the new tranche.
(5) Four years after reaching the age at which the participant changed age bracket, 100% of its total balances must remain in the Fund corresponding to the new tranche.

207. The contributions and deposits subsequent to the allocations that are made in the aforementioned opportunities must be paid in the type of Fund that corresponds to the age bracket to which the affiliate belongs. In turn, the allocation established above will not be made for those balances for which the affiliate has expressly chosen a Fund.

The Administrators must send information to their affiliates regarding the possibilities of choice and with respect to the allocation of Funds, according to what the Superintendency establishes in a general norm.

The affiliates and the Administrators may agree that each of the balances for mandatory contributions, indemnity savings accounts, voluntary savings accounts, agreed deposits and voluntary contributions be assigned to two types of Funds. In addition, future transfers may be agreed between types of Funds, and the same balance must not be distributed in more than two types of Funds. A general rule, issued by the Superintendency, shall regulate the manner in which the options referred to in this paragraph are to be exercised. The Administrators who choose to enter into these agreements must sign them with all their affiliates who request it.

The Administrators will collect the corresponding contributions and voluntary deposits made by the worker – those that do not have the character of social security contributions – by paying them in the respective individual capitalization accounts and in the voluntary savings accounts of their affiliates, as appropriate, and will invest these resources in accordance with the law.

However, the PFAs whose assets are equal to or greater than 20.000 UF, may provide other Administrators with the services referred to in the previous paragraph, in accordance with the instructions issued subject to this law by the Administrator who commissions the service. This service will not be able to include the investment of the pension resources of other Administrators.

Chapter 3. Tender for the Administration of Individual Capitalization Accounts

208. In accordance with the reform established by Law 20.255, by itself or through the contracting of third-party services, the Superintendency will carry out public tenders to award the administration service of the individual capitalization accounts of the persons who must enter the system. The tenders will be carried out every twenty-four months, awarding the administration to the entity that meets the entailed requirements and offers to charge the lowest commission for deposit of periodic quotations at the time of submission of the offers. However, the Superintendency may refrain from bidding in a given period when there is technical background that merits it.

The period of permanence in the winning Administrator will be established in the respective bidding bases and may not exceed twenty-four months, counted from the date of incorporation of the affiliate to the winning Administrator.

Existing PFAs and those national or foreign legal entities that are not yet constituted as such may participate in the bidding process. The latter must have the provisional certificate of authorization established in Law 18.046 and the approval of the Superintendency to participate in said process, and must comply with the technical, economic, financial and legal requirements that allow it to be constituted as Administrator in case of awarding the tender.

The commission offered in the tender for active affiliates must be lower than the lowest contribution deposit fee in force in the system at the time of submission of bids. In the event that any Administrator has communicated a modification to it, the modified contribution deposit fee will be considered, for the purposes of determining the lowest commission in the system.

The award of the service will be decided by means of a well-founded resolution of the Superintendency. The successful bidder must accept all new members of the system, under the conditions stipulated in the offer under which the tender was awarded.

Workers who have joined the awardee Administrator may only be transferred to another during the period of permanence in the awardee Administrator, when it is in any of the following situations:

(1) Breach of the established obligation, on minimum required capital.
(2) Failure to comply with the obligation established with respect to the minimum return for any type of Fund.
(3) Cessation of payments of any of its obligations or in a state of notorious insolvency or when it is requested or declared the commencement of liquidation proceedings.
(4) In liquidation process.
(5) That the commission charged for deposit of contributions is higher than that charged by another Administrator, for two consecutive months. In this case, affiliates may only decide to be transferred to an Administrator that charges a lower commission for deposit of contributions than the successful bidder.

(6) That the commission for deposit of contributions is increased at the end of the period established.

(7) That the lower commission for deposit of contributions charged does not compensate for the higher profitability that the affiliate would have obtained in another Administrator during the period between the date of affiliation to the Administrator awarded the tender and the date on which the transfer is requested. In this case, the workers may only be transferred to that other Administrator. The calculation procedure for exercising this right shall be determined by the Superintendency.

Chapter 4. Pension Financing

209. A contribution is understood as being the representative amount of an affiliate's accumulated contributions deposited in his or her individual capitalization account.

If the affiliate has deposited in that account 10% of an IP paid in accordance with a First Medical Report, in UF, the received pension's amount is multiplied by the corresponding number of months, and then divided by 9.

Contributions must be paid over social previtional taxable received remuneration or declared income corresponding to: (i) the month before the medical leave's beginning, or (ii) the opportunity determined in the corresponding contract.

Such taxable remuneration or income will be adjusted at the same time and percentage as the subsidy is adjusted. Entities in charge of a subsidy's payment are obliged: (i) to retain corresponding percentages, and (ii) to deposit retained amounts in corresponding institutions.

§1. General Contributions

210. Affiliates less than 65 years of age for men and 60 years of age for women are obliged to contribute to their individual capitalization account 10% of their social taxable remuneration or rents. They also have to make an additional contribution – determined by the concerned PFA – intended for its financing — including the insurance premium payment needed for the fulfilment of PFA financial obligations. As a general rule, its amount will be the same for all affiliates.

In cases of dependent workers, the part of this contribution devoted to the insurance premium payment will be paid by their employers, except in cases of young workers entitled to social welfare subsidies while they are receiving those subsidies.

During labour disability periods, affiliates and their employers have to continue paying corresponding contributions. In turn, in those periods, affiliates also have to pay health contributions calculated based on health social welfare taxable remuneration and rents.

§2. Heavy Work Contributions

211. Affiliates performing heavy work also have to deposit a 2% contribution above their social welfare taxable remuneration. The same contribution must be also paid by their employers. Heavy work includes those types of work that accelerate physical, intellectual, or psychological deteriorization to the majority of workers performing such work, even though it does not constitute an occupational disease or labour accident, thus provoking their premature ageing. The ENC is in charge of determining jobs that constitute heavy work, taking into account the nature and conditions in which such work is performed. This Commission can reduce the contribution to 1% in consideration of lower deteriorization levels of some types of heavy work.

§3. Additional Contribution

212. It is understood that an additional contribution is the difference between capital needed to finance the reference pension plus a death payment and the total accumulated capital and recognition bonus existing at the time of death or when the total invalidity report comes into force.

§4. Old-Age Pension, Invalidity Pension, Survivor Pension

213. Old-age pensions, IPs, and SPs are financed with the balance of affiliates' individual capitalization accounts.

Nevertheless, if legal requirements are met, partial IPs due after the First Medical Commission's Report are financed by the PFA with which the concerned worker is affiliated.

Chapter 5. Old-Age Pension

214. The balance of an affiliate's individual capitalization account will be constituted by accumulated capital resulting from the following four items:

(1) The worker's contributions.
(2) An additional contribution (the difference between capital needed to finance the reference pension plus the death payment and the total accumulated capital existing in the individual capitalization account at the time of death, or when the total invalidity medical report comes into force).
(3) A recognition bonus is afforded to those workers who are covered by the old social welfare system and decided to affiliate with a PFA at the beginning of the new system. This can be accompanied by a complementary amount.
(4) Transfers to an individual capitalization account from an affiliate's social welfare savings account.

Chapter 6. Invalidity and Survivor Pensions

215. In such cases, the balance of an affiliate's individual capitalization account will be constituted by accumulated capital resulting from the following five items:

(1) Thc worker's contributions.
(2) An additional contribution (the difference between capital needed to finance the reference pension plus a death payment and the total accumulated capital existing in the individual capitalization account at the time of death, or when the total invalidity medical report comes into force). In turn, a contribution is understood to be the amount representing deposited contributions that the affiliate should have accumulated in the corresponding individual capitalization account if he or she has deposited in that account 10% on an invalidity pension paid as a result of the First Medical Report.
(3) A recognition bonus is afforded to those workers who were covered by the old social welfare system but decided to affiliate with a PFA at the beginning of the new system. It can be accompanied by a complementary amount.
(4) Transfers to an individual capitalization account from an affiliate's social welfare savings accounts.
(5) An additional PFA contribution (in case of invalidity declared by the First Medical Report).

For this kind of pension, needed capital is understood as being the capital requested to cover the following:

(1) All affiliate's reference pensions and those of his or her family group, as of the time: (i) that death occurs, or (ii) the Medical Report declaring total invalidity comes into force. This capital ends when the affiliate's right to receive a pension (as well as each one of the beneficiaries' right to receive a pension) totally ceases.
(2) Death payment.

Needed capital will be jointly determined by SPAP and SPAVI, taking into account technical data and mortality and life expectancy tables, plus interest rates determined by SPAVI.

§1. Invalidity Pension

216. Regarding partial invalidity declared in a Medical Commission's First Report, an affiliate's reference pension will be equivalent to:

(1) 70% of the basic income of affiliates who have died or have been declared totally invalid.
(2) 50% of the basic income of affiliates entitled to a partial invalidity pension.

Basic income is understood to be the resulting amount after dividing by 120 the total amount of social welfare taxable remuneration and declared rents in the last ten years before the affiliate's death, or the declaration of total or partial invalidity, duly actualized in connection with Consumer Price Index's variations.

Concerning affiliates with less than ten years of affiliation who have died as a result of an accident, the total received remuneration and declared rents will be divided by the number of months existing between their affiliation and the month before death or invalidity occurs or is declared. However, for workers affiliated before reaching 24 years of age who have died or declared invalid before reaching 34 years of age, the basic income will be the higher one resulting from the application of the above-mentioned rules. In this case, an accident is understood to be a sudden, violent, and traumatic event that causes death or invalidity.

Special rules were established regarding the situation of public employees affiliated with the new pension system before 1 January 1988.

In cases of affiliates receiving IPs in periods considered to calculate basic income, it is understood that those pensions have the conditions of social welfare taxable remuneration and rents.

Basic income will be expressed in UF as valued on the last month's day before the date of death or declaration of partial or total invalidity.

217. The concerned PFA will be responsible for the payment of partial IPs originating from the first invalidity report and also, for entering the additional contribution to the corresponding individual capitalization accounts of affiliates declared totally invalid, and non-pensioned affiliates that have died, in the following cases:

(1) Affiliates that are contributing.
(2) Dependent workers' affiliates who were not in service because of the termination or suspension of their labour relations, Chilean law establishes that they will also be entitled to this benefit if: (i) death or an invalidity declaration takes place within twelve months of that termination or suspension, and (ii) they have made at least six months of contributions in the year previous to the month when termination or suspension took place.

To this end, the legal presumption is applied that an affiliate was contributing: (i) if death or an invalidity declaration takes place while a dependent worker is in service; (ii) if an IW has paid obligatory contributions for social welfare taxable yearly rents, whose amount is not less than the equivalent of seven months of Monthly Minimum Income. In that case, the IW will have a yearly coverage as of 1 May of the year in which those contributions were paid, until 30 April of the following year. If contributions paid are less than that amount, the concerned affiliate will be covered during the number of months resulting from multiplying by 12 the existing relation between the number of contributions equivalent to the Monthly Minimum Income and 7 (counted from 1 May of the paid contributions' year). Nevertheless, whichever contribution should be paid, the concerned worker will always be covered in May of the year when contributions were paid; or (iii) if a voluntary affiliate has paid the above-mentioned contribution the month before the date of death or an invalidity declaration.

The additional contribution basic income will be calculated considering the maximum social welfare taxable remuneration or rent: 60 UF legally readjusted.

218. Regarding affiliates under partial IPs: (i) that are in a transitional period or in terms taking place between the First and Second Medical Report, or (ii) for which a Second Medical Report is still pending, the corresponding PFA will be only responsible and obliged to enter the additional contribution related to those affiliates who die or become entitled to an IP through a Second Medical Report, if the above-mentioned conditions are present.

To these effects, the affiliate's monthly amount of money deposited in the concerned PFA, multiplied by 10, after deducting corresponding commissions, will be considered social welfare taxable income. This income cannot be inferior to a minimum monthly income.

219. To guarantee the financing of PFA legal obligations, Law 20.255 established that all PFA must jointly agree on an insurance contract, assigned through public tender, which will be convened considering two separate gender groups as a means to overcome discrimination against women.

This jointly agreed-upon insurance must totally cover PFA financial obligations related to: (i) pensions of affiliates declared partially invalid in a First Medical Report; (ii) additional contributions when affiliates become entitled to an IP through a Second Medical Report or through an affiliate being declared totally invalid; (iii) additional contributions due when an affiliate who has been declared partially invalid in a First Medical Report dies; (iv) additional contributions due when a non-pensioned affiliate dies; and (v) contributions due when an affiliate who has been declared partially invalid in a First Medical Report is not entitled to an IP in a Second Medical Report.

Another means considered with the same purpose by Law 20.255 is that if a gender difference exists between an insurance contribution and the contribution needed to finance it, the PFA has to deposit the difference in corresponding individual capitalization accounts.

220. Invalidity and SPs ruled by LD 3.500 and its modifications are different, separate, and incompatible with invalidity and SPs ruled by Law 16.744 and any other legal regulation related to occupational diseases and labour accidents. Moreover, IPs ruled by LD 3.500 and its modifications are also incompatible with subsidies due for labour incapacity related to the same causes that produced invalidity.

Non-pensioned affiliates not fulfilling requisites to receive an old-age pension can receive an IP if, as a consequence of an illness or a weakness of physical or intellectual strength, they suffer a permanent diminution of their capacity to work, according to the following:

(1) A total invalidity pension if the loss of capacity to work is at least two-thirds.
(2) A partial invalidity pension if the loss of capacity to work is no more than 50% and less than two-thirds.

A Medical Commission has to verify the fulfilment of these requisites and to make a report declaring or denying the existence of total or partial invalidity. A First Medical Report declaring total invalidity has the character of being final and unique. If the Report declares partial invalidity, after three years, the Medical Commission has to pronounce a Second Report, ratifying, changing, or denying the declaration made in the first one.

If the affiliate does not attend the Commission's written summons to re-evaluate the invalidity after three months of being issued, the pension's payment will be suspended as of the fourth month.

If the affiliate does not attend this summons within six months after it was issued, it is understood that the invalidity has ceased.

However, an affiliate who has been declared partially invalid and reaches the age to be pensioned for old age can request a Second Report in the period of three years after having reached that age. If the affiliate does not use this option, he or she will maintain the right to receive the additional contribution if an invalidity re-evaluation takes place after he or she reaches that age.

Affiliates who have been declared invalid through a Second Medical Report and are not old-age pensioners (and thus are not entitled to that pension) will be entitled to a total IP if the loss of capacity to work is at least two-thirds.

221. If legal conditions are present and the corresponding legal presumption is applicable, the concerned PFA will be responsible:

(1) To pay partial pensions originating from the First Medical Report.
(2) To enter in the corresponding individual capitalization accounts the additional contribution: (i) to affiliates declared totally invalid, and (ii) to non-pensioned affiliates that have died.

This responsibility cannot be altered in the insurance contract. In the application of the preceding regulations, it is understood that:

(1) An additional contribution is the difference between capital needed to finance the reference pension (plus the death payment) and the total accumulated capital (plus the recognition bonus) existing at the time of death or when the total invalidity report comes into force.
(2) The contribution is the representative amount of an affiliate's accumulated contributions deposited in his or her individual capitalization account, if the affiliate has deposited in that account 10% of invalidity pensions paid in accordance with a First Medical Report, in UF. To this end, a pension's amounts received are multiplied by the corresponding number of months, and then divided by 9.

To calculate the above-mentioned additional contribution to finance the pension, the following will not be considered an affiliate's accumulated capital:

(1) Contributions paid before the total invalidity is declared.
(2) The retained balance (30% of the existing balance in the individual capitalization account when the Second Medical Report comes into force, including the recognition bonus and its complement, if any).

In turn, to calculate the retained balance, not taken into account are contributions paid in the transitional period existing between the First and Second Medical Reports.

222. Affiliates declared partially invalid by a First Medical Report will be entitled to receive IPs. Their amount will be UF and cannot be lower than:

(1) 100% to a reference pension (70% of the basic income of workers who have died and were entitled to benefits).
(2) 50% to workers entitled to receive a partial invalidity pension and who are also entitled to benefits.

If an IP's amount is lower than 100% of a basic solidarity OAP (and the affiliate is not entitled to be a beneficiary of the Solidarity Pension System), he or she can request that the pension be adjusted to a basic solidarity pension using his or her individual capitalization account.

Affiliates declared partially invalid who are not in the situation referred to in paragraph 418 will be entitled to receive a pension, according to the First Medical Report. Such pensions will be received in the modality of Programmed Withdrawals (PW) and will be equivalent to 70% of those withdrawals.

A resulting pension will not be affected by commissions legally charged by a concerned PFA over an individual capitalization account's periodic deposits and withdrawals. An affiliate cannot retire his or her 'free disposal surpluses' until the IP is paid, according to a Second Medical Report.

223. Once the Second Medical Report is in force, affiliates declared partially invalid by a First Medical Report will be entitled to receive IPs under any modality (Immediate Life Rent (ILR), temporal rent with Deferred Life Rent (TR-DLR), PWs, or ILR with PWs).

However, to finance the pension, the retained balance cannot be considered, which will be used either:

(1) To recalculate the current pension amount.
(2) To finance a new pension if the pensioned affiliate continues working as a dependent worker when: (i) invalidity becomes total, (ii) the affiliate reaches the age established to be pensioned, or (iii) the affiliate becomes an old age pensioner under rules governing the anticipated retirement.
(3) To adjust the pension to 100% of a basic solidarity OAP, if he or she is not entitled to be a beneficiary of the Solidarity Pension System.

In turn, a retained balance is understood as being 30% of an existing individual capitalization account's balance when a Second Medical Report came into force, including the bonus recognition and its complement, if any). To calculate that retained balance, contributions paid in the transitory three-year period since the affiliate became a partial invalidity pensioner through a First Medical Report will not be considered.

Affiliates declared partially invalid and entitled to a pension by a Second Medical Report cannot withdraw free disposal surpluses, as established in relation to pension modalities of ILR, ILR with PWs, TR-DLR, and programmed LR, unless they make use of their retained balance.

Regarding the retained balance and in relation to the option and destination of any AFP type of fund, the affiliate will no longer be considered a pensioner.

§2. Survivor Pension

224. Beneficiaries of an SP are the members of the deceased insured's family group: the surviving spouse, children – including adopted ones – parents, and the father or mother of a child born outside of marriage.

As a general condition, each affiliate has to prove the existence of corresponding beneficiaries in his or her PFA.

The particular conditions are:

(1) The survivor spouse has to have been married to the deceased affiliate at least six months before the spouse's death, or three years if the deceased affiliate was an old age or invalidity pensioner. These rules are not applicable if the survivor spouse is pregnant or if there are children in common.

(2) Children have to fulfil one of the following requisites: (i) to be minors less than 18 years of age; (ii) to be minors less than 24 years of age but older than 18 years of age if they are students of regular courses of a basic, medium, technical, or superior level. The condition of being a student must be accomplished when the affiliate dies or has to be acquired before the beneficiary becomes 24 years of age; or (iii) to be an invalid of any age. The invalidity can result after the affiliate's death but before the beneficiary becomes 24 years old.

(3) The mother or father of children born outside marriage has to fulfil the following two requisites: (i) to be a single or widowed, and (ii) to have lived at the expense of the deceased affiliate.

If none of the above-mentioned beneficiaries exists, the SP is to be paid to parents of the deceased affiliate if, at the time of death, they were entitled to receive family allowances.

§3. Minimum Invalidity and Survivor Pensions

225. To be entitled to a minimum IP, the affiliate has to fulfil the following requisites at the First Medical Report's date:

(1) To not have the right to a minimum old age State-guaranteed pension.
(2) To have at least two years of contributions – in the five years previous to the invalidity declaration's date – in any social welfare system; or to be contributing at that date if invalidity is declared as a result of a labour accident that occurred after the affiliation to the system; or to have completed ten years of effective contributions in any social welfare system; or to have at least sixteen months of contributions after the affiliate began his or her first labour relation.

To be entitled to a minimum SP, a beneficiary can apply, if, at the affiliate's date of death, at least one of the following requisites was fulfilled:

(1) The affiliate was a pensioner.
(2) The affiliate had at least two years of contributions in the previous five-year period, or was contributing (if death was due to a labour accident), or had completed ten years of effective contributions in any social welfare system, or had at least sixteen months of contributions after the beginning of his or her first labour relation.

This State guarantee is also applicable to:

(1) Pensioners who have withdrawn 'free disposal surpluses' from their individual capitalization accounts. However, in this case, a deduction will be made according to the percentage of the pension that could be financed if that withdrawal should not have been made. The same deduction will apply to survivor's pensions if the beneficiaries, as an inheritance, have withdrawn funds from corresponding individual capitalization accounts.
(2) Pensioners receiving an 'anticipated old-age pension'. However, in this case, a deduction will be made amounting to the pension's percentage that could be financed with the capital utilized to pay pensions until the age of 65 years for men and 60 years for women.
(3) Additional contributions, in other words, existing amounts resulting from differences between capital needed to cover reference pensions and death payments, and capital accumulated by the affiliate plus a recognition bonus, if the affiliate dies or a Report declaring definitive invalidity becomes accountable. In the case of partial invalidity, contributions paid since the corresponding Report's date are not a part of the accumulated capital, or the retained balance existing in the individual capitalization account of those affiliates declared partially invalid by a Medical Commission's Second Report.
(4) PFA obligations: (i) to pay partial invalidity pensions originating from a First Medical Report; (ii) to deposit additional contributions to corresponding individual capitalization accounts of affiliates declared totally invalid; or (iii) to

deposit additional contributions to corresponding individual capitalization accounts of deceased pensioned affiliates.

(5) Pension modalities of ILR and TR-DLR.

(6) A death payment of 15 UF to the widow, or father or mother, or son or daughter having paid funeral expenses. If those costs were paid by someone not having legal family ties, the death payment will amount to real costs paid, up to UF 15. This payment will be charged to the affiliate's individual capitalization account.

Chapter 7. Modalities of Old Age, Invalidity, and Survivor Pensions

226. Affiliates over 65 years of age for men and 60 years of age for women, as well as those entitled to be pensioned before that age (anticipated pension and pension for heavy work), and affiliates declared totally invalid or partially invalid (in a Second Medical Report), have the option to be pensioned in any of following modalities: (i) Immediate Life Rent; (ii) Temporal Rent with Deferred Life Rent; (iii) Programmed Rent and or ILR with PW.

Under Law 19.934 (2004), to facilitate an appropriate selection of the pension modality, affiliates are entitled to previously receive information, guidance, and advice from: (i) the Pension Amount's Consultation and Offer System (with interconnected electronic services provided by PFAs and life insurance companies; (ii) banks' filial societies providing social welfare advisory services; and (iii) social welfare advisers duly authorized by the Superintendency of Values and Insurance.

§1. Immediate Life Rent and Immediate Life-Rent with Programmed Withdrawal

I. Immediate Life Rent

227. ILR is only available to affiliates entitled to contract a rent at least equivalent to a basic solidarity old-age pension. ILR contracts operate as of the affiliate's written acceptance date of the LIC's offer.

ILR is the pension modality agreed upon between an affiliate and a LIC. A concerned one assumes the obligation to pay a monthly rent as of the time the contract is signed and until the affiliate's death, as well as to pay SPs to legal beneficiaries of the familiar groups: the survivor spouse, children (born within marriage or in a non-marriage relation or adopted), the father and mother, and the father or mother of children born outside of marriage.

An ILR contract cannot be revoked and must be adjusted to general rules established by the Superintendency for Values and Insurance (SVI). Those rules have the objectives: (i) to safeguard the social prevention character of this insurance contract, and (ii) to ensure an appropriate relation between received pensions and LIC-offered pensions.

Monthly rent is to be calculated considering a total individual capitalization account's balance (except surpluses legally retired by the affiliate). The resulting monthly rent amount can be constant or variable. A constant amount must be expressed in UF, while variable amounts can be expressed in a legal national or foreign currency, or an investment portfolio's index as authorized by the (SVI).

II. Immediate Life Rent with Programmed Withdrawal

228. Immediate Life Rent with Programmed Withdrawal (ILR-PW) is a pension modality in which an affiliate agrees to an ILR contract with a LIC, utilizing a portion of an individual capitalization account's balance while the remaining balance is destined to finance a PW.

This mixed modality is only available to affiliates entitled to receive an ILR at least equivalent to a basic solidarity social welfare pension.

In this modality, affiliates receiving a pension at least equivalent to 100% of a maximum pension with a solidarity contribution, and 70% of the average paid remuneration or declared rent, will be entitled to retire any 'free disposal surplus' existing in their individual capitalization accounts. Regarding affiliates declared invalid, this will only be considered 70% of their basic income.

Affiliates selecting this modality and contracting a constant ILR amount can decide to invest resources corresponding to PW in any fund administered by the concerned PFA.

Affiliates can also request their PFA to reduce selected programmed rent amounts, as well as amounts received from PW – together with received ILR amounts – adjusted to 100% of the basic solidarity pension, if they are not entitled to be a beneficiary of the Solidarity Pensions System.

Average paid remuneration is determined by dividing by 120 the amount of duly actualized paid remuneration or declared rents in the last ten years before the affiliate's death, or the First Medical Report's date declaring partial invalidity or a Medical Report's date declaring total invalidity, if periods not covered by contributions are less than sixteen months.

If this is not the case, the above-mentioned remuneration will be divided by the number resulting from deducting from 120 the number of months without contributions exceeding sixteen months.

If, during the above-mentioned ten-year period, affiliates have received IPs, the corresponding pensions' amounts – together with social welfare taxable paid remuneration or declared rents – will be taken into account to calculate basic income.

Received remuneration and declared incomes must be actualized. For that purpose, the SVI has to publish monthly the corresponding actualization factors, according to: (i) variations experienced by the Consumer Price Index and established by the National Statistics Institute, and (ii) the existing factors at the end of month when remuneration was received or income was declared as compared with the existing at the end of the month previous to the actualization.

§2. Temporal Rent with Deferred Life Rent

229. TR-DLR is a pension modality agreed upon by an affiliate and a LIC to receive a monthly rent at the starting date fixed in the contract, but maintaining in the individual capitalization account sufficient funds to obtain from the PFA a temporal rent. This temporal rent will be received as of the beginning date of this modality until DLR began to be paid by the LIC.

The DLR's amount cannot be inferior to 50% of the temporal rent's first monthly payment, nor superior to 100% of that payment.

The following rules established for ILR are also applicable to DLR:

(1) An LIC is obliged: (i) to pay a monthly rent until the affiliate's death, and (ii) to pay SPs to legal beneficiaries.
(2) Insurance contracts cannot be revoked and have to be in compliance with the Supervisory Public Agency for Values and Insurance's general rule aimed at preserving the social welfare nature of these contracts, particularly with reference to monthly rents' determination.
(3) The option for an ILR with PW is only available to affiliates entitled to contract a rent at least equivalent to the basic old-age solidarity pension.
(4) Once an insurance contract is in force, the concerned PFA has to transfer the corresponding individual capitalization account's funds to the concerned LIC, which will be obliged to pay agreed-upon LRs and survivor's pensions.

Nevertheless, at any time, the contracting parties can anticipate the beginning of an LIC's obligation to pay DLR through one of the following methods:

(1) Decreasing the amount of insured rent (but not an amount lower than a basic solidarity old-age pension).
(2) Paying in advance an additional insurance premium utilizing funds from an individual capitalization account, or with voluntary contributions.
(3) A combination of the above-mentioned methods.

Temporal Rent (TR) is understood as a withdrawal – agreed upon between the affiliate and his or her PFA – from a corresponding individual capitalization account after the contracting of a DLR.

TR is expressed in UF and is paid in twelve monthly instalments.

During the TR period, an affiliate can decide to withdraw a lower amount or to adjust that rent to 100% of the amount of a basic old-age solidarity pension, if the affiliate is not entitled to be a beneficiary of the Solidarity Pension System.

If the affiliate has contracted for a DLR at least equivalent to 100% of the maximum pension with a solidarity contribution, and equivalent to 70% of the average received remuneration or declared rents (or basic income, in the case of those declared invalid), he or she can decide to use 'the freely disposal right' to retire existing surpluses in the individual capitalization account, thus making it possible to finance the agreed-upon TR.

§3. Programmed Withdrawal

230. A PW is a pension modality consisting of a yearly withdrawal (expressed in UF) from an affiliate's individual capitalization account. Every year, its amount is determined by dividing the individual capitalization account's balance by the capital needed to pay the affiliate's pension, or to pay legally established percentages to survivors.

'Needed capital' is the individual capitalization account's portion destined for PW after being transferred to an LIC and whose actual value must be at least equivalent to yearly payments due during the PW period, duly actualized and with interest rates jointly fixed by the Ministry of Finance and the MLSP.

The needed capital determination has to take into consideration mortality and life expectancy tables, jointly established by SOP and the SVI. To this end, both supervisory bodies will annually interchange data on LR and PW pensions' modalities.

A yearly amount so determined will be paid in twelve monthly instalments duly adjusted by a factor established by SVI by means of a general rule, if one of these circumstances is present: (a) the referenced self-financed pension is superior to the maximum pension with a solidarity contribution, or (b) the affiliate is not entitled to be a Solidarity Pension System beneficiary. The mentioned factor has to be able to soften the pension's amount changes resulting from the re-calculations of PW.

Nevertheless, an affiliate can decide: (i) to withdraw an inferior amount, or (ii) to adjust monthly withdrawals to 100% of a basic solidarity old-age pension, if he or she is not entitled to be a Solidarity Pension System beneficiary.

Affiliates whose individual capitalization account balance is superior to the minimum balance required to apply for the PW option can freely withdraw, resulting in surpluses. The 'minimum balance required' is understood to be capital needed to pay corresponding affiliate and SP's equivalent to 70% of the average received social prevention taxable remuneration or basic income, if the affiliate has been declared invalid.

The minimum balance required must be at least equal to the needed capital to pay 100% of the maximum pension with a solidarity contribution. In any case, the minimum balance cannot be inferior to the required balance to receive a pension as described above.

Chapter 8. Anticipated Pensions

231. If legal requirements are met, the Chilean pension system allows affiliates to be pensioned before the established ages fixed for men and women. To this end, it distinguishes between a general right and a particular right to anticipated pensions.

§1. General Right to an Anticipated Pension

232. Under reforms approved from 1990 to 2008, two different situations must be distinguished: (i) affiliates selecting any legal pension modality, and (ii) affiliates selecting the PW pension modality.

I. Affiliates Selecting Any Legal Pension Modality

233. In this modality, the petitioner has to be in one of these two situations:

(1) to be entitled to receive a pension at least equivalent to 80% of the maximum pension with the solidarity contribution existing when the pension is requested; or
(2) to be entitled to receive a pension at least equivalent to 70% of the average social prevention taxable received remunerations or declared incomes.

In the second situation, affiliates receiving a pension at least equivalent to 100% of a maximum pension with a solidarity contribution, and up to 70% of the average paid social welfare taxable remuneration or declared income, will be entitled to retire existing 'free disposal surpluses' in their individual capitalization accounts. Regarding affiliates declared invalid, only 70% of their basic income will be considered.

The above-mentioned average remuneration will be determined by dividing by 120 the total amount of received social welfare taxable remuneration and declared incomes in the last ten years before the pension's date, if the total number of months without contributions is not more than sixteen. If this is not the case, the above-mentioned total amount of remuneration and rents will be divided by 120, less the number of months without a contribution exceeding sixteen.

If, in that period, the affiliate has received IPs, they will be added to social welfare taxable remuneration or declared incomes. In this case, the maximum limit of this addition is not applied (the basic income considered to determine the initial IP). For all these purposes, pension amounts are expressed in UF, as valued on the last month's day in which those pensions were paid.

The above-mentioned remuneration and incomes have to be actualized as determined by the SOP, through factors published monthly, fixed in line with the Consumer Price Index's variations experienced between the last month's day when remuneration was received or rents were declared and the last month's day before the corresponding actualization date.

Affiliates entitled to receive a recognition bonus (and its complement, if any), and who are also able to finance the pension with said bonus – or with said bonus plus the individual capitalization account's balance – can: (i) give up their rights over those documents endorsing them, or (ii) transfer the bonus after its amount has been recalculated by the SPI and transferred to the Republic General Treasury. In both cases, the bonus will be paid at its expiration date.

II. Affiliates Selecting the Programmed Withdraw Pension's Modality

234. Affiliates selecting the PW pension's modality and not giving up their bonus rights or transferring them, as referred to in the previous paragraph, have to fulfil the following two requisites:

(1) To be entitled to a pension at least equivalent to: (i) 70% of the average social welfare taxable received remuneration or declared rents; and (ii) 80% of the maximum pension with a solidarity contribution existing when the pension is requested. In this case, the pension's amount will be calculated considering the existing individual capitalization account's balance plus the recognition bonus' value (and its complement, if any), actualized on the day that the pension is requested, plus the interest rate established by the SOP.
(2) To have an individual capitalization account balance sufficient to finance the pension mentioned until he or she reaches the needed age to be pensioned and the recognition bonus must be paid.

§2. Particular Right to an Anticipated Pension

235. Affiliates carrying out work qualified as heavy works – or having carried them out – and who do not fulfil the previously mentioned age requisites to be pensioned, can obtain a reduction in the legally required number of years to receive an old-age pension.

Under the reform introduced by Law 19.404 (1995), besides the obligation to pay the 10% general contribution, affiliates performing heavy work also have to pay an additional 2% contribution beyond their social welfare taxable remuneration. Employers are also obliged to pay the same contribution.

Heavy work includes those types of work for which performance accelerates physical, intellectual, or psychological degeneration in the majority of workers performing them, thus provoking their ageing, even though they do not constitute an occupational disease or labour accident.

The ENC has to determine which types of work are considered heavy work due their nature and the conditions in which they are performed. The same Commission can reduce the 2% contribution to 1%, keeping in mind the existence of a relatively lower level of degeneration.

These contributions are not applied if a concerned worker is on a medical leave. If these requisites are met, there is a two-year reduction for each of five years in which the 2% additional contribution has been paid, with a limit of ten years, if at the time of being pensioned, the affiliate has twenty years of contributions or services in any social welfare system.

If the additional contribution has been reduced to 1%, there is a deduction of one year per every five worked years, with a limit of five years. Fractions of five-year periods in which 2% contributions have been made will entitle the worker to a proportional age reduction.

Chapter 9. Pensioners' Right to Work and Late Survivor Pension Beneficiaries

§1. Pensioners That Continue Working as Dependent Workers (Wage Earners)

236. A pensioner who continues working as a dependent worker must continue depositing his or her 7% health contribution calculated over the social welfare taxable remuneration but will be exempted from paying the general 10% old age, invalidity, and survivor insurance contribution.

In turn, the corresponding employer will also be exempted from paying contributions to finance the insurance established to guarantee the accomplishment of PFA obligations.

Affiliates pensioned for partial invalidity who reach the age to be pensioned for old age but continue working as dependent workers are obliged to pay: (i) the 7% health contribution, and (ii) the above-mentioned general 10% contribution. In turn, the corresponding employer will be obliged to pay contributions to finance the insurance established to guarantee the accomplishment of PFA obligations.

Contributions paid by an affiliate receiving a pension for partial invalidity due to a Second Medical Report, and who decides to continue working as a dependent worker, will increase his or her retained balance, which could be used to increase the pension amount.

The pensioner's health contributions will be calculated over his or her remuneration. However, regarding the remuneration limit of social welfare taxable remuneration, in this particular case, the calculation is to be made by deducting the corresponding pension amount.

A pensioner making voluntary contributions will increment the corresponding individual capitalization account in the PFA with which it is affiliated or decides to affiliate.

Once a year, in the same month in which an affiliate becomes a pensioner, affiliates with an ILR or a DLR can transfer his or her individual capitalization account's balance to the LIC that is paying, or has to pay, the LR, thus being entitled to contract another LR or PW.

§2. Late Survivor Pensions Beneficiaries

237. If, after the individual capitalization account balance of an affiliate has been determined, a survivor appears whose rights as such were not timely certified, the PFA has to verify that condition and, if it corresponds, has to include that person as a beneficiary.

If, after the payment of a pension has been initiated, the PFA certifies that a late claimer is a legal survivor, it is necessary to recalculate corresponding SPs and to pay corresponding new pension amounts as of the time of the new beneficiary's request date.

Chapter 10. Pensions for Wage Earners (Dependent Workers)

238. Chilean legislation regulates three kinds of pensions for dependent workers (WEs) and independent persons (self-employed): (i) old-age pensions, (ii) invalidity pensions, and (iii)) survivor pensions. The first two are ruled by common regulations and other specific regulations related to their nature.

§1. Field of Application

I. Territorial Field of Application

239. As has been mentioned, Chilean legislation establishes equal treatment for national and foreign workers, thus making Chilean legislation applicable to all workers residing in any national territorial location, regardless of their nationality.

Nevertheless, for pension matters, there are some modalities incorporated in bilateral or multilateral international agreements and conventions, or in specific laws such as Law 18.156, which states that foreign technicians and professionals are exempted from paying pension contributions in Chile, if the following conditions are met:

(1) They demonstrate that they are affiliated to a social security or social welfare regime outside of Chile – of any nature – that protects them at least in cases of illness, invalidity, old age, and death.
(2) Their corresponding labour contracts contain a compromise to maintain the workers' affiliation to a social security or social welfare regime outside of Chile.

II. Personal Field of Application

240. The Chilean pension system ruled by LD 3.500 and its amendments are applicable to all WEs and self-employed persons affiliated with an AFP. To those persons that, in due time, decided to remain affiliated with the old pension system institutions, the corresponding legislation is applicable.

§2. Old-Age Pension

I. Conditions

241. Dependent and independent affiliate men over 65 years of age or women over 60 years, have the right to an old-age pension. Affiliates who do not exercise their right to an old-age pension cannot request to receive an IP. In that case, the PFA has no obligation or responsibility for corresponding SPs.

II. Calculation

242. A pension amount directly depends on the amount of funds accumulated in the corresponding individual capitalization account. If needed, the pension amount can be supplemented with the newly established Solidarity Pension Fund, created by Law 20.255 (2008).

§3. Invalidity Pension

243. It must be remembered that invalidity and SPs ruled by LD 3.500 and its modifications are different, separate, and incompatible with invalidity and SPs ruled by Law 16.744 and to any other legal regulation related to occupational diseases and labour accidents. IPs governed by LD 3.500 are also incompatible with subsidies due for labour incapacity related to the same causes that produced invalidity.

I. Beneficiaries

244. The right to an IP is afforded to WEs and self-employed affiliates that are (i) non-pensioned under LD 3.500; (ii) not fulfilling requisites to obtain an old-age pension; and (iii) suffering a permanent diminution of their capacity to work as a result of a disease or weakness of their physical or intellectual strengths.

Under Law 20.255, non-pensioned affiliates older than 60 years and younger than 65 years are also entitled to an IP and to the additional contribution for the corresponding survivor.

II. Conditions

245. In addition to the above-mentioned conditions, the following ones must also be fulfilled:

(1) The capacity to work's loss has to be two-thirds, at least, for a worker to receive a total invalidity pension.
(2) The capacity to work's loss has to be less than two-thirds and at least 50% for a worker to receive a partial invalidity pension.

The capacity to work's loss has to be verified and evaluated by corresponding Regional Medical Commissions. These Commissions are integrated by three medical surgeons designated by the SOP. If needed, in certain regions, more than one Commission can be established. There is also a Central Medical Commission.

In the verification and evaluation process, concerned affiliates: (i) will be advised, without cost, by a medical surgeon designated by the Regional Medical Commission, but they can also be advised, at their own cost, by a medical surgeon designated by them; and (ii) must follow all procedures legally laid down, regarding First and Second Medical Reports, especially those including their obligation to attend legally fixed medical examinations. For instance, if the affiliate does not attend the Commission's written summons to re-evaluate the invalidity after three months of being issued, the pension's payment will be suspended as of the fourth month.

If the affiliate does not attend this summons within six months after it was issued, it is understood that the invalidity has ceased.

A First Medical Report declaring total invalidity has the character of being final and unique. After three years of this declaration, the Medical Commission has to pronounce a Second Report ratifying, changing, or denying the declaration made in the first Report.

However, an affiliate declared partially invalid who reaches the age to be pensioned for old age can request a Second Report in the three-year period of having reached that age. If the affiliate does not use this option, he or she will maintain the right to receive the additional contribution if an invalidity re-evaluation takes place after he or she has reached that age.

Affiliates declared invalid through a Second Medical Report and who are not old-age pensioners (and are not entitled to that pension) will be entitled to a total IP if the loss of capacity to work is at least two-thirds.

§4. CALCULATION

246. Regarding partial invalidity declared in a Medical Commission's First Report, an affiliate's reference pension will be equivalent to: (i) 70% of the basic income of affiliates that have died or have been declared totally invalid, or (ii) 50% of the basic income of affiliates entitled to a partial IP.

Basic income is understood to be the resulting amount after dividing by 120 the total amount of social welfare taxable remuneration and declared rents in the last ten years before the affiliate's death or a Medical Report declaring total or partial invalidity, duly actualized in connection with the Consumer Price Index's variations.

In the case of affiliates: (i) with less than ten years of affiliation, and (ii) those who have died due to an accident, total received remuneration and declared rents will be divided by the number of months existing between their affiliation and the month before death or invalidity occurs or invalidity prior is declared. However, for workers affiliated before being 24 years old and who have died or declared invalid before being 34 years old, basic income will be the higher amount resulting from the application of the above-mentioned rules. In this case, an accident is understood to be a sudden, violent, and traumatic event that causes death or invalidity.

As established in LD 3.500 (Article 54, as amended), the corresponding PFA will be responsible for paying partial IPs originating from the First Medical Invalidity Report and also to enter the additional contribution to the corresponding individual capitalization account of: (i) affiliates declared totally invalid, and (ii) non-pensioned affiliates that have died, in the following cases:

(1) Affiliates that are contributing.
(2) Dependent workers' affiliates that were not in service because of the termination or suspension of their labour contracts, Chilean law establishes that they

will be also entitled to this benefit if: (i) death or an invalidity declaration takes place within twelve months of that termination or suspension, and (ii) they have made at least six monthly contributions in the year previous to the month when termination or suspension took place.

(3) Self-employed (independent workers) having paid obligatory contributions for social welfare taxable yearly rents, which amount is not less than the equivalent of seven months of Minimum Income.
(4) Voluntary affiliates having paid the above-mentioned contribution the month before the death or invalidity declaration's dates. In this case, the additional contribution will be calculated considering the maximum social welfare taxable remuneration or rent: 60 UF legally readjusted.

Regarding affiliates with partial IPs: (i) that are in the transitional period or terms having been placed between the First and Second Medical Reports, or (ii) for which a Second Medical Report is still pending, the corresponding PFA will be only responsible and obliged to enter the additional contribution related to those affiliates that have died or became entitled to an IP through a Second Medical Report, if conditions mentioned above are present.

To these effects, the affiliate's monthly amount of money deposited in the concerned PFA will be considered social prevention taxable income, multiplied by 10, after deducting corresponding commissions. This income cannot be inferior to the Minimum Monthly Income.

247. If conditions are present and the corresponding law presumption is applicable, a concerned PFA will be responsible:

(1) To pay pensions originating from the First Medical Report.
(2) To enter into a corresponding individual capitalization account the additional contribution: (i) to affiliates declared totally invalid, and (ii) to non-pensioned affiliates that have died.

In the application of the preceding regulations, it is understood that:

(1) An additional contribution is the difference between needed capital to finance the 'reference pension' (plus the death payment), and the total accumulated capital (plus the recognition bonus) existing on the date of death or when the total invalidity report comes into force.
(2) The contribution is the representative amount of the accumulated affiliate's contributions deposited in his or her individual capitalization account, if the affiliate has deposited in that account 10% of IPs paid in accordance with a First Medical Report, expressed in UF. To this end, pension amounts received are multiplied by the corresponding number of months, and then divided by 9.
(3) To calculate the individual capitalization, the following are not considered: (i) contributions paid before the total invalidity is declared, and (ii) the 'retained balance' (30% of the existing balance in the individual capitalization amount when the Second Medical Report enters into force, including the recognition bonus and its complement, if any). In turn, to calculate the retained balance,

contributions paid in the transitional period existing between both Medical Reports will not be taken into account.

Affiliates declared partially invalid by a First Medical Report will be entitled to receive IPs.

If the IP's amount is lower than 100% of a basic solidarity OAP (and the affiliate is not entitled to be a beneficiary of the Solidarity Pension System), he or she can request that pension to be adjusted to a basic solidarity pension using his or her individual capitalization account.

Affiliates declared partially invalid who are not in the situation referred to in paragraph 418 will be entitled to receive a pension, according to the First Medical Report. Such pensions will be received in the modality of a PW and will be equivalent to 70% of that withdrawal.

The resulting pension will not be affected by Commissions legally charged by the concerned PFA over individual capitalization accounts' periodic deposits and withdrawals. Affiliates cannot retire their 'free disposal surpluses' until the IP is paid according to a Second Medical Report.

248. Once the Second Medical Report is in force, affiliates declared partially invalid by a First Report will be entitled to receive IPs under any modality (ILR, Temporal Rent with Referred LR, PWs, or ILR with PWs).

To finance the pension, the retained balance cannot be considered, which will be used either:

(1) To recalculate the current pension amount.
(2) To finance a new pension if the pensioned affiliate has continued working as a dependent worker, and if: (i) invalidity becomes total; (ii) the affiliate reaches the age established to be pensioned; or (iii) the affiliate becomes an old-age pensioner under rules governing the anticipated retirement.
(3) To adjust the pension to 100% of the basic solidarity OAP, if he or she is not entitled to be a beneficiary of the Solidarity Pension System.

In turn, 'retained balance' will be understood to be 30% of the existing individual capitalization account's balance when the Second Report comes into force, including the recognition bonus and its complement, if any. To calculate that retained balance, contributions paid in the transitory three-year period, since the affiliate became a partial invalidity pensioner through a First Medical Report, will not be considered.

Affiliates declared partially invalid and entitled to a pension by a Second Report cannot withdraw 'free disposal surpluses', unless they make use of the above-mentioned retained balance.

Regarding the retained balance and in relation to the affiliate option and destination to any PFA, he or she will not be considered a pensioner.

§5. SURVIVOR PENSION

I. Beneficiaries

249. Beneficiaries of a SP include the following family group members of a deceased affiliate: a surviving spouse; children, including adopted ones and those born outside of marriage; and parents, including an unmarried father or mother.

II. Conditions

250. As a general condition, each affiliate has to prove the existence of corresponding beneficiaries in his or her PFA

Particular conditions are:

(1) The survivor spouse has to be married to the deceased affiliate at least six months before the spouse's death, or three years, if the deceased affiliate was an old-age pensioner or an invalidity pensioner. These rules are not applicable if the survivor spouse is pregnant or there are children in common.
(2) Children have to fulfil at least one of the following requisites: (i) to be minors less than 18 years of age; (ii) to be minors less than 24 years of age but older than age 18, if they are students of regular courses of basic, medium, technical, or superior educational levels. The condition of being a student is to be accomplished when the affiliate dies or before the beneficiary becomes 24 years of age; or (iii) to be an invalid of any age. The invalidity can be pronounced after the affiliate's death but before the beneficiary becomes 24 years old.
(3) The mother or father of a person born outside marriage has to fulfil the following two requisites: (i) to be a single person or a widow, and (ii) to have lived at the expense of the deceased affiliate.
(4) If none of the above-mentioned beneficiaries exists, the SP is to be paid to the parents of the deceased affiliate if, at the time of death, they were entitled to receive family allowances.

III. Calculation

251. Registered SPs' beneficiaries are entitled to receive the following pension percentages:

(1) 70%: Survivor's spouse.
(2) 50%: Either the married mother or father of a child entitled to a survivor's pension. This percentage increases to 60% when the children's right to a pension ceases.
(3) 36%: The mother or father of a person born in a non-marriage relationship but has been recognized by her or him. This percentage increases to 36% when such a child's right to a pension ceases.

(4) 50%: The mother and father if no other beneficiary exists and they were entitled to a family subsidy when the affiliate died.

(5) 15%: Each non-married child meeting at least one of these requisites: (i) a minor less than 18 years of age; (ii) a major older than 18 years of age and a minor less than 24 years of age but studying regular basic, medium, technical or, superior recognized courses when the affiliate's death occurs; or (iii) a non-pensioned invalid not of the age requisite to receive an old-age pension but suffering a permanent reduction of his or her ability to work due to an illness or weakness of his or her physical or intellectual strength. This percentage decreases to 11% for children declared partially invalid when they become 24 years old.

Chapter 11. Pensions for the Self-Employed

252. The Chilean pension system covers both WEs and the self-employed. Thus, referred regulations regarding old age, invalidity, and SPs are also applicable to self-employed affiliates to a PFA, even though there are some legal differences related to particular circumstances.

Under LD 3.500, the affiliation of independent (self-employed non-WEs) workers was not compulsory. To improve the coverage of these workers and their gradual integration into the reformed social prevention system, Law 20.255 established special rules regarding: (i) recognition of two affiliation categories of IWs; (ii) contributions to the pension fund; (iii) health services and contributions; (iv) occupational diseases and labour accidents social insurance; and (v) services to the family allowances and affiliation to a CCAF.

253. Law 20.255 recognizes the following two categories of IWs: (i) those considered such by the Tax Law, for whom now it is compulsory to be affiliated and to pay contributions, and (ii) those IWs not included in Article 42 Number 2 of the Income Tax Law: their affiliation will remain voluntary.

According to the Chilean Labour Code, an IW is one performing activities without dependency or subordination to any employer, and who does not have any worker under his or her dependence. After reforms introduced by Law 20.255, independent affiliate is any natural person who, without being subordinated to an employer, individually exercises an activity through which he obtains income from work and who must join the Chilean pension system.

The first contribution made to a PFA by an independent person produces his affiliation to the System and his affiliation to the Fund for which he chooses. If that person, simultaneously, receives such incomes and also remunerations from one or more employers, all taxable income and taxable remuneration will be added for the purposes of applying the annual maximum contribution limit established in LD 3.500.

Self-employed workers who in the year receive taxable income – corresponding to 80% of all gross income taxed by the Income Tax Law, obtained by the independent affiliate in the previous calendar year – are subject to the contributions established in Title III of LD 3,500 and the 7% destined to finance health benefits.

The pensions and health contributions made by these independent and voluntary affiliates will have the character of social security contributions for the purposes of the Law on Income Tax. With regard to health contributions, these shall be calculated on the basis of the income declared monthly to the respective social security health institution, which for these purposes may not be less than a minimum monthly income or higher than the maximum taxable limit.

The aforementioned persons will be entitled to the Pension System of this law and to the health benefits established in DFL 1 of 2006 of the MH, which establishes the consolidated, coordinated and systematized text of LD 2.763, of 1979, and of laws 18.933 and 18.469.

§1. The Self-Employed Affiliates

254. Self-employed who join the System established by this law will continue to be subject to the Single System of Family Benefits and Unemployment Allowance schemes when, on the date of their incorporation, they have been affiliated to a pension scheme that provides for the benefit of family allowance or the benefit of unemployment benefit, while they carry out the activity that gave them the quality of imposing of said pension regime.

The commission to which the PFA will be entitled to the compulsory social security contributions paid annually by the IWs affiliated with them will correspond to the average percentage of the commissions that the administrator to which the affiliate belongs has received in the year prior to the payment of said contributions.

For the purposes of disability and survivors' insurance, a self-employed person who has made his compulsory contributions has annual coverage of that insurance from 1 July of the year in which he paid the contributions until 30 June of the year following that payment.

§2. The Voluntary Affiliates

255. Articles 92-J to 92-N of LD 3.500, as reformed, establish that any natural person who does not exercise a remunerated activity may pay social security contributions in a voluntary individual capitalization account of an administrator. The resources held in said account shall be unattachable and the rights and obligations with respect thereto shall be governed, as appropriate, by the rules established in DFL 3,500 for the individual capitalization account.

The additional contribution charged for the administration of the resources of this account will be calculated on the equivalent of the income obtained.

Affiliation to the system must be made by the interested parties by subscribing to the corresponding application. With respect to those who are already affiliated because they have been dependent or IWs, the first contribution as voluntary affiliates determines the opening and maintenance by the PFA of voluntary individual capitalization accounts.

Mandatory individual capitalization accounts and voluntary individual capitalization accounts must be maintained in the same PFA.

The contributions that are paid on account of a voluntary affiliate may be made by the latter or by another on their behalf and will not have the character of social security contributions for the purposes of the Income Tax Law.

It is up to the voluntary affiliate to choose the type of Fund in which their contributions will be deposited, and they may also make additional voluntary savings established in Article 21 of LD 3.500.

The amount of money quoted monthly in the PFA will be considered taxable income of these affiliates, discounting the amount corresponding to commissions, multiplied by ten, according to what is determined by a general rule of the Superintendence. This income may not be less than a minimum monthly income, and the taxable ceiling shall not be applied to them. When members make contributions through a single payment for more than one income or monthly earnings, taxable income will be considered to be derived from the monthly contribution made by these affiliates. This contribution will be determined by the PFA as a result of dividing by twelve the total amount quoted once discounted the amount corresponding to the additional contribution. In the event that the result of the indicated operation is less than the contribution equivalent to a minimum monthly income, the number of contributions must be adjusted so that in each month, the contribution amount is at least equivalent to that corresponding to a minimum income.

Voluntary members are covered for the risk of disability or death if they have contributed in the calendar month prior to such claims. For the purposes of determining the additional contribution, the calculation of the base income will be carried out considering the maximum taxable limit.

256. Dependent workers whose spouse or civil partner has the status of voluntary affiliate, may authorize their respective employers to deduct from their remuneration, under the legally established rules, the sums they allocate to contributions for the voluntary individual capitalization account of their spouse or civil partner, including the additional contribution. The employer shall pay this contribution in the PFA in which the voluntary member is incorporated or in which his dependent worker is affiliated, as determined by him. The aforementioned obligation will cease in each of the months in which a payment of contributions of the worker through an entity paying subsidies proceeds.

Chapter 12. Special Cases

257. Pension amounts of older and lower income pensioners result in increments with the payment of special payments decided by the government, such as 'winter bonuses', 'nativity bonuses', and 'Independence Day bonuses'.

As a material compensation to victims (and their families) of the dictatorship period (September 1973 to March 1990), two sets of benefits – including social welfare benefits – were established after the publication of the Rettig Report and the Valech Commission Report on Violations of Human Rights.

In summary, those benefits relate to: (i) increments of pension amounts; (ii) pensions to parents of victims; (iii) 'reparation pensions' to victims; and (iv) payment of special bonuses.

Part IX. Handicapped Persons

Chapter 1. Social Integration

258. As a tool of social integration, in Chile, the expression 'handicapped persons' has been – replaced by 'persons with disability' – *personas con discapacidad* – in Spanish.

Laws 20.422 (2010), 21.275 (2020), 21.303 (2021) and 21.403 (2021) have amended the Labour Code and its complementary legislation in matters related to the labour activities of persons with incapacity, establishing the following main rules:

(1) A person with disability is one who has one or more physical or mental incapacity or limitation, whether this consists in a psychological, intellectual, or sensorial type, of a temporary or permanent nature, when interacting with various barriers present in the environment. As a result of them, he is prevented or restricted from participating fully and effectively in society, on equal terms with others.
(2) Equal opportunities for persons with disabilities are understood as the absence of discrimination based on disability, as well as the adoption of positive-action measures aimed at avoiding or compensating for the disadvantages of a person with disabilities in order to participate fully in political, educational, labour, economic, cultural and social life.
(3) In order to guarantee the right to equal opportunities for persons with disabilities, the State shall establish measures against discrimination, which shall consist of accessibility requirements, the making of necessary adjustments and the prevention of harassment.
(4) Comprehensive rehabilitation is the set of actions and measures whose purpose is that persons with disabilities achieve the highest degree of participation and ability to exercise one or more essential activities of daily life, in consideration of the deficiency caused by the disability.

To achieve these purposes, the State:

(1) Shall promote and apply positive action measures to encourage the elimination of architectural barriers and promote universal accessibility.

(2) Shall adopt the necessary measures to ensure to women with disabilities and persons with mental disabilities, whether for psychological or intellectual reasons, the full enjoyment and exercise of their rights under conditions of equality with others, especially with regard to their dignity, the right to constitute and be part of a family, and their sexuality and reproductive health.
(3) Shall also take measures to ensure that children with disabilities fully enjoy and exercise their rights, in particular respect for their dignity, the right to be part of a family and to maintain their fertility, on an equal basis with other persons.
(4) Shall adopt the necessary measures to prevent situations of violence, abuse and discrimination against women and children with disabilities and persons with mental disabilities because of their status.

259. Besides these actions, current legislation has established:

(1) Any person or institution, public or private, that offers educational services, training, or employment, requiring the taking of exams or other similar requirements shall make the necessary adjustments to adapt the mechanisms, procedures and practices of selection in everything that is required to safeguard the equality of opportunities of persons with disabilities who participate in them.
(2) Applicants who present a disability that causes them an impediment or difficulty in the application of the selection instruments that are administered for this purpose must inform it in their application, for their adaptation.
(3) Chilean Sign Language is the natural, original language and intangible heritage of deaf people, as well as the essential element of their culture and individual and collective identity. The State recognizes its status as the official language of deaf persons. The State recognizes and undertakes to promote, respect and ensure respect, in accordance with the Constitution, the laws and international treaties ratified by Chile and in force, the cultural and linguistic rights of deaf persons, ensuring their access to public and private services, education, the labour market, health and other areas of life in society in sign language. The teaching of sign language shall preferably be carried out by qualified deaf persons. A regulation issued by the Ministry of Education and the Ministry of Social Development and Family shall regulate the conditions, requirements and qualifications necessary for the teaching of sign language.
(4) Deafblindness is recognized as a unique disability and promotes the full social inclusion of deafblind people. In this regard, it defines as a deafblind person one who, due to their reduced or non-existent auditory and visual functionalities, simultaneously present, constitutes a unique disability, which, when interacting with various barriers present in the environment, is prevented or restricted in its communication, mobilization, full and effective participation in society, access to information and the environment on equal terms with others. At the same time, it calls as 'interpreter guide' the person who performs the role of interpreter and guide of deafblind people, with extensive knowledge of the official communication systems adjusted to their needs.

260. In its single article, it incorporates in Law 20.422 – on equal opportunities and social inclusion of people with disabilities – the following other main rules:

(1) Public and private institutions will establish the conditions for people with disabilities to access, attend and appear before them with interpreter guides after accreditation of this condition.
(2) The State shall promote, within the scope of its competencies, in accordance with its powers, means and budgets, the continuous coaching and training of interpreter guides in accordance with the standards determined by the regulations issued for this purpose by the Ministry of Social Development and Family.
(3) The State recognizes dactylology, the Braille system, orientation and mobility techniques and other recognized alternative communication systems as official communication systems, in accordance with established in the regulations issued for this purpose by the Ministry of Education and the Ministry of Social Development and Family. Deafblind people will be free to choose the system or systems they wish to use to communicate in their daily lives. (Law 21.403 of 2021)

261. Enterprises with one hundred or more workers have to contract or maintain as contracted workers, at least 1% of persons with incapacity, or that are titulars of an IP of any social security regime. Benefitted persons must be in possession of official certificates of qualifications.

Those labour contracts and their modifications have to be duly registered by the employers and also reported to the Directorate of Labour, which will be supervising the application of these regulations.

If due to the nature of services to be performed or the lack of interest of possible workers, the enterprise cannot totally or partially accomplish the above-mentioned obligation, they will be obliged to apply one of these alternatives: (i) to celebrate contracts of services with enterprises that have contracted persons with incapacity and have to pay them, at least, an amount equivalent to twenty-four minimum monthly incomes; or (ii) to make a donation in cash to projects or programmes of associations, corporations or foundations which their social objective is the capacitation, training, rehabilitation, promotion or encourage the job creation, employment or labour inclusion of persons with incapacity. In this case, donations are not exempted from tax payments.

Chapter 2. Benefits and Conditions

262. As mainly remembered in Parts III and VI, invalidity and SPs ruled by LD 3.500 and its modifications are different, separate, and incompatible with invalidity and SPs ruled by Law 16.744 and any other legal regulation related to occupational diseases and labour accidents.

Moreover, IPs ruled by LD 3.500 and its modifications are also incompatible with subsidies due for labour incapacity related to the same causes that produced invalidity.

In other words, incapacity to work due to an accident or disease may be common or caused by work, directly or indirectly.

263. Non-pensioned affiliates not fulfilling requisites to receive an old-age pension can receive an IP if, as a consequence of an illness or a weakness of physical or intellectual strength, they suffer a permanent diminution of their capacity to work, according to the following:

(1) A total IP if the loss of capacity to work is at least two-thirds.
(2) A partial IP if the loss of capacity to work is more than 50% and less than two-thirds.

A Medical Commission has to verify the fulfilment of these requisites and to make a report declaring or denying the existence of total or partial invalidity. A First Medical Report declaring total invalidity has the character of being final and unique. If the Report declares partial invalidity after three years, the Medical Commission has to pronounce a Second Report, ratifying, changing, or denying the declaration made in the first one.

If the affiliate does not attend the Commission's written summons to re-evaluate the invalidity after three months of being issued, the pension's payment will be suspended. If the affiliate does not attend this summons within six months after it was issued, it is understood that the invalidity has ceased.

However, an affiliate who has been declared partially invalid and reaches the age to be pensioned for old age can request a Second Report in the period of three years after having reached that age. If the affiliate does not use this option, he or she will maintain the right to receive the additional contribution if an invalidity re-evaluation takes place after he or she reaches that age. Affiliates who have been declared invalid through a Second Medical Report and are not old-age pensioners (and thus are not entitled to that pension) will be entitled to a total IP if the loss of capacity to work is at least two-thirds.

264. If legal conditions are present and the corresponding legal presumption is applicable, the concerned PFA will be responsible:

(1) To pay partial pensions originating from the First Medical Report.
(2) To enter in the corresponding individual capitalization accounts the additional contribution: (i) to affiliates declared totally invalid, and (ii) to non-pensioned affiliates that have died.

This responsibility cannot be altered in the insurance contract. In the application of the preceding regulations, it is understood that:

(1) An additional contribution is the difference between capital needed to finance the reference pension (plus the death payment), and the total accumulated capital (plus the recognition bonus) existing at the time of death or when the total invalidity report comes into force.
(2) The contribution is the representative amount of an affiliate's accumulated contributions deposited in his or her individual capitalization account, if the affiliate has deposited in that account 10% of IPs paid in accordance with a First Medical Report, in UF. To this end, a pension's amounts received are multiplied by the corresponding number of months and then divided by 9.

To calculate the above-mentioned additional contribution to finance the pension, the following will not be considered an affiliate's accumulated capital:

(1) Contributions paid before the total invalidity is declared.
(2) The retained balance (30% of the existing balance in the individual capitalization account when the Second Medical Report comes into force, including the recognition bonus and its complement, if any).

In turn, to calculate the retained balance, not taken into account are contributions paid in the transitional period existing between the First and Second Medical Reports.

265. Affiliates declared partially invalid by a First Medical Report will be entitled to receive IPs. Their amount will be UF and cannot be lower than:

(1) 100% to a reference pension (70% of the basic income of workers who have died and were entitled to benefits).
(2) 50% to workers entitled to receive a partial IP and who are also entitled to benefits.

If an IP's amount is lower than 100% of a basic solidarity OAP (and the affiliate is not entitled to be a beneficiary of the Solidarity Pension System), he or she can request that the pension be adjusted to a basic solidarity pension using his or her individual capitalization account.

Affiliates declared partially invalid who are not in the situation referred to in paragraph 418 will be entitled to receive a pension, according to the First Medical Report. Such pensions will be received in the modality of PWs and will be equivalent to 70% of those withdrawals.

A resulting pension will not be affected by commissions legally charged by a concerned PFA over individual capitalization accounts, periodic deposits and withdrawals. An affiliate cannot retire his or her 'free disposal surpluses' until the IP is paid, according to a Second Medical Report.

Once the Second Medical Report is in force, affiliates declared partially invalid by a First Medical Report will be entitled to receive IPs under any modality (ILR, Temporal Rent with DLR, PWs, or ILR with PWs).

266. However, to finance the pension, the retained balance cannot be considered, which will be used either:

(1) To recalculate the current pension amount.
(2) To finance a new pension if the pensioned affiliate continues working as a dependent worker when: (i) invalidity becomes total, (ii) the affiliate reaches the age established to be pensioned, or (iii) the affiliate becomes an OAPer under rules governing the anticipated retirement.
(3) To adjust the pension to 100% of a basic solidarity OAP, if he or she is not entitled to be a beneficiary of the Solidarity Pension System.

In turn, a retained balance is understood as being 30% of an existing individual capitalization account's balance when a Second Medical Report comes into force, including the bonus recognition and its complement, if any). To calculate that retained balance, contributions paid in the transitory three-year period since the affiliate became a partial invalidity pensioner through a First Medical Report will not be considered.

267. Affiliates declared partially invalid and entitled to a pension by a Second Medical Report cannot withdraw free disposal surpluses, as established in relation to just mentioned pension modalities, unless they make use of their retained balance.

Part X. Minimum Income Benefit: Solidarity Pension System and Universal Guaranteed Pension

Chapter 1. Solidarity Pension System

268. As has been mentioned, a solidarity pension system was established by Law 20.255 (2008), financed with State contributions. The system contained: (i) a basic solidarity pension for old age (BSPOA); (ii) a basic solidarity pension for invalidity (BSPI); (iii) a solidarity contribution to pension for old age (SCOA); and (iv) a solidarity contribution for invalidity (SCI).

Law 21.419 (2022), which established the UGP, modified Law 20.255 and provided that the solidarity system grants benefits of basic solidarity disability pensions and solidarity disability pension contributions.

§1. Basic Solidarity Pension for Invalidity

269. Beneficiaries of the basic solidarity disability pension (BSPI) are those declared as a disabled person by a Medical Commission, according to LD 3.500, and not entitled to any other pension, if they meet the following requirements:

(1) To be aged 18 years and minor than 65 years
(2) To be a member of a family ranked in the poorest 60% of the population. For this purpose, it is understood that a family group is composed of the eventual beneficiary and the persons who have the following qualities with respect to it: (i) their spouse or civil partner; (ii) their children under 18 years of age; and (iii) their children over that age, but under 21years of age, who are students of regular basic, middle, technical or higher education courses.

    The eventual beneficiary may request that persons who have the following qualities be considered in his family group, provided that they share with him the family budget: (i) the mother or father of his/her children; and (ii) his/her disabled children, over 18 years of age and under 65, and their parents over 65years of age, in both cases when they cannot access the benefits of the solidarity system because they do not meet the corresponding residence requirement.

In any case, the eventual beneficiary may request that the persons indicated in the first paragraph not be considered in their family group, when they do not share the family budget with him. For the purposes of accessing the benefits of the solidarity system, the family group that the petitioner has at the time of submission of the respective application will be considered.

(3) To have accredited residence in the Chilean territory during a period of no less than five years in the six-year period prior to the presentation of the request. In any case, foreigners may not access the pension or the solidarity contribution for disability when the cause of the main impairment that causes the disability comes from an accident that occurred outside the territory of the Republic of Chile.

The foregoing, provided that the foreigner does not have the status of resident in Chile, in accordance with the provisions of LD 1,094 of 1975, when such event was verified. The time in which Chileans must remain abroad due to the fulfilment of diplomatic missions, consular representations and other official functions of Chile will be considered a period of residence in the country. Likewise, for persons included in the definition of exiles, contained in Law 18,994, who have been registered as such by the National Return Office, the time in which they remained abroad for that reason will be considered a period of residence in the country. For this purpose, the Ministry of Justice will issue the corresponding certification with respect to those who meet said quality, in the manner determined by the Regulations. The exceptions established above shall apply, where appropriate, to applications for access to the pension and solidarity contribution for disability, or to the child bonus for women, established in Title III of Law 20,255.

To access the basic solidarity disability pension, the corresponding application must be submitted to the SPI.

The basic solidarity pension for total or partial disability shall be of equal value to that of the UGP, shall accrue from the date of submission of the corresponding application indicated above, and shall be incompatible with any other pension of any pension scheme.

§2. Solidarity Contribution for Invalidity

270. The following shall be beneficiaries of the solidarity disability pension contribution: (i) whose disability has been declared by a Medical Disability Commission; (ii) who are affiliated to the pension system established in LD 3,500; (iii) who do not receive pensions from other social security schemes; and (iv) who meet the following requirements:

(1) Those established in numerals (i), (ii) and (iii) of the immediately preceding paragraph.

(2) Be entitled to a disability pension in accordance with the provisions of LD 3,500, if the sum of the amount of said pension plus any other received from said system is an amount lower than the basic solidarity disability pension.

Likewise, disabled persons who are only entitled to a survivor's pension in accordance with the provisions of LD 3.500, and who meet the requirements indicated above, will be beneficiaries of the aforementioned pension contribution, provided that the amount of said pension is less than the basic solidarity disability pension.

The solidarity pension contribution for disability will be to the amount obtained by deducting the amount of the pension or sum of pensions received by the disabled person from LD 3.500, from the value of the basic solidarity disability pension.

The application to access this contribution may be submitted from the date of obtaining the disability pension granted in accordance with LD. 3.500 and will accrue from the date of said application.

The beneficiary of the basic solidarity disability pension or the solidarity disability pension contribution, as the case may be, shall receive this benefit until the last day of the month in which he reaches 65 years of age. From that date, he/she will be able to access the UGP.

Without prejudice to the foregoing, persons who are beneficiaries of the basic solidarity disability pension or the solidarity disability pension may apply for the UGP from the date on which they reach 64 years of age. In this case, the aforementioned UGP will accrue from the first day of the month following the completion of sixty-five years of age, provided that the petitioners meet the requirements to be beneficiaries of said pension.

271. With regard to beneficiaries of the basic solidarity disability pension or the solidarity pension contribution for disability who have not applied for the UGP within the periods indicated in the previous paragraph and until the quarter prior to reaching 65 years of age, the SPI will process ex officio and, if applicable, the application for a UGP. For this, the Institute will use the background of the Social Security Data Information System and those provided by public and private organizations. In this case, the UGP will accrue at the opportunity indicated above. For applications processed ex officio, the Social Security Institute may require the holder of the application to provide the background information necessary to prove compliance with the requirements for access to the UGP. If within a period of six months from the date the request is made, the information is not delivered, the application processed ex officio shall have no effect.

With respect to persons who have received the basic solidarity disability pension or the solidarity disability pension contribution for a period of twenty years or more, whether continuously or discontinuously, the residence requirement to access the PGU will be understood to have been met.

Chapter 2. Universal Guaranteed Pension

§1. Concept

272. In Article 8 of Law 12, 419 (January 2022), was created the benefit called 'Universal Guaranteed Pension' (PGU, in Spanish), in the form and conditions established by this law, which will be financed with State resources. For the purposes of this law, the concept of 'Universal Guaranteed Pension' shall have the meaning of a non-contributory benefit, which will be paid monthly and may be accessed by people who meet the requirements established in Article 10, whether or not they are affected by any pension regime. The monthly pension amounts to a maximum of CLP 193,917, yearly adjusted in the month of February.

§2. Beneficiaries

273. Articles 10 and 11 provide that beneficiaries of the UGP will be people who meet the following copulative requirements:

(1) Have reached 65 years of age.
(2) Not to integrate a family group belonging to the richest 10% of the population aged 65 or over in Chile, in accordance with the provisions of Article 11 of this law. It will be understood that the possible beneficiary and the persons who have the following qualities with respect to it compose a family group: (i) spouse or civil cohabitant; (ii) sons or daughters under 18years of age; or (iii) sons or daughters over 18 of age, but under 24of age, who are students of regular courses of basic, secondary, technical or higher education. However, the eventual beneficiary may request that the following qualities be considered in his family group, for the purposes of this law, provided that they share the family budget with him: (i) mother or father of their sons or daughters, not included in letter a), and (ii) disabled sons or daughters, over 18 years of age and under 65, and parents over 65 years of age, in both cases when they cannot access the benefits of the solidarity system for not complying with the corresponding residence requirement indicated in letter c) of Article 16 of Law 20.255. In any case, the eventual beneficiary may request that the just mentioned persons not be considered in their family group, when they do not share the family budget with the family group. For the purposes of accessing the benefit, the family group that the petitioner has at the time of submission of the respective application will be considered.
(3) To prove residence in the territory of the Republic of Chile for a period of not less than twenty continuous or discontinuous years, counted from the time the petitioner has reached the age of twenty and, in any case, for the period of not less than four years of residence in the last five years immediately prior to the date of submission of the application to benefit from this law. For the purposes of compliance with this requirement, the period of residence in the country shall be considered the time in which Chileans must remain abroad due to

the fulfilment of diplomatic missions, consular representations and other official functions of Chile. Likewise, for persons who have the status of exiles, in accordance with Article 2 (a) of Law 18.994, who have been registered as such by the National Office of Return, the time they remained abroad for that reason shall be considered a period of residence in the country. To this end, the Ministry of Justice and Human Rights will issue the corresponding certification with respect to those who comply with this quality, in the manner determined by the regulations. The requirement of Article 10 (c) shall also be deemed to have been met in respect of persons who register twenty years or more of contributions in one or more of the pension systems in Chile.

(4) Have a basic pension less than the higher pension.

§3. Meanings

274. Article 9 provides that the concepts indicated below shall have the meanings indicated in each case:

(1) Lower pension: The value of the lower pension will be CLP 630,000, which will be used to calculate the amount of the UGP.
(2) Superior Pension: The value of the superior pension will be CLP 1,000,000, which will be used to calculate the amount of the UGP according to Article 12.
(3) Base pension: That which results from adding the self-financed pension of reference of the applicant plus the survivor's pensions that he or she is receiving according to LD 3.500, the pensions granted for any reason in accordance with the schemes administered by the Social Security Institute and the survivor's pensions under Law 16.744. All amounts will be expressed in legal tender.
(4) Self-financed reference pension: (i) in the case of affiliates in the LD. 3.500 system: The reference self-financed pension that will be considered for the calculation of the base pension will be calculated as an immediate life annuity of LD 3.500, without special conditions of coverage, considering the age, the family group and the total of the accumulated balance in the individual capitalization account that the beneficiary has at the date of the legal age to retire for old age, regardless of whether he or she has requested the pension or not, according to the aforementioned LD. For this calculation, the average interest rate implicit in old-age annuities, granted in accordance with LD. 3.500, in the last six months immediately prior to that in which the beneficiary has reached that age will be used. In the case of disability pensioners, the reference self-financed pension will be that established in the second paragraph of Article 23 of Law 20.255. The amount of the reference self-financed pension will be expressed in UF (Units of Foment) at the value it has on the date on which the beneficiary reaches the legal pension age.

The balance indicated in the previous paragraph shall not include transfers of the balance of the Individual Unemployment Account referred to in Article 19 of Law

19.728, transfers of the voluntary savings account, voluntary contributions, voluntary pension savings deposits, collective voluntary pension savings, or the agreed deposits referred to in LD 3.500; (ii) for the imposing of the schemes administered by the Social Security Institute: The self-financed pension of reference of the imposing of any of the schemes administered by the Social Security Institute will be calculated considering the variables that are required for the determination of the old age or retirement pension, seniority or any other of a homologous nature, according to the former provident fund to which the imposing belongs. The aforementioned pension will be calculated on the date on which the imposing person reaches 60 years of age if it is a woman and 65 years if it is a man. This self-financed pension will only be considered for the calculation of the basic pension as long as the imposing is not pensioned for old age; (iii) for those who retire early in accordance with Article 68 of LD 3.500: The reference self-financed pension will be calculated as an immediate life annuity without special conditions of coverage, considering the age and family group, both at the date of completion of 60 years for women and 65 for men, and the total of the accumulated balance in the individual capitalization account that the beneficiary has at the date of pension in accordance with the aforementioned Article 68. For this calculation, the average interest rate implicit in old-age annuities, granted in accordance with said Law-Decree, in the last six months immediately prior to that in which the beneficiary has retired for old age will be used.

The balance indicated in the previous paragraph will be expressed in instalments to the value it has at the date of obtaining the pension and will be added, if applicable, to the amount of the pension contributions that the person has made after that date, also expressed in instalments. This balance will not include transfers of the balance of the Individual Account for Unemployment referred to in Article 19 of Law 19.728, transfers of the voluntary savings account, voluntary contributions, voluntary pension savings deposits, collective voluntary pension savings or agreed deposits of LD. 3.500. When the applicant reaches the age of 60 in the case of women or 65 years in the case of men, the reference self-financed pension shall be expressed in UF of the value it has at the date of reaching that age and; (iv) All values expressed in legal tender in this article shall be adjusted in accordance with Article 17. This balance: (a) will be expressed in instalments to the value it has at the date of obtaining the pension and will be added, if applicable, to the amount of the pension contributions that the person has made after that date, also expressed in instalments, and (b) will not include transfers of the balance of the Individual Account for Unemployment referred to in Article 19 of Law 19.728, transfers of the voluntary savings account, voluntary contributions, voluntary pension savings deposits, collective voluntary pension savings or agreed deposits of LD. 3.500.

When the applicant reaches the age of 60 in the case of women or 65 years in the case of men, the reference self-financed pension shall be expressed in UF of the value it has at the date of reaching that age.

§4. SPECIAL SITUATIONS

275. Articles 12, 13, 23 and 24 of Law 12.419 regulate the following special situations:

(1) Persons who meet the requirements established in Article 10 will receive a UGP that will reach the following amounts: (i) for those beneficiaries who have a basic pension less than or equal to the lower pension, the benefit will reach the maximum amount of the UGP; (ii) for those beneficiaries who have a base pension greater than the lower pension, the amount of the benefit will be calculated as follows: (a) the maximum amount of the UGP multiplied by the determination factor; (b) this factor shall correspond to the difference between the higher pension and the basic pension, divided by the result of the difference between the higher pension and the lower pension; (c) however, the recalculation of the benefit will be carried out at the same time as the higher pension; (d) the lower pension and the maximum amount of the UGP are readjusted or increased. Similarly, this benefit and the base pension will be recalculated when the beneficiary begins to receive a new survivor's pension, in accordance with LD. 3.500, and when it is appropriate to grant a survivor's pension to a beneficiary of the aforementioned legal body, who had acquired that quality after the date of the original calculation.
(2) Without prejudice to these provisions, with respect to those who retire early in accordance with Article 68 of LD. 3.500, the reference self-financed pension shall be calculated in accordance with Article 9.
(3) Persons who retire under Article 68 bis of LD. 3.500 (anticipated pension), who receive one or more pensions granted in accordance with said LD, of an amount less than the maximum of the UGP, will be entitled to a supplement that allows reaching the maximum value of said Guaranteed Pension. This supplement shall be received at the age resulting from subtracting from 65 the number of years of reduction of the legal age for retirement in accordance with the aforementioned Article 68 bis and provided that they meet the requirements indicated in points b) and c) of Article 10. The beneficiaries of the aforementioned supplement will receive it until the last day of the month in which they reach 65 years of age, and Articles 17, 18 and 19 will be applicable to them.
(4) Pensioners under Article 68 bis of LD. 3.500, when they meet the requirements established in Article 10, will be entitled to the UGP, in accordance with the provisions of Article 12. For the purposes of the previous paragraph, the reference self-financed pension to determine the amount of the base pension and the benefit, will be calculated as an immediate life annuity of LD. 3.500, without special conditions of coverage, considering the age, the family group and the total balance accumulated in the individual capitalization account, which the beneficiary has at the date of retirement for old age according to the aforementioned LD, plus the actual interest accrued on the same date of the balance. For this calculation, the average interest rate implicit in old-age annuities, granted in accordance with LD. 3.500, in the last six months immediately prior to that in which the beneficiary has retired for old age will be used.

The balance indicated in the previous paragraph will not include the transfers of the balance of the Individual Account for Severance referred to in Article 19 of Law 19.728, the transfers of the voluntary savings account, voluntary contributions, voluntary pension savings deposits, collective voluntary pension savings, or the agreed deposits referred to in LD. 3.500.

The amount of the reference self-financed pension shall be expressed in UF at the value it has at the date on which the beneficiary retires for old age. However, the recalculation of the benefit of this law will be carried out at the same time as the UGP, the lower or higher pension, is readjusted or increased.

276. Anyone who receives the benefit of this law and does not cause the right to a mortuary contribution or death allowance in any social security regime, will be entitled to the payment of a mortuary fee for those who prove to have taken charge of the funeral expenses, and for these purposes, the respective request for reimbursement must be submitted to the SPI. That Institute must pay to whom it corresponds, the effective amount of the benefit until the concurrence of its expense, with a limit of 15 UF, which will be financed with State resources.

For the beneficiaries of this law, affiliated to the Pension System governed by LD. 3.500, whose balance is zero or does not reach to finance the entire mortuary quota, the benefit of the State charge will correspond to the missing difference with the limit of 15 UF.

Persons who enjoy the benefit established by this law shall not cause family allowance. However, they may be beneficiaries of this benefit in relation to their descendants who live under their care under the terms contemplated in the Single System of Family Benefits.

§5. Beginning, Extinction and Suspension of Benefits

277. All matters about the beginning of the benefits payments and the extinction or suspension of them, is regulated in Articles 16, 18 and 19 of the law, as follows:

(1) The benefit of this law will accrue from the month following the fulfilment of the 65 years of age or the date of the presentation of the application if it is later than the fulfilment of the aforementioned age.
(2) The benefit of this law will be extinguished in the following cases: (i) for the death of the beneficiary. In this case, the benefit will be extinguished on the last day of the month of death; (ii) for the beneficiary remaining outside the territory of the Republic of Chile for a period exceeding one hundred and eighty continuous or discontinuous days during a calendar year; (iii) for having delivered the beneficiary incomplete, erroneous or false records, in order to prove compliance with the requirements to access the benefit of this law; and (iv) because the beneficiary no longer fulfils the requirement laid down in Article 10 (b).

The person who has had the right to receive the UGP extinguished, who wishes to request again the benefit of this law, must prove residence in the territory of the Republic of Chile for the period not less than two hundred and seventy days in the year immediately prior to the date of the application.

(3) The UGP shall be suspended in the following cases: (i) if the beneficiary does not collect the UGP during the period of six continuous months. However, the beneficiary may request that the measure be annulled, until the period of six months from the date on which the suspension was ordered. Once the period has elapsed without the request having been verified, the extinction of the benefit will operate, and (ii) when the beneficiary does not provide the background to prove compliance with the requirements that are necessary for the maintenance of the benefit, required by the Social Security Institute, within three calendar months following the respective requirement.

(4) In the cases indicated in Article 10 (b), the request must be made to the beneficiary in the manner determined by the regulations, and if the beneficiary does not deliver the background or does not appear, as appropriate, within a period of six months from said request, the extinction of the benefit will operate.

278. At the same time, Articles 15 and 18 to 22 and Law 21,419 regulate the competence, power and guidelines referred to the SPI, created as a consequence of the profound reform of 2008. For the purposes of Law 21.419, the SPI will have all the powers established in Article 56 of Law 20.255 (2008).

This Institute shall administer the UGP. In particular, it shall be responsible for granting, extinguishing, suspending or modifying it, where appropriate. The regulations will control the processing, application, form of operation and payment of the UGP and the necessary rules for its application and operation. As provided for in the second paragraph of Article 16, payment is made by that Institute, which may agree with one or more public or private entities that guarantee national coverage, 'provided that these do not involve direct transfers of public resources that finance the UGP to the contributory pension paying entities of LD. 3.500'.

279. To access the UGP established by this law, people must submit the corresponding application to the SPI from the date on which the petitioner reaches 64 years and 9 months of age. At the time of making the request, the petitioner must provide the necessary information to establish the means of payment among those available.

Anyone who, in order to receive the benefit of this law, for himself or for third parties, knowingly provides, declares or delivers false, incomplete or erroneous data or records, shall be punished with the penalties established in Article 467 of the Criminal Code. In addition, it must return to the SPI the sums unduly received, readjusted in accordance with the variation experienced by the Consumer Price Index determined by the National Institute of Statistics, between the month prior to the one in which they were received and the one that precedes the restitution. The amounts thus readjusted shall also accrue the monthly criminal interest established in Article 53 of the Tax Code. The National Director of the SPI shall be responsible for exercising the powers established in Article 3 of LD 3.536 (1981), reporting to the SOP.

The SPI may review compliance with the requirements at any time and must terminate the benefit when there has been a cause of extinction. Notwithstanding the foregoing, the Institute must carry out a general annual review of compliance with the requirements regarding the benefits in force with seniority greater than three years from their granting.

280. Public or private entities in the social security field or that pay pensions of any kind, or that administer pension contributions of any kind, must provide the Social Security Institute with all the information necessary for the granting and payment of the benefit established in this law or that which is required to evaluate this and other pension benefits, being these entities obliged to provide it within the deadlines to be established. The information collected under this law will be part of the Pension Data Information System referred to in Article 56 of Law 20.255. For these purposes, the SOP shall be empowered to issue particular or general instructions to those entities.

Part XI. Claims and Adjudication

281. Chilean social prevention legislation establishes many different rules to process claims and to resolve controversies, taking into account the nature of risks and benefits involved. Many of these processes take place at the administrative level. In this regard, is important to note that: (i) administrative adjudications can be reviewed by tribunals, and (ii) tribunals are authorized to apply fines and other sanctions – including arrest and prison terms – in cases of serious infringements, such as non-appropriate or fully and timely compliance with rules governing the discount and deposit of contributions in the relevant institutions.

The main procedural rules are related to pensions, health, occupational diseases and labour accidents, family allowances, and unemployment. This chapter will only examine some judicial claims and adjudications referred to as pensions.

Chapter 1. Claims

§1. Introduction of Claims

282. Respect claims related to the SOP's exercise of its faculties and functions, we must remember that among other faculties and functions, SOP is authorized to apply sanctions and to rule upon the revocation of the authorization given for the existence of a PFA, its related societies, and administrators of its social prevention resources' portfolio. Moreover, SOP can also order the sale of investments if a PFA has not met its obligations and requisites set forth in LD 3.500, as amended, regarding the creation and functioning of said societies administrating the PFA portfolio of social welfare resources.

To this end, SOP has to previously inform and notify the PFA of facts that constitute an infringement upon laws governing them. The concerned PFA has a ten-workday period to present its defence, with accompanying documentation refuting the allegation together with a deposit representing 25% of the fine ordered by SOP. The concerned PFA and the filial societies and administrative societies of its social prevention resources portfolio can present a claim against the SOP resolution.

The claim is to be presented in the corresponding Court of Appeals. The court has to decide if the claim: (i) is admissible and, (ii) has been presented within the legal deadline.

If the claim is declared admissible, the court will notify its decision to SOP, which has a fifteen-day period to oppose the court's decision. With or without SOP opposition, the court has to resolve the claim presented. Its decision has to be made within thirty days.

SOP civil servants' declarations will be presented through written reports that will have the effect of legal presumptions about the facts reported.

PFA and related social directors and representatives have solidarity responsibility with respect to fines imposed by SOP for facts and infringements resulting from their fault or negligence. Affected persons can present a claim under the same rules.

283. Procedural rules that have just been summarized are also applicable to other claims, for instance, those presented by a PFA against other SOP resolutions, such as:

(1) Designation of a delegated inspector to protect the pension funds' security.
(2) Replacement of a director of a society, designated by the concerned PFA as a society's shareholder.
(3) Obligatory reimbursement of loss suffered by affiliates' individual capitalization accounts resulting from the PFA non-fulfilment of its legal obligations or to instructions given by the affiliate.

284. For all legal purposes, a court adjudication constitutes an executive title and will produce its legal effects fifteen days after its notification (if it is not opposed), or fifteen days after the opposition is finally resolved. If the court adjudication accepts the claim, the deposited 25% fine will be reimbursed.

285. In reference to claims related to IPs, we must also remember that reports presented by a Medical Commission regarding the declaration of the existence of a total or partial invalidity, can be claimed by the concerned affiliate, the Social Welfare Institute, and concerned insurance companies.

A written claim must be presented to the concerned Regional Medical Commission within a fifteen-workday period as of the time that it was notified. The claim does not require a lawyer's participation.

Within a five-day period after receiving the claim, that Commission will send it to the Central Medical Commission, accompanied by all background information taken into account in the claimed report. The Central Medical Commission will study the claim without a judicial procedure and can order that new examinations and analyses have to be made within a period of no more than sixty days. The Central Medical Commission must pronounce its decision ten days after receiving those examinations and analyses, or ten days after receiving the claim if new examinations and analyses were not ordered.

All matters regarding the above-mentioned examinations and analyses, including the claimant's financial responsibilities, are regulated by LD 3.500 as reformed as of 2009.

If a claimed issue relates to consideration of an invalidity that derives from an occupational disease or labour accident, consequently, Law 16.744 has to be applied. The Central Medical Commission will also be represented by a medical surgeon designated by SUSESO, who will preside over its deliberations and will make the final decision in case of a tie in voting. SUSESO will also designate a lawyer to participate in the study of the case, but without the right to vote, who can be accompanied by a lawyer designated by SOP. In turn, the concerned administrative agency established by Law 16.744 can also designate a medical surgeon as an observer.

The Central Medical Commission can request corresponding entities to send records and reports within a ten-day period. The same request can be made to the concerned employer. If, within a fifteen-workday period, the employer does not provide the requested information, the Directorate of Labour will apply a fine of 2 to 19 UF.

Adjudications of Medical Central Commission have to be notified to: (i) the affiliate; (ii) the corresponding PFA; (iii) the concerned insurance company; and (iv) the entity responsible for paying the professional IP under Law 16.744. The pension has to be paid by the corresponding entity if the claim is not accepted.

Concerned persons and institutions can present to SUSESO a claim against the adjudication.

The presentation of such a claim does not suspend payments ordered in the adjudication.

If the Medical Central Commission's final decision rules that invalidity derives from an occupational disease or labour accident, the PFA will cease payments of an IP ruled by LD 3.500 and its modifications. The corresponding entity ruled by Law 16.744 must reimburse the PFA amounts paid to the concerned affiliate since the Medical Central Commission's adjudication date. At same time, the entity has to pay for services and benefits established by Law 16.744.

However, if the Medical Central Commission's final decision rules that invalidity does not derive from an occupational disease or labour accident, the PFA will continue paying the IP as ruled by LD 3.500 and its modifications. If the PFA was paying a Basic Solidarity Invalidity Pension (BSIP), it is obliged to make corresponding settlements.

§2. Protection Against Seizure and Transfer

286. The Labour Code (Article 57) declares that wages and social security contributions cannot be subject to seizure if they do not exceed 56 UF. Thus, the wage or social security contribution portions exceeding this limit can be seized.

In turn, LD 3.500 (Article 34), as modified by Law 19.641 (1999), establishes that the patrimony of each pension fund administered by an PFA cannot be seized, except for the portion related to individual voluntary contributions deposited in the corresponding savings account.

§3. Legal Capacity to Receive Benefits

287. The legal capacity to receive monetary benefits derived from a claim presented belongs to the claimant or to corresponding inheritors if the claimant has died.

Nevertheless, the claimant can authorize a third person (a proxy) to receive those benefits in his or her capacity of representation, by means of a legally written authorization made in the presence of a Notary Public.

Chapter 2. Adjudication

288. Labour procedure legislation has been reformed in recent years to assure access to justice, to obtain adjudications duly funded, and to make it possible for adjudications to be appropriately put into effect.

Thus, principally Laws 20.023, 17.322, and 20.087 and the Labour Code and the Civil Procedure Code establish current legal procedure to execute labour adjudications, including those related to social welfare credits.

Once legal requisites for adjudications being enforceable are accomplished, the relevant tribunal will initiate procedures to put the adjudication into effect, including the intervention of tribunals for the collection of labour and social prevention debts. To assure the payment of debts, the tribunal can order the Republic General Treasury Office to retain the corresponding debt amounts from any pending payment to the debtor. This measure is called a special protective tool.

If payment is not made, the tribunal orders the seizure of sufficient debtor's funds, properties, and resources to be auctioned.

Affected affiliates and social welfare institutions are entitled to prosecute for payment of social welfare debts. Workers are not obliged to act with a lawyer in these judicial procedures. A debtor can be arrested if legal requisites are present.

Annexes

Annex 1. Oiss: The Iberoamerican Social Security Multilateral Convention (Summary Of Its Content)

I. Initial Considerations Of States Parties Of The Convention General Rules And Determination Of The Applicable Legislation.

General rules

(1) Definitions.
(2) Personal field of application.
(3) Material field of application (economic benefits for disablement, old age, survivors, labour accidents and occupational diseases).
(4) Equal treatment.
(5) Addition of periods.
(6) Conservation of rights and payment of benefits out of country.
(7) Readjustment of pensions.
(8) Relations between this Convention and other instruments for coordinating social security.
(9) Determination of the applicable legislation.
(10) Especial rules.
(11) Exceptions.
(12) Voluntary insurance.

II. Particular Rules Related To Different Categories Of Benefits.

Disablement, old age and survivors

(1) Determination of benefits.
(2) Periods under one year.
(3) Amounts owed taking into account periods of voluntary insurance.
(4) Coordination of regimens and legislations based on savings and capitalization.
(5) Regime of benefits.
(6) Transfer of fund.
(7) Benefits in case of labour accidents and occupational diseases.
(8) Determination of the right to benefits.

III. Mechanisms For Administrative Cooperation.

Medical expert examinations.
Information exchanges.
Claims and documents.
Exemptions.

IV. Administrative Technical Committee.

Composition and functioning.
Committee functions.

V. Transitory rules.

VI. Final rules.

Implementation Agreement.
Conference.
Dispute settlement.
Signature.
Ratification, acceptance, approval or adhesion.
Coming into force.
Amendments.
Repeal.
Languages.
Receiver.
Annexes.

Annex 2. Principal Normative Development (September 1924- September 1973)

1924

L. 4.055, regulating labour accidents.

1925

DL LD 857, creating the White-Collar Insurance Board of Private Sector Employees (Caja de Previsión de Empleados Particulares), for: (i) the administration of a retirement fund and of the indemnity payment for years of service, and (ii) the use of amounts collected as a collateral guarantee for housing purposes. It is important to note that at that time labour law provisions made a distinction between blue and white collar workers taking into account the predominance of physical or intellectual efforts in the performance of the job established in each individual labour contract. An especial tripartite labour administration institution (the Blue and White Collars Workers Classification Board) was in charge to solve doubts or conflicts in the recognition of either condition and also the existence of a labour relation.

1930

DFL. 1.340 (ML), establishing the new text of DFL.767 (1925), on the creation of the Public Employees and Journalists Social Prevention Institution. (LD. 454–1925)

1936

L. 5.802, establishing that the Ministry of Health will be named Ministry of Health, Social Prevention and Social Assistance.

1937

L. 6.020, regulating social prevention matters like family allowances, unemployment and indemnity for years of service (white collar workers in the private sector).

L. 6.037, creating the Social Prevention Entity for Chilean Maritime Seamen.

1938

L. 6.174, establishing Preventive Medical Services, given and administered by each insurance body. There main purposes were to prevent occupational and common diseases. Under this system, special leaves could be afforded.

1940

L. 6.457, establishing a tax law.

L. 6.527, reforming L. 6.020.

L. 6.612, reforming L. 6.020 thus allowing white collar worker in the bank sector to receive both: the old age pension and he indemnity for years of services.

L. 6.676, reforming L. 6.612.

L. 6.733, regulating the application of L. 6.527 to teachers and white collar workers in educational and welfare institutions.

1941

L. 7.064, reforming L. 6.020.

1942

L. 7.280, establishing a revised text on legislation for private white collar workers, including modifications to Labour Code.

1943

L. 7.390, recognizing an indemnity for years of services to blue-collar workers in local government (town council).

1944

L. 7.753, establishing a special bonus for workers in the public administration.

1945

L. 8.307, applying L. 7.753 to employees in semi-public entities.

1950

L. 9.588, regulating benefits to maritime seamen.

1952

L. 10.343, readjusting remunerations in the public sector.

L. 10.383, creating the Social Insurance Service (Servicio de Seguro Social) for blue-collar workers, thus replacing the Obligatory Social Insurance Body. It allowed the affiliation of employed and self-employed blue-collar workers and established: (i) pensions for survivors (widows, children, orphans); (ii) death and funeral payments; (iii) subsidies and other aids for housing. (iv) family allowances, and (v) health benefits.

L. 10.475, establishing a comprehensive social protection system for white-collar worker in the private sector, partially financed by the indemnization payment for years of service.

L. 10.662, reforming L. 6.037: old age and death, readjustment of pensions, social prevention continuity.

L. 10.986, establishing the right to transfer funds and years of services between social insurance bodies, thus assuring the continuity and enlargement of old age pensions. It also authorized to cover periods of non affiliation, known as 'lagunas previsionales' (social prevention uncovered periods).

1953

L. 1.161, creating a professional association named Nurse's College.

DFL. 243 and DFL. 245 (ML), establishing and improving: (i) indemnization for years of service; (ii) subsidies in case of unemployment, and (iii) family allowances.

1957

L. 14.428, re-establishing the five-yearly readjustment to armed forces.

1960

DFL. 286 (MF), regulating the Employees National Medical Service, and other matters like preventive medicine.

DFL. 338 (MIA), fixing the Administrative Statute for Public Administration employees, including social prevention regulations.

1962

L. 14.972, regulating amounts of fines applicable in case of social legislation infringements.

1963

L. 15.076, regulating social prevention benefits for surgeons, pharmacists, chemist-pharmaceuticals. biochemists, chemists and dentists.

L. 15.358, establishing the staff of Undersecretaries of Labour and Social Prevention (Ministry of Labour), and of the Labour Directorate.

L. 15.382, establishing a system for the readjustment of all pensions, thus assuring the maintenance of consuming power of pensions in inflationary periods.

L. 15.386, establishing the Pension Revalorization Fund and the Pension Revalorization Commission; new pension's regulations; a minimum pension limit, benefits for Social Security Service's affiliates, and a termination of employment indemnity for employees in the private sector and maritime seamen.

L. 15.467, recognizing the legal condition of white collar workers to 'lathe operators', 'die-stamp workers' and 'milling machine operators'.

1964

L. 15.477, reforming Labour Code' regulations of occupational diseases.

1965

L. 16.250, readjusting wages of white and blue-collar workers in the public and private sectors and applying to agricultural workers same minimum wage established to blue-collar workers employed in commerce and industry.

L. 16.386, recognizing the legal condition of white collar workers to fitters.

1966

L. 16.395, creating the Supervisory Public Agency of Social Security.

L. 16.426, modifying L. 16.250.

L. 16.455, regulating the termination of labour relations, including some related social prevention matters.

L. 16.464, readjusting remunerations of white and blue-collar workers in private and public sectors; contributions to public agencies and entities; various social prevention regulations, and prices stabilization.

L. 16.469, reforming L. 15.467.

L. 16.494, reforming regulations on old age pension of women employed in the public and private sectors thus modifying L. 10.343 (1952) and L. 10.475 (1952).

1967

L. 16.634, establishing anticipated pension and especial benefits to white and blue-collar workers labouring in environments classified as toxics.

L. 16.640, regulating the agriculture reform, including some social prevention matters.

DFL. 2 (ML), establishing the Labour Directorate structure, functions and staff.

1968

L. 16.744, replacing the 1924 standards on occupational diseases and labour accidents. It is presided over by the principle of 'objective responsibility' of employers. It is still in force with amendments, specially enlarging its coverage.

L. 16.781, regulating the Curative Medicine system, covering medical and dental assistance to active and pensioned affiliated persons and beneficiaries of survivors' pensions.

L. 16.840, readjusting remunerations in public and private sectors and establishing some allowances.

DFL. (MA), fixing a new structure of the Mechanized Agricultural Equipment Service.

1970

L. 17.322, establishing an executive judicial procedure to enforce the payment of social prevention contributions, including the application of fines.

L. 17.373, welfare pension to former workers of an enterprise.

L. 17.393, regulating the incorporation of newspaper sellers and distributors to the social insurance system for blue-collar workers.

L. 17.395, extending the date to improve the remuneration scale for 'semi-public workers', raising remunerations of lower income workers.

L. 17.396, distributing surpluses funds collected through family allowances contributions, among white-collar workers members of the corresponding social prevention system.

1971

L. 17.403, modifying procedures to obtain a pension, making it more easy and fast.

L. 17.416, readjusting wages and: (i) imposing an special tax on pensions over a fixed maximum amount; (ii) establishing and extraordinary readjustment of family allowances for blue-collar workers; (iii) fixing a new higher ceiling of wages subject to social insurance contributions in the public sector; (iv) establishing an special bonus in case of multiple births, and (v) raising the amount of minimum pensions for blue-collar workers.

L. 17.417, transferring more resources to the pension fund for blue-collar workers.

L. 17.425, establishing pension benefits for accountants.

L. 17.487, regulating the application of a recognition bonus to workers under L. 10.383 (Article 38).

1972

L.17.655, improving the unemployment subsidy of affiliates to the White Collar Workers Social Prevention Institution.

L. 17.663, suppressing the readjustment of habitational credits.

L. 17.665, improving procedures to accelerate the access to social prevention benefits.

L. 17.671, descentralizing the administration of the Social Security Service.

L. 17.676, establishing the exclusive participation of affiliates representatives in the administration of social prevention institutions.

L. 17.687, readjustion social prevention assistencial pensions.

L. 17.688, allowing a readjustment of contributions made to the Public Employees and Journalists Social Prevention Institution.

L. 17.689, financing welfare programs of the Merchant Seamen Social Prevention Institution.

L. 17.690, establishing special benefits to affiliates White Collar Workers Social Prevention Institution (Atacama and Coquimbo provinces).

L. 17.691, readjusting pensions of affiliates to the Bank Employees Social Security Body.

L. 17.713, establishing a general readjustment of pensions.

L. 17.716, establishing special benefits in housing mortgage to unemployed.

L. 17.720, raising State contributions to the Merchant Seamen Social Prevention Institution.

1973

L. 17.730, establishing benefits to State Insurance Institute employees.

L. 17.742, readjusting remunerations.

L. 17.779, improving benefits to newmen.

L. 17.890, readjusting and increasing benefits to affiliates in all social prevention institutions.

L. 17.900, favouring familiars of victims of the 'Santa Fe' shipwreck.

L. 17.901, incorporating workers of the Agrarian Reform Corporation (CORA) to the social prevention system of public employees.

L. 17.902, abolishing old regulations that have established the loss of social prevention rights as a punishment.

L. 17.907, reforming the readjustment of pension system, especially raising the level of minimum pension amount.

L. 17.908, establishing the immediate implementation of the habitational programme for the police and other affiliates to DIPRECA.

Annex 3. Principal Normative Development (September 1973-March 1990)

1973

LD. 6, declaring of 'temporary nature' the employment of all persons employed in the public administration, except those working in the Judiciary Power and the Republic General Comptroller Office.

LD. 98, declaring in reorganization the whole public administration and other institutions.

LD. 139, authorizing 'Delegated University's Deans' to decide the termination of labour relations of personnel under their dependency.

LD. 194, authorizing the existence of private security guards in important enterprises.

1974

LD. Establishing a unique remuneration scale.

LD. 446, readjusting remuneration in the public and private sector.

LD. 479, recognating years of service of some employees: LD. 249 (1973).

LD. 720, recognating of social prevention rights to employees in the semi-public institutions: DFL. 338 (1960).

LD. 762, establishing the applicability to Chilean universities the regulations established in LD. 139 (1973).

LD. 764, modifying LD. 534 (1974) and LD. 666 (1974).

1975

LD. 857, modifying L. 11.161.

LD. 869, establishing welfare pension system for invalids and elderly persons without incomes.

LD. 889, establishing especial regulations applicable in six territorial regions.

LD. 1.228, on administrative opinions of the Labour Directorate over labour matters in particular situations.

LD. 1.270, modifying L. 7.295 (abolition of its Article 58).

1976

LD. 1.321, extending validity of LD. 762 (1974).

LD. 1.446, approving the Training and Employment Statute.

1977

LD. 2.071, abolishing L. 12.855.

1978

LD. 2.200, regulating the individual labour contract and workers protection.

LD. 2.306, regulating recruitment and mobilization of armed forces.

LD. 2.327, creating the 'teaching career' and regulating its exercise.

LD. 2.405, dissolving the Agrarian Reform Corporation (CORA); modifying L. 16.640, and establishing an indemnity for CORA workers.

LD. 2.444, on revalorization of social prevention pensions.

LD. 2.347, declaring illicit associations or groups of persons assuming the representation of workers sectors without having legal capacity to do so, accordingly to labour law or common law.

DFL. 42 (ML), establishing the general statute of Family Allowances Compensation Institutions (CCAF).

DFL. 44 (ML), regulating incapacity labour's subsidies for dependent workers (public sector).

1979

LD. 2.448, modifying labour pensions regimes.

LD. 2.547, revalorization of pensions (Social Prevention Body for the Armed Forces and Social Prevention Body for the Police): LD. 2.444.

LD. 2.756, establishing regulations on trade union organization.

LD. 2.759, establishing regulations on collective bargaining.

LD. 2.763, reorganizing the Ministry of Health and establishing the Health Service, the National Health Fund, the Public Health Institute and the Central Supply Central for the National Health Services System.

1980

LD. 3.161, establishing special indemnizations for personnel of the Armed Forces 'Defence Ministry' whose labour relation terminated in 1980.

LD. 3.355, modifying LD. 2.756 and LD. 2758 (both of 1979) as well as other labour law regulations.

LD. 3.380, increasing the amount of social prevention and welfare pensions.

LD. 3.476, regulating private educational institutions receiving State's subsidies.

LD. 3.500, establishing a new pension system.

LD. 3.501, establishing a new social prevention's contribution system.

LD. 3.502, creating the Social Prevention Normalization Institute.

DFL. 3 (MTT), establishing new regulation in the collective bargaining system (State Railways Enterprise).

DFL. 3 (MH), regulating medical care and other health's services and benefits.

DFL. 3 (ME), regulating the Chilean universities' remunerations.

DFL. 36 (MH), regulating agreements between social prevention health services and other entities.

DFL. 101 (ML), on the statute of the Supervisory Public Agency of AFP.

1981

LD. 3.607, abolishing LD. 144 (1973) and establishing new regulations on private security guards.

LD. 3.625, modifying LD. 3.501 (1980) and LD. 889 (1975).

LD. 3.636, modifying LD. 3.607 (1981).

L. 18.008, reforming DFL. 338 (1960).

L. 18.011, reforming regulations on seamen.

L. 18.018, reforming LD. 2200 (1978).

L. 18.020, establishing a family subsidy for low income persons.

L. 18.052, establishing regulations to harbour workers.

1982

L. 18.099, on maritime workers and reforming L. 18.018.

L. 18.152, interpreting the constitutional property guarantee in relation with pension's readjustments.

L. 18.198, reforming LD. 2.200 (1978) and LD. 2758 (1979).

unique text on family allowances and unemployment subsidies system in the public and private sectors (LD. 307 and LD. 603, both of 1974).

1984

L. 18.263, readjusting pensions.

L. 18.372, reforming LD. 2.200 (1978).

1985

L. 18.379, authorizing the reprogramming of employers' social security debts with social prevention institutions, originated by the application of LD. 3500 and LD. 3.502, both of 1980.

L. 18.398, modifying LD. 3.500 (1980).

L. 18.413, replacing the readjustment of pensions' system, the unemployment subsidy system and other matters (only for 1980).

L. 18.418, trespassing the financing of maternal leaves to the Unique Fund of Family Allowances.

1986

L. 18.420, modifying LD. 3.500 (1980) and L. 13.398.

L. 18.423, regulating the social prevention situation of AFP affiliates that are engaged in military obligations.

L. 18.458, establishing the social prevention regime for the 'national defence' (armed forces) personnel.

L. 18.478, readjusting remunerations in the public sector.

L. 18.520, modifying LD. 3.500 (1980).

L. 18.521, modifying L. 18.008.

L. 18.549, on readjustments in the 'passive' sector.

L. 18.566, on taxes over 'health contributions' (LD. 3.501).

L. 18.575, on general basis of the State Administration.

L. 18.588, on nativity bonus.

1987

L. 18.591, on complementary rules of finances administration in relation with budgetary and personnel matters.

L. 18.611, establishing a regionalized budget of family allowances and welfare pensions.

L. 18.626, modifying of the employment bonus regime to labour contracts in the extreme Chilean regions.

L. 18.631, modifying L. 18.225 about des-affiliation from new social prevention institutions of the new pension system (AFP).

L. 18.646, modifying LD. 3.500 (1980).

L. 18.647, readjusting remunerations in the public sector and establishing a minimum income.

L. 18.669, establishing the Budget Law 1988.

L. 18.675, readjusting remunerations in the Judiciary Power; establishing an additional contribution for pensions, and increasing the amount of contributions to finance pension benefits.

L. 18.681, regulating 'EMPART' loans. (EMPART refers to the old Private White Collar Workers Social Prevention regime.)

1988

L. 18.689, merging the Social Prevention Normalization Institute with old social prevention institutions.

L. 18.694, modifying L. 18.263 and establishing rules on pensions readjustments.

L. 18.711, readjusting remunerations in the public sector.

L. 18.747, regulating the anticipated payment of indemnizations due to labour relations termination. (Public Sector.

L. 18.751, modifying rules on recruitment and mobilization of armed forces (LD. 2306–1978).

L. 18.753, modifying LD. 3500 (1980).

L. 18.754, establishing a common 7% health contribution over pensions given by entities supervised by the Supervisory Public Agency of Social Security, and modifying L. 16.744.

L. 18.766, regulating nativity bonus, pension readjustment and educational allowance.

L. 18.768, establishing complementary rules of finances administration in relation with budgetary and personnel matters.

1989

L. 18.774, on remuneration readjustment in the public sector, and establishing a new amount of minimum income (LD. 3500, and L. 18.647).

L. 18.779, modifying L. 18.681 and L. 18.747.

L. 18.781, modifying L. 18.689 (INP statute and staff).

L. 18.806, regulating family allowances, readjustment of pensions of the old social prevention institutions and minimum income readjustment.

L. 18.811, modifying rules on employers' mutual: DFL. 285 (1968) and L. 16.744.

L. 18.812, modifying L. 17.322.

L. 18.816, authorizing the Family Allowances Compensation Bodies (CCAF) to establish agreements with the National Health Fund (FONASA).

L. 18.833, establishing a new general statute for the Family Allowances Compensation Bodies (CCAF, thus modifying DFL. 42 (1978)-L. 18.834, approving the new Administrative Statute (public administration employees).

L. 18.835, establishing differences between indemnizations paid and the price of shares acquired with them.

L. 18.848, regulating old age pension in the Judiciary Power.

L. 18.867, modifying L. 18.768 and establishing rights to leaves and to subsides subsidies in case of adoption of children.

L. 18.868, authorizing the selling of real state properties of the Social Prevention Normalization Institute.

L. 18.870, readjusting remunerations in the public sector.
L. 18.880, establishing new rules on old age pension in the Judicial Power.
1990
L. 18.889, on private guards' hours of work: LD. 3607 (1981).

Annex 4. Normative Development (March 1990-2013)

1990

L. 18.980, granting labour stability to teachers of private educational establishments.

L. 18.933, establishing the Supervisory Public Agency of Health Institution, modifying DFL 3 (1981) on ISAPRES.

L. 18.981, readjusting minimum income amounts. The assigned one to minors of 18 years will also be the minimum income for no remuneration purposes.

L. 18.987, increasing the family subsidy amount as well the amount of all welfare pensions and minimum pensions.

L. 19.104, readjusting remunerations (public sector) and other matters.

L. 19.007, readjusting remunerations, allowances, benefits and other monetary payments to workers in the public sector, as well as a nativity bonus payment.

L. 19.010, replacing regulation on individual labour relation termination: indemnity benefits and years of services considered; protected workers; judicial claims, and additional indemnizations.

1991

L. 19.028, regulating the application of labour regulation (private sector) to technical and auxiliary personnel in the Medical and Dental Service of DIPRECA.

L. 19.035, increasing FONASA percentages' contribution to childbirth (Group D).

L. 19.049, recognizing freedom of association to constitute union's central.

L. 19.056, establishing the Budget Law for 1991.

L. 19.058, authorizing the INP Director to judicially or extra judicially give way to claims related to the devolution of rent's thus allowing the recalculation of corresponding pensions.

L. 19.060, increasing the minimum monthly income.

L. 19.069, reforming regulations on trade union organizations and collective bargaining thus strengthening both collective labour relations rights.

L. 19.073, increasing amounts of family and maternal allowances as well as family subsidies.

L. 19.084, regulating labour tribunals.

L. 19.104, readjusting remunerations (public sector), nativity bonus to public employees and pensioners, and matters of monetary content.

L. 19.108, raising FONASA bonus to medical care costs.

1992

L. 19.112, regulating remunerations of professionals and workers of the health sector; establishing the compatibility of wages and pensions, and correcting problems derived from L. 15.086.

L. 19.116, regulating the XVI National Population Census.

L. 19.117, regulating health services of social prevention health institutions and CCAF; payments to local government (Town Council) or corporate employer.

L. 19.123, creating the National Reparation and Reconciliation Corporation.

L. 19.125, replacing LD. 249 (1973)

L .19.129, regulating labour employability, labour training, labour implements and tools, compensatory indemnity's payment and other matters about coal miners.

L. 19.136, declaring that properties of CAPREDENA and DIPRECA cannot be seized.

L. 19.142, readjusting the minimum monthly income's amount.

L. 19.152, modifying L. 18.987 and readjusting familiar and maternal allowances as well as the family subsidy.

L. 19.163, regulating the Independence Day bonus to INP; Social Prevention Institutions, and Employers' Mutual pensioners.

L. 19.173, modifying L. 19.129.

L. 19.177, modifying LD. 3.500: recognition bonus, heavy works.

L. 19.181, readjusting pensions' amounts (L. 2.448 and L. 2.547), and welfare pensions.

L. 19.185, readjusting remunerations, allowances, benefits and other monetary social prevention taxable's payments: health and pensions in the public sector, plus nativity allowance in to public employees and pensioners.

1993

L. 19.195, incorporating the National Gendarmerie's Penitentiary Officials and Guards to CAPREDENA.

L. 19.200, readjusting pensions.

L. 19.228, readjusting the amounts of family and maternal allowances, family subsidy and welfare pensions.

L. 19.234, establishing special benefits for victims of dismissals for political reasons during the Pinochet regime.

L. 19.260, modifying L. 17.322 and LD. 3.500 (1980).

L. 19.262, modifying rules about readjustments of some pensions.

L. 19.281, regulating housing loans in CCAF institutions.

1994

L. 19.299, modifying the DFL. 44 (1978) and L. 18.867, on maternal subsidies.

L. 19.284, establishing rules for the social integration of disabled persons.

L. 19.307, readjusting the minimum monthly income; family allowances, and welfare non-contributory pensions.

L. 19.301, modifying regulations on market values; administration of mutual funds, investment funds and pension funds; insurance companies, and other matters.

L. 19.310, modifying LD. 2.763 (1979).

L. 19.345, extending Law 16.744, on occupational diseases and labour accidents to workers in the public sector.

1995

L. 19.381, modifying L. 18.933 (1990).

L. 19.404, regulating 'heavy works'.

L. 19.950, establishing and modifying various social security regulations.

L. 19.392, readjusting minimum monthly income; family and maternal allowances, and welfare pensions.

L. 19.399, modifying rules on pension's funds, mutual funds, investments funds, market of values, insurance companies.

L. 19.394, modifying Law 16.744 on occupational diseases and labour accidents.

L. 19.398, modifying LD. 828 and Law 18.502, and establishing an extraordinary readjustment of some pensions.

L. 19.403, establishing an extraordinary readjustment to pensions for widows and other pensions.

L. 19404, modifying Law-Decree 3.500 and establishing rules on old age pensions in case of 'heavy jobs'.

L. 19.405, modifying Law 19.378 on the Statute of Local Government Primary Medical Care System.

1996

L. 19.454, modifying Law 19.020 on family subsidy and establishing readjustments and bonuses to some pensioners.

L. 19.457, readjusting the minimum monthly income, family and maternal allowances and familiar subsidy.

DFL. 192 (ML), extending Law 16.744 on occupational diseases and labour accidents to company associates and businessmen.

1997

L. 19.502, readjusting the minimum monthly income and some allowances.

L. 19.505, establishing a special leaves in case of serious diseases of children.

1998

L. 19.539, establishing an extraordinary readjustment to some pensions.

L. 19.564, readjusting the minimum monthly income, family and maternal allowances, family subsidy and other benefits.

L. 19.582, modifying L. 19.234, on especial benefits for victims of dismissals for political reasons during the Pinochet regime.

L. 19.591, modifying Labour Code regulations on maternity protection.

L. 19.595, readjusting remunerations, family allowances and maternity allowances, family subsidy and other benefits in the public sector.

1999

L. 19.631, establishing the payment of owed social insurance contributions as a fundamental requisite to dismiss a worker.

L. 19.649, readjusting wages, family and maternal allowances, family subsidy and other benefits in the public sector.

2001

L. 19.703, readjusting wages, family and maternal allowances, family subsidy and other benefits (public sector).

L. 19.720, authorizing extraordinary agreements between social security institutions and employers to pay owed contributions.

L. 19.728, establishing the unemployment insurance.

L. 19.729, readjusting the minimum monthly income.

2002

L. 19.775, readjusting wages, family and maternal allowances, family subsidy and other benefits in the public sector.

L. 19.799, establishing special rules for victims of VHS and a bonus for catastrophic diseases.

L. 19.785, reforming Law 17.322 and other social security legal provisions.

L. 19.775, modifying investments regulations established in LD. 3.500

L. 19.811, readjusting the minimum monthly income.

L. 19.795, modifying investment rules established in LD. 3.550.

L. 19.843, readjusting remunerations, family allowances and pregnancy benefits in the public sector.

2003

L.19.881, extending the period to claim especial benefits to victims of political dismissals during Pinochet regime.

L. 19.883, readjusting the minimum monthly income.

L. 19.895, establishing protective rules for persons incorporated to ISAPRE, AFP, and insurance companies.

L. 19.917, readjusting wages, family and maternal allowances, family subsidy and other benefits in the public sector.

2004

L. 19.934, establishing the modality of life pensions, thus modifying Law-Decree 3.500.

L. 19.965, readjusting the minimum monthly income.

L. 19.969, extending the validity of the extraordinary contribution to social insurance for occupational diseases and labour accidents established by law 19.758.

L. 19.985, readjusting wages, family and maternal allowances, family subsidy and other benefits in the public sector.

2005

L. 19.966, establishing a system of guaranteed medical care benefits.

L. 20.039, readjusting the minimum monthly income.

L. 20.047, establishing a parental leave.

L. 20.077, re-establishing a subsidy in case of 'catastrophic diseases'.

L. 20.079, readjusting remunerations, family allowances and pregnancy benefits in the public sector.

2006

L. 20.101, extending definition of labour accident contained in Law 16.744 on occupational diseases and labour accidents.

L. 20.102, establishing an extraordinary readjustment of lower pensions.

L. 20.123, regulating labour under subcontracting, the functioning of transitory labour's enterprises; individual labour contract of transitory labour, and solidarity responsibility in case of occupational diseases y labour accidents.

2007

L. 20.143, readjusting remunerations, family allowances and pregnancy benefits in the public sector.

L. 20.146, establishing especial rules for claiming resolutions in cases of disablement.

L. 20.172, reforming the family allowances system.

L. 20.204, readjusting the monthly minimum income.

L. 20.210, reforming LD. 3.500 on foreign investments in the AFP system.

L. 20.233, readjusting remunerations, family allowances and pregnancy benefits (public sector).

2008

L. 20.255, Social Prevention Reform (particularly on pensions).

L. 20.262, establishing a special bonus for lower income sectors.

L. 20.269, establishing a special bonus for a pensioned sector and a contribution to the Local Government (Town Councils) Common Fund.

L.20.279, readjusting the minimum monthly income amount.

L. 20.282, increasing the retirement bonus's amount (L. 20.209).

L. 20.288. Reforming some social security matters.

L. 20.301, establishing new rules on the funerary allowance of Basic Solidarity Pension of Invalidity beneficiaries.

2009

L. 20.305, improving economic conditions of public employees' retirement.

L. 20.326, establishing investment's incentives, an extraordinary bonus for low income's families and other measures to support investment and employment.

L. 20.328, improving the Obligatory Unemployment Insurance and other matters.

L. 20.338, regulating an unemployment subsidy.

L. 20.399, regulating the use of cradle rooms by male workers.

2010

L. 20.416, establishing especial labour regulations for low sized enterprises.

L. 20.446, facilitating the payment of social security debts due to the earthquake and tsunami of February 27.

L. 20.459, facilitating the access to basic solidarity pensions (old age and invalidity).

2011

L- 20.482, modifying Article 195 (Labour Code) related to father's leave due a childbirth.

L. 20.530, creating the Ministry of Social Development.

L. 20.545, modifying regulations on maternity protection.

2012

L. 20.595, establishing bonus and conditioned transfers to families in extreme poverty, and creating a subsidy for the employment of women (ethical family's income)

L. 20.605, ordering the payment of a solidarity bonus for alimentation.

L. 20.614, readjusting the amount of the monthly minimum income.

2013

L. 20.647, allowing that workers of municipal's health establishments be incorporated to welfare benefits, and the constitution of separated welfare services in each administrative entity.

L. 20.665, regulating a solidarity bonus to low income and vulnerable families.

L. 20.682, establishing the right of pregnant and puerperial women to be exempted of civic obligation related to public electoral processes.

L. 20.691, creating the Intendency (Public Body) of Safety and Health at Work and strengthening the function of the Supervisory Public Agency of Social Security.

Annex 5. Normative Development (January 1, 2014 To April 30, 2023.

2014

Law 20.739 (24.3.2014). Extends extraordinary contributions for social insurance for accidents at work and occupational diseases.

Law 20.761 (22.7.2014). It extends to working male parents the right to feed their children and improves standards of maternity protection.

Law 20.764 (16.7.2014). It modifies rules on maternity, paternity and family life.

2015

Law 20.829 (25.4.20159). It modifies the unemployment insurance established in Law 19.728 (2001), increasing the amount of benefits and the number of payments.

Law 20.850 (6.6.2015). It created a financial protection system for high-cost diagnoses and treatments.

Law 20.864 (15.10.2015). It modified Law 20.531, exempting those over 65 -totally or partially- from the obligation to make health contributions. It also facilitated the processing of old-age benefits and granted other benefits.

Law 20.883 (2.12.2015). Readjusts salaries in the public sector, taxable or not for health and pensions. In addition, it establishes certain benefits for pensioners, including a winter bonus for those 75 years of age or older. At the same time, it established the Solidarity Unemployment Fund and the National Employment Exchange.

2016

Law 20.891 (1.26.2016). Improves postnatal parental leave and the exercise of the right to a nursery for the civil servants indicated.

Law 20.894 (1.26.2016). It extends the obligation to contribute for self-employed workers and adapts the social security regulations indicated.

Law 20.919 (6.13.2016). Grants bonus for voluntary retirement to personnel governed by Law 19.378, which establishes statute of municipal primary health care.

Law 20.921 (6.15.2016). It grants bonus for voluntary retirement to the officials of the health sector that it indicates.

Law 20.948 (9.3.2016). Grants an additional bonus and other retirement incentive benefits for public service officials indicated and modifies Title II of Law 19.882.

Law 20.949 (9.17.2016). Modifies the Labour Code to reduce the weight of manual handling loads.

Law 20.952 (9.21.2016). Grants a bonus to the lowest-paid education assistant staff indicated.

Law 20.964 (10.29.2016). Grants bonus for voluntary retirement to the assistant staff of the education indicated.

Law 20.970 (12.3.2016). Grants extraordinary adjustment to the Basic Solidarity Pension.

2017

Law 21.010 (4.28.2017). Extends and modifies the extraordinary contribution for social insurance against risks of accidents at work and occupational diseases and creates the fund that will finance the insurance for the accompaniment of children.

Law 21.012 (6.9.2017). Ensures worker safety in situations of risk and emergency.

Law 21.015 (6.15.2017). Encourages the inclusion of people with disabilities, as a general rule in companies with 100 or more workers: at least 1% of their quotas should be reserved for people with disabilities. If there are any impediments, there are alternative ways to comply with this rule.

Law 21.018 (6. 20.2017). Confers jurisdiction on the labour courts to hear disputes in which the successors in title of the worker seek to enforce the employer's liability, derived from accidents at work or occupational diseases.

Law 21.023 (7.22.2017). Eliminates the benefit of the AFP in terms of interest on social security contributions owed.

Law 20.894 (1. 9.2017). It establishes that the classification of a certain job as heavy work will produce effects whether it is performed by workers hired directly by the employer or under a subcontracting regime or made available by temporary services companies.

Law 21.054 (12.23.2017). Eliminates the distinction between manual workers and white-collar employees in the field of accidents at work and occupational diseases, entering into force from 1.1.2019.

Law 21.063 (30.12.2017). It creates an insurance for the accompaniment of Children (SANNA) who suffer from certain diseases such as cancer, solid organ transplant, terminal phase or state, and serious accident with risk of death or serious and permanent functional sequelae. In addition, it amends the Labour Code in order to adjust the leave so that the father or mother of the minor can be absent from work with the right to subsidy (substitute income).

Law 21.133 (2.2.2019). It modifies the rules for the incorporation of self-employed workers into social protection schemes, originally included in a mandatory but gradual manner, by Law 20.255 of 2008. Regulations that oblige since 2019 independent workers who issue fee slips to contribute totally or partially to the pension, health, serious illnesses of children, work accidents and occupational diseases regimes. These are the independent persons subject to the tax rules of the Income Law.

2019

Law 21.129 (1.17.2019). Modifies various legal bodies, establishing a maternal immunity for female officials of the Armed Forces, Order and Public Security, in accordance with the provisions of Article 201 of the Labour Code, during the period of pregnancy and up to one year after the expiration of maternity leave (postnatal rest), excluding the period of parental postnatal leave. The worker will enjoy labour fuero. In the event that the father makes use of these permits, he will also enjoy that protection

Law 21.155 (5.2.2019). Establishes measures to protect breastfeeding and its exercise, whose main objectives are: (i) to recognize the fundamental value of motherhood and the right to breastfeeding, as a right of childhood; (ii) enshrine the right of children to access human milk and the right of mothers to freely breastfeed their children, and (iii) guarantee the free exercise of nursing and free breastfeeding, punishing any arbitrary discrimination that causes deprivation, disturbance or threat to these rights.

Law 21.168 (7.27.2019). Creates the Right to Preferential Care, guaranteeing that all persons over 60 years of age, as well as people with disabilities, have the right to be treated preferentially and in a timely manner by any type of health action provider, whether in the public or private sectors.

Ley 21.190 (12.11.2019). Improves and establishes new benefits in the solidarity pension system.

2020

Law 21.220 (3.26.2020). Modifies the Labour Code on remote work. It establishes specific regulations for teleworking, as well as the indications to be considered as prevention against accidents at work, maintaining the employer's duty of effective protection towards its workers.

Law 21.225 (4.2.2020). Establishes measures to support families and micro, small and medium-sized enterprises due to the impact of the Covid-19 disease. It provides for the payment of a COVID-19 Bonus equivalent to CLP 50,000 per family burden for groups belonging to the poorest 60% of the population.

Law 21.227 (4.6.2020). Authorizes access to unemployment insurance benefits of Law 19.728, in exceptional circumstances, establishing the possibility that in the event of the suspension of labour relations as a result of the contingency caused by COVID-19, workers may obtain benefits from the Unemployment Insurance funds, both from individual accounts and from the solidarity fund. The obligation of the employer to pay contributions in the terms indicated by law shall subsist. Additionally, a benefit is contemplated for domestic workers in the periods of mandatory quarantine, to access a benefit charged to the compensation fund that must be constituted by the employer with a mandatory monthly contribution since the contract comes into force.

Law 21.218 (4.3.2020). Creates a subsidy to achieve a guaranteed minimum income.

Law 21.227 (4.6.2020). Establishes employment protection standards.

Law 21.230 (5.16.2020). Grants an emergency family income.

Law 21.232 (6.1.2020). Modifies Law 21.227, authorizing access to unemployment insurance benefits of Law 19.728 in exceptional circumstances, in the matters indicated.

Law 21.242 (6.24.2020). Establishes a benefit for the self-employed.

Law 21.243 (6.23.2020). Modifies Law 21.230 and extends and increases IFE (emergency family income).

Law 21.247 (7.27.2020). Establishes benefits for parents (fathers or mothers) and caregivers of children, under the conditions indicated.

Law 21.248 (7.30.2020). Introduce a constitutional reform that allows the exceptional withdrawal of accumulated funds of individual capitalization under the conditions indicated.

Law 21.251 (8.3.2020). Modifies Law 21.230, to facilitate and expand access to emergency family income.

Law 21.252 (8.1.2020). Establishes a financing with fiscal contribution for the protection of the income of the middle class in the cases indicated.

Law 21.258 (9.2.2020). Creates the national cancer law, which pays posthumous tribute to Dr Claudio Mora.

Law 21.260 (9. 2. 2020). Modifies the Labour Code to enable remote work or teleworking of pregnant workers, in the event of a constitutional state of emergency of catastrophe, due to public calamity, on the occasion of an epidemic or pandemic due to a contagious disease, and establishes other exceptional rules that it indicates.

Law 21.263 (9.4.2020). Relaxes access requirements and improves unemployment insurance benefits and benefits of Law 21.227.

Law 21.269 (9.21.2020). Incorporates domestic workers to unemployment insurance of Law 19.728.

Law 21.288 (12.14.2020). Creates the Covid-19 transitional emergency fund.

Law 21.295 (12. 10.2020). Establishes a single and extraordinary withdrawal of pension funds under the conditions indicated.

2021

Law 21.309 (2.1.2021). Establishes benefit that indicates for affiliates and pensioners classified as terminally ill.

Law 21.312 (2.15.2021). Extends validity of benefits established in laws 21.227 and 21.263.

Law 21.322 (4.21.2021) Establishes the comprehensive social protection network system.

Law 21.323 (4.6.2021). Establishes a new middle-class bond and a solidarity loan for the protection of the income of the middle class.

Law 21.325 (4.20.2021) lays down rules on migration and aliens (Article 16).

Law 21.330 (4.28.2021). Modifies the Constitution, to establish and regulate an exceptional mechanism for the withdrawal of pension funds and advance of life annuities, under the conditions indicated.

Law 21.339 (5. 8.2021). Establishes a new tax charge bonus, under the conditions indicated.

Law 21.342 (6. 1.2021). Establishes occupational health safety protocol for the gradual and safe return to work within the framework of the health alert decreed on the occasion of Covid-19 in the country.

Law 21.337 (6.4.2021). Establishes the reciprocal quality of family burden between both spouses, for the purposes of health benefits and family allowances.

Law 21.351 (6.14.2021). Modifies Ley 21.247, granting exceptional benefits to dependent, independent and public sector workers who have made use of one or more preventive parental medical leave under the conditions indicated.

Law 21.350 (6.14.2021). Regulates the procedure for modifying the base price of health plans.

Law 21.360 (7.12.2021). It readjusts the amount of the minimum monthly income, as well as the family and maternal allowance, and the family subsidy, and grants extraordinary aid for families in the context of Covid-19.

Law 21.371 (9.29.2021). It establishes special measures in the event of gestational or perinatal death.

Law 21.375 (10.21.2021). It enshrines palliative care and the rights of people suffering from terminal or serious illnesses.

Law 21.391 (11.24.2021). Establishes a modality of remote work or teleworking for the care of children and people with disabilities, in the cases indicated.

2022

Law 21.403 (1.3.2022). It recognizes deaf blindness as a unique disability and promotes the full social inclusion of deafblind people.

Law 21.419 (1.29.2022). Creates the universal guaranteed pension and modifies various legal bodies.

Law 21.424 (2.11.2022). Modifies Law 18,056 on the granting of grace pensions to children of people who have died from Covid-19.

Law 21.430 (3.15.2022). It establishes guarantees and comprehensive protection of the rights of children and adolescents.

Law 21.431 (3.11.2022). Modifies the Labour Code regulating the contract of workers of companies of digital service platforms.

Law 21.441. (5.9.2022). Extends the duration of work leave in the event of the death of the father, mother or child in pregnancy.

Law 21.456 (5.26.2022). Readjusts the amount of the Minimum Monthly Income, the Family and Maternal Allowance and the Family Subsidy. In addition, it grants a compensatory contribution of the increase in the value of the basic food basket.

Law 21.471 (8.19.2022). Authorizes the General Director of Pledge Credit to forgive default interest on collateral credits accrued during the period indicated.

Law 21.474 (7.27.2022). Creates Extraordinary Bonus Chile Supports Winter and extends parental postnatal leave.

Law 21.475 (9.6.2022). It declares 29 April of each year as the National Day of Workers of the Chilean Health System.

Law 21.498 (11.15.2022). Modifies Article 202 of the Labour Code, allowing teleworking to pregnant women during the state of health alert due to Covid-19, decreed by the competent authority.

Law 21.509 (11.25.2022). It authorizes the active search for cases in the community and the early diagnosis of Covid-19, in people over 14 years of age, without the consent of parents or curators.

Law 21.510 (11.24. 2022). It temporarily extends paternal postnatal leave.

Law 21.512 (12.14.2022). Regulates the final disposal of personal protection elements of a sanitary nature, prohibits and sanctions their elimination in public places.

Law 21.513 (12.6. 2022). It considers the health and user care goals fulfilled, by the health officials indicated, for the purposes of paying the corresponding allowances and bonuses, on the occasion of the state of catastrophe due to the Covid-19 pandemic.

Law 21.526 (12.28.2022). It readjusts salaries to public sector workers, grants bonuses that it indicates, grants other benefits that it indicates and modifies various legal bodies.

2023

Law 21.530 (2.2.2023). It establishes a right to reparatory rest for health workers in the private sector, in recognition of their work during the Covid-19 pandemic, under the conditions and with the effects indicated.

Law 21.531 (2.10.2022). It creates a law for cases of fibromyalgia and chronic non-oncological pain.

Law 21.538 (1.26.2023). Modifies Law 21.419, which creates the Universal Guaranteed Pension and modifies the legal bodies indicated.

Law 21.541 (3.17.2023). It authorizes health providers to provide care through telemedicine.

Law 21.545 (3.10.2023). It promotes the right to health protection of people with autism and similar neurodevelopmental situations, also promoting the inclusion and protection of their rights.

Law 21.550 (3.25.2023). Granted an extraordinary contribution of to each beneficiary of the Permanent Family Contribution regulated by Law 20.743 and increased the amounts of the family and maternal allowance and the Single Family-Allowance, automating this subsidy.

Law 21.551 (4.19.2023). Exempts from the medical requirement those who request the performance of the preventive mammogram examination.

Selected Bibliography

General Introduction

Bertranou, Fabio y Marinakis, Andre (Editores): Reflexiones sobre el trabajo. Visiones desde el Cono Sur de América Latina en el Centenario de la OIT. Oficina Internacional del Trabajo. Santiago, 2019. [Reflections about labour. A view from de South Cone of Latin America].

Bowen, Alfredo. *Introducción a la seguridad social* [*Introduction to Social Security*]. 3rd edition. Santiago: Chilean Legal Publishing House, 1991.

Cheyre, Hernán. *La previsión en Chile ayer y hoy [Chilean Social Welfare: Yesterday and Today].* Santiago: Centre of Public Studies, 1991.

Cifuentes-Lillo, Hugo. 'Características generales del sistema de seguridad social chileno' ['Chilean Social Security System: General Characteristics']. In *Revista Laboral Chilena* [*Chilean Labour Review*], edited by Mario Soto-Venegas. Santiago, 1996.

Cifuentes-Lillo, Hugo. 'Necesaria reforma a la seguridad social chilena. Algunas consideraciones preliminares' ['Necessary Reform to Chilean Social Security. Some Preliminary Considerations']. In *Revista Laboral Chilena* [*Chilean Labour Review*], edited by Mario Soto-Venegas. Santiago, 2005.

Cifuentes-Lillo, Hugo, Arellano-Ortiz, Pablo, Walker-Errázuriz, Francisco. Seguridad Social. Parte General y Pensiones. [Social Security. General Part and Pensions]- Librotecnia. Santiago. Diciembre 2013.

Humeres-Noguer, Héctor. *Derecho del Trabajo y de la Seguridad Social. Tomo III. Derecho de la Seguridad Social [Labour and Social Security Law. Volume III Social Security Law].* Santiago: Chilean Legal Publishing House, 2007.

Humeres-Noguer, Héctor. *La seguridad social en la Constitución Política chilena. I parte* [Social security in the Chilean Constitution. Part I]. In *Revista Laboral Chilena* [Chilean Labour Review], edited by Mario Soto-Venegas. Santiago, 1998.

Humeres-Noguer, Héctor. 'La seguridad social en la Constitución Política chilena. II parte' ['Social Security in the Chilean Constitution. Part II']. In *Revista Laboral Chilena* [*Chilean Labour Review*], edited by Mario Soto-Venegas. Santiago, 1998.

ILO/International Labour Conference, 111th.Session: Advancing Social Justice. Report of the Director General.

International Labour Office: The value of essential work. World Employment and Social Outlock. 2023.

Selected Bibliography

International Labour Office: World Social Protection Report 2020–2022.

International Labour Office: World Employment and Social Outlock. 2021.

Legislation enacted since March 1990.

Morgado-Valenzuela, Emilio. 'La Seguridad Social en las Constituciones de Iberoamérica' ['Social security in the Ibero-American Constitutions']. In *CIVITAS Revista Española de Derecho del Trabajo* [*CIVITAS, Spanish Review of Labour Law*]. Number 46. Madrid, 1991.

Morgado-Valenzuela, Emilio. 'Presente y tendencias de la seguridad social' ['Social Security: Present and Tendencies']. In Academia *Iberoamericana de Derecho del Trabajo y de la Seguridad Social (AIADTSS) y Gobierno del Estado de Sinaloa México: Memorias del Duodécimo Encuentro Iberoamericano de Derecho del Trabajo y la Seguridad Social* [*Iberoamerican Academy of Labour Law and Social Security & Government of Sinaloa State (Mexico): Twelfth Iberoamerican Meeting of Labour Law and Social Security's Report*]. Sinaloa, 2001.

Novoa, Patricio. Derecho de la Seguridad Social [Social Security Law]. Santiago: Chilean Legal Publishing House, 1977.

Organización Iberomericana de Seguridad Social (OISS). *Banco de información de los sistemas iberoamericanos de seguridad social. Edición 1997* [*Information Bank on the Ibero-American Social Security Systems*]. Presentación de Adolfo Jiménez-Fernández, Secretario General de la OISS [Foreword by Adolfo Jiménez-Fernández (OISS's Secretary General)]. Madrid: Iberoamerican Social Security Organization (OISS), 2007.

Organización Internacional del Trabajo [International Labour Office]. *Las normas internacionales del trabajo: Un enfoque global 75 aniversario de la Comisión de expertos en Aplicación de Convenios y Recomendaciones* [*International labour standards: A global viewpoint on the 75th Anniversary of the Commission of Experts in the Application of Conventions and Recommendations*]. Geneva: ILO, 2001.

Organización Internacional del Trabajo [International Labour Office]. Oficina Regional para América Latina y el Caribe: *Panorama Laboral 2008. América Latina y el Caribe* [*Regional Office for Latin America and the Caribbean: Labour Overview 2008: Latin America and the Caribbean*]. 1st edn. Lima, 2008.

Organización Internacional del Trabajo [International Labour Office]. *Aplicación de las normas internacionales del trabajo, 2009 (II)* [*Application of international labour standards, 2009 (II)*]. Conferencia Internacional del Trabajo, 98ª reunión, 2009. Documento informativo sobre ratificaciones y actividades normativas hasta el 31 de diciembre de 2008) [International Labour Conference, 98th meeting, 2009). Information paper about ratifications and normative activities until 31 December 1998]. Geneva, 2009.

Piñera, José. *El cascabel al gato: La batalla por la Reforma Provisional* [*Placing the Bell on the Cat: The Battle for Social Welfare Reform*]. Santiago: Zig-Zag Publishing Company, 1991.

United Nations Development Program. *Human Development Report.* 2007/2008 Edition. New York, 2007.

Selected Bibliography

Part I. The Institutions

Arellano-Ortíz, Pablo. 'Las AFP's no son un producto de exportación verdaderamente chileno' ['The AFPs Are Not a True Chilean Exportation Commodity']. In *Revista Laboral Chile* [*Chilean Labour Review*], edited by Mario Soto-Venegas. Santiago, 2007.

Cifuentes-Lillo, Hugo. 'Modificaciones introducidas a la Ley 18.933 sobre instituciones de salud previsional, y Análisis de la Ley 19.381' ['Modifications to Law 18.933 on Social welfare health institutions and Law 19.381 Analysis']. In *Revista Laboral Chilena* [*Chilean Labour Review*], edited by Mario Soto-Venegas. Santiago, 1995.

Legislation enacted since March 1990.

Superintendency of Social Security (SUSESO): Rules issued by the Superintendency of Social Security in Covid-19. In: SUSESO Bulletin N° 2. April 2020.

Superintendency of Social Security (SUSESO): SUSESO Yearbook 2019. December 2019.

Superintendency of Social Security (SUSESO): SUSESO Yearbook 2018. December 2018.

Superintendency of Social Security (SUSESO): Description and evolution of subsidies. December 2020.

Part II. Contributions and Financing

Gumucio-Rivas, Juan-Sebastián. 'Nociones sobre financiamiento de la seguridad social' ['Notions on Social Security Financing']. In *Revista Laboral Chilena* [*Chilean Labour Review*], edited by Mario Soto-Venegas. Santiago, 1995.

Gumucio-Rivas, Juan-Sebastián. 'De reparto a capitalización: La experiencia previsional chilena. I. Parte' ['From Share-Out to Capitalization: The Chilean Experience. Part I]. In *Revista Laboral Chilena* [*Chilean Labour Review*], edited by Mario Soto-Venegas. Santiago, 1996.

Gumucio-Rivas, Juan-Sebastián. *De reparto a capitalización: La experiencia previsional chilena. II. Parte* [From Share-Out to Capitalization: The Chilean Experience. Part II]. In *Revista Laboral Chilena* [*Chilean Labour Review*], edited by Mario Soto-Venegas. Santiago, 1996.

Errázuriz, Francisco Walker, Hugo Cifuentes-Lillo & Ricardo Liendo. 'La factibilidad de hacer obligatoria la cotización al sistema de pensiones de parte de los trabajadores independientes. I Parte' [Feasibility to Make Obligatory the Self-employed Contributions to the Pension System. Part I]. In *Revista Laboral Chilena* [*Chilean Labour Review*], edited by Mario Soto-Venegas. Santiago, 2005.

International Labour Office: World Social Protection Report 2020–2022.

Legislation enacted since March 1990.

Superintendency of Social Security (SUSESO): SUSESO Yearbook 2019. December 2019.

Superintendency of Social Security (SUSESO): SUSESO Yearbook 2018. December 2018.

Selected Bibliography

Part III. Health Care

Cifuentes-Lillo, Hugo. Modificaciones introducidas a la Ley 18.933 sobre instituciones de salud previsional, y Análisis de la Ley 19.381 [Modifications to Law 18.933 on Social Prevention Health Institutions and Law 19.381 Analysis]. In *Revista Laboral Chilena* [*Chilean Labour Review*], edited by Mario Soto-Venegas. Santiago, 1995.

Verdugo-Ernst, Lucía. 'Las instituciones nacionales de seguridad social: Principales reformas de los últimos 14 años' ['Social Security National Institutions: Principal Reforms in the Last 14 Years']. In *Revista Laboral Chilena* [*Chilean Labour Review*], edited by Mario Soto-Venegas. Santiago, 1994.

Legislation enacted since March 1990.

Superintendency of Social Security (SUSESO): Independent workers before social security: occupational health. July 2021.

Superintendency of Social Security (SUSESO): New psychosocial risk assessment questionnaire. March 2023.

Superintendency of Social Security (SUSESO): Psychosocial risk in Chile. September 2022.

Part IV. Family Allowances

Cifuentes-Lillo, Hugo. 'Las prestaciones familiares' ['Family Benefits']. In *Revista Laboral Chilena* [*Chilean Labour Review*], edited by Mario Soto-Venegas. Santiago, 1997.

Cifuentes-Lillo, Hugo. 'Los pensionados y su afiliación a las Cajas de Compensación de Asignación Familiar' ['Pensioners' Affiliation to Family Allowances Compensation Institutions']. In *Revista Laboral Chilena* [*Chilean Labour Review*], edited by Mario Soto-Venegas. Santiago, 1998.

Cifuentes-Lillo, Hugo. 'Extensión de los derechos laborales y de seguridad social de la madre trabajadora al padre y los adoptantes, en espacial el fuero' ['Mothers' Labour and Social Security Rights Extension to Fathers and Step-Mothers and Step-Fathers, Especially in Relation to 'Fuero' Protection]. In *Revista Laboral Chilena* [*Chilean Labour Review*], edited by Mario Soto-Venegas. Santiago, 2000.

Cifuentes-Lillo, Hugo. 'Permiso para el padre trabajador por nacimiento de un hijo' ['Fathers' Leave due to Childbirth']. In *Revista Laboral Chilena* [*Chilean Labour Review*], edited by Mario Soto-Venegas. Santiago:, 2005. Cifuentes-Lillo, Hugo. 'Imputación de responsabilidad por los siniestros del trabajo y su prevención' ['Imputation of Responsibility for Labour Risks and Their Prevention']. In *Revista Laboral Chilena* [*Chilean Labour Review*], edited by Mario Soto-Venegas. Santiago, 2007.

Cifuentes Hugo, and Francisco Walker. 'Aspectos generales de la Ley 20.255: Reforma de la Previsión Social' ['General Aspects of Law 20.255: Social Welfare Reform']. In *Revista Laboral Chilena* [*Chilean Labour Review*], 4/2008, number 165, edited by Mario Soto-Venegas. Santiago, 2008.

International Labour Office: World Social Protection Report 2020–2022.

Legislation enacted since March 1990.

Verdugo-Ernst, Lucía. 'Revisión de la legislación vigente sobre salas cuna' ['Revision of Chilean Legislation about Day Nurseries']. In *Revista Laboral Chilena* [*Chilean Labour Review*], edited by Mario Soto-Venegas. Santiago, 1995.

Superintendency of Social Security (SUSESO): Five years of validity of the insurance for accompaniment of children. SANNA. January 2023.

Superintendency of Social Security (SUSESO): Study of the sustainability of the Insurance Fund for the Accompaniment of Children. SANNA. December 2020.

Superintendency of Social Security (SUSESO): Guide to serious illness of a child under one year of age. 2021.

Superintendency of Social Security (SUSESO): Extension of paternal postnatal leave. July 2023.

Part V. Incapacity to Work

International Labour Office: World Social Protection Report 2020–2022.

Legislation enacted since March 1990.

Part VI. Industrial Accidents and Occupational Diseases

Central Unitaria de Trabajadores (CUT): Informe final de la Comisión CUT sobre Seguridad y Salud de los Trabajadores [Final Report of the Unitarian Central of Workers- CUT, on the Health and Security at Work]. En:: Revista Laboral Chilena [*Chilean Labour Review*], Santiago, Abril 2011.

Gajardo-Harboe, M. Cristina: Obligaciones en materia de higiene y seguridad en Chile: los cambios de la Ley de Subcontratación [Obligations on Higyene at Work: changes in the Law of subcontracting] and. En: Revista Laboral Chilena [*Chilean Labour Review*], Santiago, Mayo 2009.

Gumucio-Rivas, Juan-Sebastián. 'Accidentes del trabajo y la indemnización por el lucro cesante' ['Labour Accidents and Non-perceived Gains' Indemnity']. In *Revista Laboral Chilena* [*Chilean Labour Review*], edited by Mario Soto-Venegas. Santiago, 2007.

Gumucio-Rivas, Juan-Sebastián & Diego Corvera-Vergara. 'Responsabilidad del empleador por accidentes del trabajo en Chile' [Employer Responsibility for Labour Accidents in Chile]. In *Revista Laboral Chilena* [*Chilean Labour Review*], edited by Mario Soto-Venegas. Santiago, 1996.

International Labour Office: World Social Protection Report 2020–2022.

Legislation enacted since March 1990.

Oficina Internacional del Trabajo [International Labour Office]. *Medio siglo al servicio de Chile: El sistema privado de mutualidades de accidentes del trabajo y enfermedades profesionales, 1957–2007 [Half a Century at the Service of Chile: The Private Mutual System of Labour Accidents and Occupational Diseases*]. Consultant: Jorge Jiménez de la Jara. Santiago: International Labour Office, 2008.

Soto-Venegas, Mario. 'Modificación al Reglamento sobre prevención de riesgos profesionales' [Modifications to Regulations on Labour Risks Prevention]. In *Revista Laboral Chilena* [*Chilean Labour Review*], edited by Mario Soto-Venegas. Santiago, 1996.

Verdugo-Ernst, Lucía. 'Deberes de la empresa en materia de higiene y seguridad en trabajo' ['Enterprise Duties on Labour Health and Security']. In *Revista Laboral Chilena* [*Chilean Labour Review*], edited by Mario Soto-Venegas. Santiago, 1995.

Part VII. Unemployment

Cifuentes-Lillo, Hugo. 'Seguro de Desempleo' ['Unemployment Insurance']. In *Revista Laboral Chilena* [*Chilean Labour Review*], edited by Mario Soto-Venegas. Santiago, 2002.

Gumucio-Rivas, Juan-Sebastián. 'Protección al desempleo en Chile: Régimen vigente y bases para su reforma' [Unemployment Protection in Chile: The Existing Regime and Bases for Its Reform]. In *Revista Laboral Chilena* [*Chilean Labour Review*], edited by Mario Soto-Venegas. Santiago, 1993.

Halpern-Montecino Cecily & Héctor Humeres-Noguer. 'Desnaturalización de las indemnizaciones por años de servicios' [Adulteration of Indemnities for Years of Services]. In *Revista Laboral Chilena* [*Chilean Labour Review*], edited by Mario Soto-Venegas. Santiago, 2000.

International Labour Office: World Social Protection Report 2020–2022.

International Labour Office: Employment and Social Outlock 2021.

International Labour Office: Employment and Social Outlock 2022.

Legislation enacted since March 1990.

Thayer-Morel, Luis Eduardo. *Las indemnizaciones por años de servicios* [Indemnities for Years of Services]. In *Revista Laboral Chilena* [*Chilean Labour Review*], edited by Mario Soto-Venegas. Santiago, 2000.

Part VIII. Pensions

Arellano-Ortíz, Luis Eduardo. *Las AFP's no son un producto de exportación verdaderamente chileno* [The AFPs Are Not a True Chilean Exportation Commodity]. In *Revista Laboral Chile* [*Chilean Labour Review*], edited by Mario Soto-Venegas. Santiago, 2007.

Asociación de Abogados Laboralistas [Association of Labour Lawyers]. 'Propuesta de la AGAL respecto de la reforma del Sistema de Pensiones' [A Proposition to Reform the Pension System]. In *Revista Laboral Chilena* [*Chilean Labour Review*], edited by Mario Soto-Venegas. Santiago, 2006.

Cifuentes-Lillo, Hugo, Arellano-Ortiz, Pablo, Walker-Errázuriz, Francisco: Seguridad Social. Parte General y Pensiones. [Social Security. General Part and Pensions]- Librotecnia. Santiago. Diciembre 2013.

Consejo Asesor Presidencial para la Reforma Previsional [Presidential Advisory Council for the Social Prevention Reform]. *El derecho a una vida digna en la vejez: Hacia un Contrato Social con la Previsión en Chile [The Right to a Decent Life in Old Age: Towards a Social Contract with Social Welfare in Chile*]. Volume I. Santiago: Diagnóstico y Propuestas de Reforma, 2006.

Elgueta-Adrovez, Patricio & Hugo Cifuentes-Lillo. 'Ahorro previsional voluntario (Características básicas)' ['Voluntary Social Welfare Saving: Basic Characteristics']. In *Revista Laboral Chilena* [*Chilean Labour Review*], edited by Mario Soto-Venegas. Santiago, 2002.

Gumucio-Rivas, Juan-Sebastián. *Evaluación del nuevo régimen de pensiones a doce años de funcionamiento. Análisis desde el punto de vista de los principios de la seguridad social* [Evaluation of the New Pension Regime after Twelve Years of Functioning: Analysis from the Social Security Principles Viewpoint]. In *Revista Laboral Chilena [Chilean Labour Review*], edited by Mario Soto-Venegas. Santiago, 1995.

International Labour Organization. *Pension Reform in Chile and the Contribution of the ILO*. ILO Sub regional Office for the Southern Cone in Latin America (Chile, Paraguay, Uruguay). Santiago, Chile, 2008.

International Labour Organization: Social Security for Social Justice and an Equitable Globalization. 100a. International Labour Conference. Geneva, 2011.

International Labour Organization: Recommendation number 202.

International Labour Office: World Social Protection Report 2020–2022.

International Labour Office: Employment and Social Outlock 2021.

International Labour Office: Employment and Social Outlock 2022.

International Monetary Fund (IMF): Assessing Chile's Pension System Challenges and Reform Options: Christopher Evans and Samuel Pienknagura. IMF Working Paper WP/21/232.

Legislation enacted since March 1990.

Oficina Internacional del Trabajo [International Labour Organization]. *Envejecimiento, empleo y protección social en América Latina* [*Ageing, Employment and Social Welfare in Latin America*], edited by Fabio Bertranoud. Santiago, 2006.

Estrada, Eduardo. *La Universalidad en el Sistema de AFP o promesas de una noche de verano* ['Summer Nights' Promises: Universality in the AFP System]. In *Revista Laboral Chilena* [*Chilean Labour Review*], edited by Mario Soto-Venegas. Santiago, 2005.

Miranda-Salas, Eduardo & Eduardo Rodríguez-Silva. *Análisis del sistema de fondos de pensiones: Perspectivas e interrogantes [Analysis of the Pension Fund System: Perspectives and Doubts*]. Santiago: Editorial Jurídica de Chile, 1995.

Morgado-Valenzuela, Emilio. 'Reforma de la seguridad social en Chile: el sistema de pensiones por vejez' ['Chilean Social Security Reform: The Old Age Pension System']. In *Academia Iberoamericana de Derecho del Trabajo y de la Seguridad Social (AIADTSS) y Organización Iberoamericana de Seguridad Social (OISS)* [*Iberoamerican Academy of Labour Law and Social Security (AIADTSS) and Iberoamerican Social Security Organization (OISS)*]. Madrid, 1998.

Schmidt-Cronosija, Romy. 'Nuevo sistema de trabajas pesados' ['New System of Heavy Works']. In *Revista Laboral Chilena* [*Chilean Labour Review*], edited by Mario Soto-Venegas. Santiago, 1996.

Soto-Venegas, Mario. 'Ley 19.234, Beneficios previsionales para exonerados políticos' ['Social Security Benefits for Politically Dismissed']. In *Revista Laboral Chilena* [*Chilean Labour Review*], edited by Mario Soto-Venegas. Santiago, 1993.

Part IX. Handicapped Persons

International Labour Office: World Social Protection Report 2020–2022.

International Labour Office: Employment and Social Outlock 2021.

Legislation enacted since March 1990.

Selected Bibliography

Superintendencia de Seguridad Social: Nuevas normas para la evaluación del grado de invalidez de los trabajadores afiliados al Nuevo Sistema Previsional (Extracto). [New regulation to evaluate the invalidity's degree of workers after changes of Law 20.255. Extract]. En: *Revista Laboral Chilena [Chilean Labour Review*], Mayo 2012.

Part X. Minimum Income Benefit

International Labour Office: World Social Protection Report 2020–2022.
International Labour Office: Employment and Social Outlock 2021.
International Labour Office: Employment and Social Outlock 2022.
Legislation enacted since March 1990.

Part XI. Claims and Adjudication

Aránguiz-Zúñiga, Tita. 'Los Tribunales y el cobro de cotizaciones provisionales' ['Courts and Judicial Prosecution of Social Welfare Debts']. In *Revista Laboral Chilena* [*Chilean Labour Review*], edited by Mario Soto-Venegas. Santiago, 2005.

Díaz-Urtubia, Paola *La ejecución laboral: Conferencia en Escuela Judicial para Jueces* [*The Labour Execution Procedure: Non Published Lecture in the Judicial School for Judges*]. Santiago, 2008.

Lanata-Fuenzalida, Gabriela. '¿Prisión por deudas? El arresto como una presión a los empleadores que no depositan las contribuciones de seguridad social descontadas' ['Prison for Debts? Arrest as a Pressure to Employers That Have Not Deposited Discounted Social Security Contributions']. In *Revista Laboral Chilena* [*Chilean Labour Review*], edited by Mario Soto-Venegas. Santiago, 2005.

Venegas, Mario Soto. 'Modificaciones a la cobranza judicial de imposiciones (Ley 19.260)' ['Modifications in the Judiciary Procedure to Enforce Payment of Social Prevention Contributions (Law 19.260)']. In *Revista Laboral Chilena* [*Chilean Labour Review*], edited by Mario Soto-Venegas. Santiago, 1994.

Index

The numbers here refer to paragraph numbers.

Index